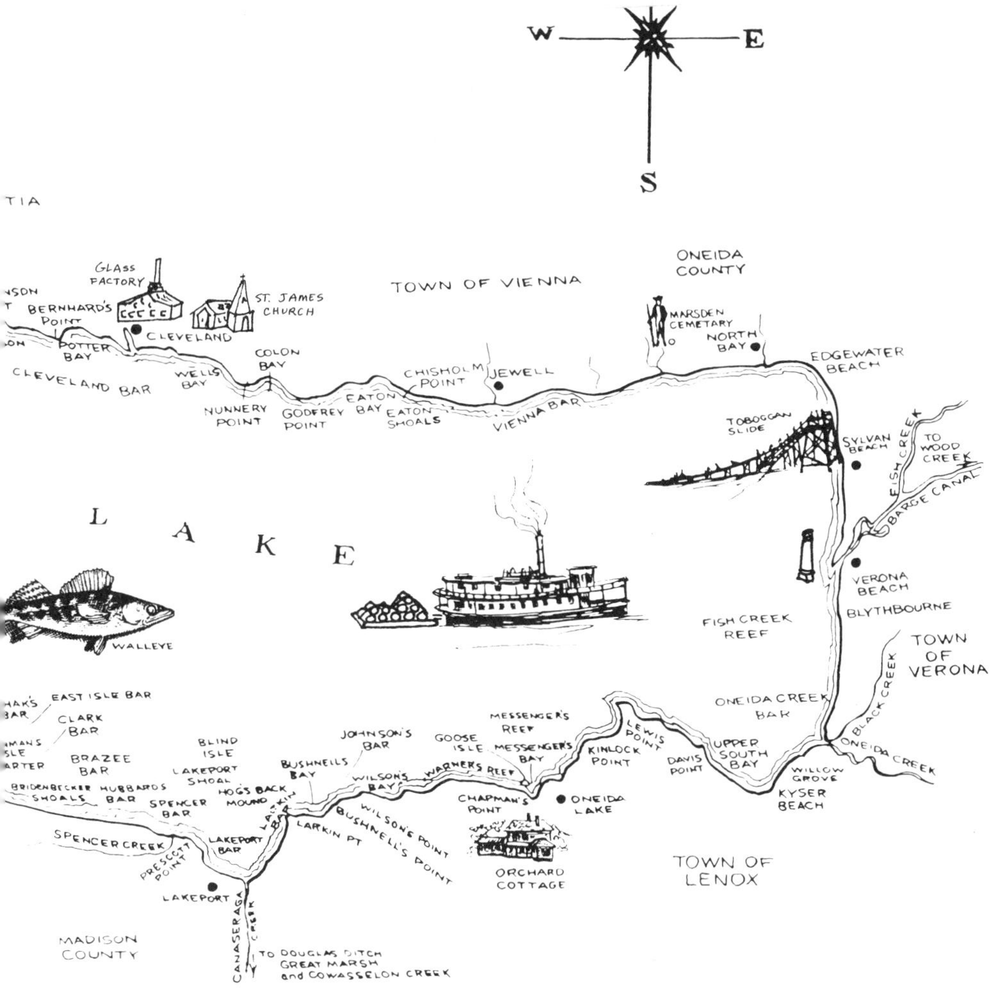
W
E
S
GLASS FACTORY
BERNHARD'S POINT
POTTER BAY
CLEVELAND
ST. JAMES CHURCH
TOWN OF VIENNA
ONEIDA COUNTY
MARSDEN CEMETARY
NORTH BAY
EDGEWATER BEACH
CLEVELAND BAR
WELLS BAY
COLON BAY
NUNNERY POINT
GODFREY POINT
EATON BAY
EATON SHOALS
CHISHOLM POINT
JEWELL
VIENNA BAR
TOBOGGAN SLIDE
SYLVAN BEACH
FISH CREEK
TO WOOD CREEK
BARGE CANAL
L A K E
WALLEYE
VERONA BEACH
BLYTHBOURNE
FISH CREEK REEF
TOWN OF VERONA
BLACK CREEK
ONEIDA CREEK BAR
EAST ISLE BAR
CLARK BAR
BRAZEE BAR
BLIND ISLE
LAKEPORT SHOAL
HOG'S BACK MOUND
BRIDENBECKER SHOALS
HUBBARDS BAR
SPENCER BAR
SPENCER CREEK
PRESCOTT POINT
LAKEPORT BAR
LAKEPORT
LARKIN BAR
LARKIN PT
BUSHNELLS BAY
JOHNSON'S BAR
WILSON'S BAY
WILSON'S POINT
BUSHNELL'S POINT
GOOSE ISLE
MESSENGER'S REEF
MESSENGER'S BAY
WARNER'S REEF
CHAPMAN'S POINT
ONEIDA LAKE
ORCHARD COTTAGE
KINLOCK POINT
LEWIS POINT
DAVIS POINT
UPPER SOUTH BAY
WILLOW GROVE
KYSER BEACH
ONEIDA CREEK
TOWN OF LENOX
MADISON COUNTY
CANASERAGA CREEK
TO DOUGLAS DITCH
GREAT MARSH
and COWASSELON CREEK

From "The Beach" to Brewerton

Stories of Oneida Lake

From "The Beach" to Brewerton

Stories of Oneida Lake

Jack Henke

North Country Books, Inc
Utica, New York

From "The Beach" to Brewerton
Stories of Oneida Lake

ISBN 0-925168-98-X

Library of Congress Cataloging-in-Publication Data

Henke, Jack.
From the Beach to Brewerton : Oneida Lake stories / Jack Henke.
p. cm.
ISBN 0-925168-98-X (alk. paper)
1. Oneida Lake (N.Y.)--History--Anecdotes. 2. Oneida Lake Region (N.Y.)--History, Local--Anecdotes. 3. Oneida Lake Region (N.Y.)--History--Anecdotes. I. Title.
F127.O52H45 2004
974.7'62--dc22

2004017906

North Country Books, Inc.
311 Turner Street
Utica, New York 13501
ncbooks@adelphia.net

This book is dedicated to the memory of:

David Maldwyn Ellis
Professor of History at Hamilton College from 1946 to 1980

David Richard Millar
Professor of History at Hamilton College from 1963 to 1991

G. Bruce Stallknecht
Curator of the Fort Brewerton Historical Society from 1988 to 2003

...scholars, teachers, and above all, friends.

Table of Contents

Prelude

Welcome to the world of Oneida Lake history. This is a book of stories about that rich past. In this book you can experience the genesis, evolution, and lifeblood of Sylvan Beach, the lake's premier resort. You can travel with colonial armies as they campaign across Oneida. You can journey with people exploring the lake region in the days of our nation's infancy, you can sense the hardships that nature's varying moods have brought to Oneida's people, and you can identify with romantics as they marvel at the lake's visual glories. In the following pages you will meet doctors and deckhands, loggers and industrialists, fish pirates and game wardens, politicians and poets, bootleggers and boat builders, lovers and liars, captains and cooks–a cross section of the Middle America that made Oneida Lake their home. You will come to know people who have lived by and with the lake, as well as those for whom it has been a great playground. And, if I have been successful, you will walk away from this book with an appreciation of their lives and of their lake and its importance to Central New York.

I write about Oneida Lake because I love being an historian and, objectivity aside, I care very deeply about this body of water. The lake has enriched and continues to enrich my life. I spend innumerable hours talking with the lake's people, researching the lake's past and, of course, enjoying the lake's superb recreational offerings (you will note the strong "fishing bias" that permeates my writing). Oneida Lake and its people have created beautiful stories that I believe must be captured, in part because of history's inherent value, but also to insure that the wondrous resource that is Oneida may be preserved for posterity.

Today, the lake's environmental integrity and unique productivity are threatened as never before. I write, in part, to expose and fight these threats, but also to understand them and place each problem within the context of the lake's history.

The data I've used comes from a web of sources as diverse as the offerings of today's Internet.

Historical societies and town historians' offices are particularly useful research sites because their collections are locally focused and regularly updated. I've logged many hours at the Onondaga, Madison, and Oneida County Historical Associations, and at the Fort Brewerton Museum/Historical Society and the Town of Sullivan's historian's office. Local historians have been extremely generous and caring. Joni Hines of the North Shore Historical Society, Lona Flynn of the Cicero Historical Society, Carol Greene and Clara Houck from the Town of Sullivan, and Bruce and Chris Stallknecht from Fort Brewerton have sent me tremendous material and always responded promptly to my requests.

County records answer many questions about the lake's people. Censuses reveal the names of family members, as well as facts about occupations, possessions, income, background, and neighbors. Property records verify land holdings and are particularly useful in documenting development trends. County map rooms are treasure chests of data because older maps often contain property owners' names next to their buildings, as well as details about businesses and place names along the lake's shore. County clerks' offices house the censuses and deeds, but also hold surprises such as unpublished manuscripts, gazetteers, collections of news articles, and interesting memories. Some older workers in the clerks' offices can recall specific landowners, as well as maps pertinent to a particular research quest. When I began an investigation of Sylvan Beach's history in 1972, for example, an elderly gentleman worked in the Oneida County Office Building's deeds room. After I told him about my research's goals, he lectured me about the Spencer family, the village's founders. Not only did he teach me about the family and their achievements, he expedited my research by directing me to the books where their property transactions were recorded.

The mail has brought a tremendous volume of unsolicited information about Oneida Lake. People who have read my books, perused articles about my work, or heard me speak about the lake's history have written scores of letters in which they've included items such as stories about their family's or friends' experiences. They've also sent newspaper clippings, photos, post cards, maps, and even souvenirs.

Eva DeMassa from Oneida, for example, penned me a fascinating letter in which she talked about hardships that Sylvan Beach folks experienced around 1900:

"I learned to row a boat as a matter of necessity. Fish Creek flooded the village in the days before the Barge Canal and, to deal with this, we tied our boat to our front steps. The flooding was terrible. I've rowed down Main Street and never grounded my boat. In the winter the snow was so deep that you could sit on the telephone wires! People cut steps – down! – to get into the post office and grocery store.

"The first street lights were oil lamps, covered with big globes. They were set on poles that were perhaps six or seven feet tall. My father contracted with the Town of Vienna to care for the lights. My brother (age nine) and I (age seven) did the work. I washed the globes and he filled the lights from two five-gallon cans of oil, pulled around in an 'express wagon.' We rode a horse around to each light in the morning and used the animal as a ladder to reach the light and turn it out."

I'm a member of the Oneida Lake Association's Board of Directors and, in this position, I've encountered fine moments of the lake's past. One of my first jobs after joining the board was indexing fifty years worth of issues of the Oneida Lake Bulletin, the association's official publication, and this led me to a wealth of data (copies of the index and the Bulletin are now a part of the Onondaga County Library's and Madison County Historical Society's collections). The board's veteran members have been particularly helpful, and encouraging, with my research. Richard Colesante, director emeritus of Constantia's Oneida Lake Fish Cultural Station (translation–"fish hatchery"), provided me with primary source documentation about his facility's nineteenth century origins. Parker Stone walked me through Clarence App's venerable Cleveland boat livery in the 1960s and Arnold Armani shared a duck-hunting story that I'll never forget. Bob Ripberger told me about the association's history and Kurt Snyder, whose family owns Wantry Island, south of Constantia, entertained me with a story about the island's waterfowling lore:

"My great uncle, Bill Hafermalz, helped start the 'North Shore Sportsmen's Club' around 1920. A mixed group of Syracuse movers and shakers that loved waterfowl hunting belonged to the club. One of their traditions involved constructing a makeshift shanty on Wantry just before duck season's opener. A few club members always spent the night before season in the shanty. They'd play pitch, enjoy the hunting camaraderie, and awaken in a perfect spot when opening day dawned.

"If you hunt on an island, however, you're at Oneida's mercy. The first few shanties were aluminum structures that measured about ten by twelve feet. When it rained, which was often, you'd experience the sensation of trying to sleep in a tin can. Club members finally remedied that problem by building a plywood shanty. When the shanty's weight made transportion to the island difficult, enterprising waterfowlers mounted the shed on floats. They towed the shanty to Wantry and slid it onto the island. Everything went smoothly, until heavy rains raised the lake's level and washed the shanty to Lord knows where.

"The third shanty was made from black plywood panels and appeared to be as lake-worthy as any. An Oneida Lake gale disagreed, however, and ripped the structure apart. Several days later my son, Matt, and I loaded our boat with the customary hunting supplies and motored to Wantry. When we neared the isle, Matt said, 'Dad, the shanty's gone!' Nothing remained of that shanty. Nothing at all.

"I sat by Bob Chabot, who lives in Sylvan Beach, at the next Oneida Lake Association meeting. I told him about the shanty. Bob asked, 'Was it made from black plywood?' When I responded affirmatively, he laughed. The shanty's panels ended up on the beach in front of his home, fifteen miles east of Wantry.

"Perhaps the lake was trying to tell us something."

Formal interviews enrich my work in bountiful ways. People who have lived Oneida Lake's history are fountainheads of invaluable knowledge. To record their memories is to preserve the lake region's past. In this book you'll hear master gardener Paul Laible discuss the manicured lawns and geometrically patterned groves of trees at Charles and Iola Brown's Xandria Estate, now the Cornell Biological Field Station at Shackelton Point. You'll listen to Chuck Rogers as he talks you through the history of the Brewerton Bait Shop (now Brewerton Sports), the oldest outdoor sports store on the lake, and shares his memories of angling during the days when copper lines and two-man row boats were considered "high tech." You'll chuckle with William "Buddy" McCarthy while he takes you speakeasy-hoppin' in Sylvan Beach during a less-than-prohibitive Prohibition era. And you'll see how a beautiful marriage, an indomitable work ethic, and a love for Sylvan Beach have made Eddie's Restaurant a seven-decade success story.

But sometimes other, less formal encounters inspire my work. For years my mother, Marion Osterhout Henke, and I observed an

Easter Sunday ritual in which we'd attend church and then take a leisurely drive to the lake for dinner and sightseeing. Every year mom insisted that we stop at the Oneida Lake Marina, on Upper South Bay where I berth my boat, so that she could "watch the water for awhile." Mom, who lived in central Utica, loved the crisp spring colors, the brilliant blues of the waves, the fresh greens of the fields and the trees, but it was the lake's cornucopia of migrating birds that fascinated her. She marveled at the hooded mergansers that performed diving shows in the marina, chasing the emerald shiners that migrated to Oneida's warming springtime shallows. The ubiquitous mallards, screaming sea gulls, and honking Canadian geese all pleased her, but it was a great blue heron that returned to the marina each April that interested her most. We joked that it was the same bird, returning for us year after year, and of course there was no way we could prove the point, but every year there was one heron in the marina and, when we parked by the water, it studied us briefly, flew nearby, and then demonstrated its stealthy fish-stalking prowess. Unlike most of its kind, this heron was a very sociable bird and often fished within Audubon range of our vehicle, so close that the subtle variations of whites, grays, and blues in its feathers were clearly visible.

After the marina, we always visited South Bay's "Pier 31" restaurant, and sat at a picture-windowed table. At dinner, Mom enjoyed the vast, beautiful expanse of water that is Oneida Lake. We'd share the delight, relive the day's avian adventure, and savor a quality Easter day. When it came time to leave, Mom always paraphrased this thought:

"What a memorable Easter Sunday. So simple, so perfect. The birds and the water and the fields. Every year...here. I'll remember these scenes all summer, Jack, and fall and winter, too. How could anyone forget them? It's easy to understand why you spend so much time by Oneida Lake."

Being an historian is a blessed job, indeed.

– Chapter 1–

A Little Geography

"We left Scriba Creek on Friday evening about six. The sky was serene and delightful. A soft breeze curled the waves and fringed them with white, while the sun sinking towards the west beautified the whole scenery. I did not witness such a grand or majestic sight since I crossed the Atlantic.

In proportion that we penetrated deeper in Oneida Lake, the beauty of this diversified prospect was more and more enhanced. The islands, the shores, the woods, the mountains seemed to vie with each other for our preference."

–Francis Adrian Van Der Kemp, 1792

Oneida Lake was created by events in the last ice age that occurred about 10,000 years ago. As glaciers slowly retreated across New York's landscape they formed a large lake that scientists called "Lake Iroquois." This body of water covered much of the state, including the Finger Lakes region and Lake Ontario. Initially, Lake Iroquois drained to the sea through the Hudson and Mohawk Valleys. When the glaciers dug the St. Lawrence Valley as they moved north, however, they opened another drainage route. The waters of Lake Iroquois receded, and Oneida Lake remained in one of the ancient lake's deeper depressions. You might call Oneida a "big puddle" left from an ancient inland sea.

Four counties border Oneida Lake. Oswego and Oneida Counties encompass the lake's North and East Shores (and, technically, the water itself), while Onondaga and Madison Counties take in the south side. No cities occupy Oneida's shores, but lands that border the lake's West End have become heavily suburbanized, largely because Interstate 81 gives commuters from Brewerton and Cicero, the lake's westernmost communities, easy access to metropolitan Syracuse. Several other villages touch the lake. Traveling from west to east on Route 49 along the lake's North Shore, motorists pass through West Monroe, Constantia, Cleveland, Jewell, and North Bay, quiet locales all. Route 31 skirts the lake's South Shore in Madison County and bisects, from west to east, Bridgeport, Lakeport, and Upper South Bay. This road is a heavily traveled, noisy highway, much busier than its North Shore counterpart. Sylvan Beach and Verona Beach stretch along Route 13 on the lake's East Shore. Early travelers marveled at these places' "shelving beaches," where the gently sloping lake bed and soft, white sands made bathing safe and pleasant.

Oneida measures about twenty-one miles in length from the Route 13 bridge over the Barge Canal at Sylvan Beach to the Route 11 bridge that spans the lake's Oneida River outlet at Brewerton. Under most circumstances, viewers at Sylvan Beach enjoy a westward expanse of lake stretching seemingly infinitely through the horizon but, on occasion, atmospheric quirks make details on the West End visible (the Brewerton water tower is a noteworthy landmark). Likewise, the lake overspreads to the east when observed from Brewerton. Sunrises at Brewerton and sunsets at Sylvan and Verona Beaches produce glorious displays of light and color. At its stoutest place, from Cleveland to Lakeport, Oneida measures five and a half miles. On average, it's a somewhat slimmer four miles wide.

Oneida Lake's surface area covers about eighty square miles. The lake drains a basin of slightly under 1,400 square miles. It has about fifty-five miles of shore. Homes and cottages occupy most of the edges, but a few blessed pockets of wooded frontage thrive. Dense forests meet the water along the entire east side of Big Bay, near Brewerton, and occasional woodlands intersperse between homes on the North and South Shores. A beautiful, expansive hay meadow once stretched from Route 31 to the lake, west of Lakeport. The meadow, the last remaining piece of agricultural land bordering Oneida, reminded observers of the region's agrarian past. Economic development, however, claimed the field in

2003-2004, and will probably take more of the lake's natural periphery as time passes.

Significant wetlands surround Oneida. The Big Bay Swamp and Toad Harbor Marsh occupy several hundred acres between the lake and Route 49. The Cicero Swamp and Great Marsh lie south of the lake and large tracks of wetlands dampen the landscape in and around the Verona Beach State Park. Construction, however, devours smaller wetlands every year. This constricts the lake basin's water-holding capacity and, thus, aggravates flooding. It also deprives waterfowl of vital habitat.

Islands punctuate Oneida's aquatic expanse and all of them rise in the lake's western half. Frenchman's and Dunham's Isles, the lake's largest, guard the northern fringe of Lower South Bay near Cicero. Both isles are densely forested. New York State owns Frenchman's and maintains a lighthouse there for Barge Canal navigation. The lighthouse has sibling beacons at Verona Beach and Brewerton. A group of isles that nineteenth century boatmen called the "duck islands" are situated south of Constantia. Among these rocky, wind-swept crests are Wantry, Long, and Little Islands. Large numbers of colonial water birds nest on the islands.

For its size, Oneida Lake is shallow. Its average depth is around twenty-two feet and its deepest area, south of Cleveland, drops to about sixty feet. Some old-time fishermen called this spot "App's Hole" for Clarence App, the former proprietor of a famous boat livery at Cleveland harbor. Others named it "catfish hole," for the large channel and "mud" cats caught there. Rock-crested shoals are common throughout the lake, especially in the western end, and provide excellent habitat for Oneida's diverse, abundant aquatic life. Several unique reefs called "Pancake Shoals" cover the lakebed near Lewis Point, Lakeport, and Constantia. These "pancakes" are small, circular rocks, sometimes likened to petrified cow manure. They are composed of iron and manganese and scientists aren't positive how they were formed.

Although the foothills of the Allegheny Mountains begin to rise five miles to the south, no hills border the lake proper (these "mountains" are, technically speaking, an eroded plateau). Oneida sits in what geologists call a "lacustrine" (lake) plain. Because the lake is unprotected and shallow, winds have a maximum effect and treacherous waves can rise within fifteen minutes. West winds are especially dangerous because the lake is located on a northwest to southeast axis. The prevailing winds in Upstate New York are westerlies and the conditions they generate on Oneida Lake have claimed many vessels and lives throughout recorded history.

Several tributaries feed Oneida. Fish Creek, the largest, empties into the Barge Canal about a half-mile east of Sylvan Beach. The creek flows through an extensive watershed that includes a large section of the southern Tug Hill Plateau. Scriba Creek meets Oneida at Constantia and Black Creek merges with the lake at Cleveland harbor. Fish, Scriba, and Black Creeks, and many unnamed clear-flowing streams, drain sandy soils north of the lake and in the Tug Hill Plateau. Oneida is a nutrient-rich lake, however, and always has been. French travelers once called it "the green lake" for the verdant algal blooms that occur every summer. The bulk of the lake's nutrients enter through the murky waters that drain lands to the south. Oneida Creek winds through the agriculturally rich Stockbridge Valley and enters the lake at Upper South Bay. Canaseraga Creek, which flows into Lakeport Bay, drains the lush "muck land" farming region between the lake and Route 5. Chittenango Creek, which enters Oneida north of Bridgeport, provides a conduit for waters from the Great Marsh and the fertile farms that border it. The phosphorus and nitrogen from these tributaries make Oneida's waters more productive that those of any comparable lakes in New York.

"Productive" is an understatement. Even after a lifetime's research, I continue to be awed by the quantity and variety of life that thrive in Oneida Lake. The lake's vast fish population sustained Native Americans for centuries before whites arrived. Tons of the lake's eels, whitefish, walleyes, and suckers were netted and subsequently smoked, salted, or iced, and exported as far as New York City in the nineteenth and early twentieth centuries. The Oneida Lake "fish pirate" became a legendary character during this era. These poachers netted tremendous quantities of the lake's bounty until enhanced law enforcement curtailed most pirating around 1940. Oneida Lake walleyed pike dinners were an extremely popular item on lakeside restaurants' menus until 1960, when these fish's sale was banned. Even today, anglers harvest and market Oneida's bullheads, sunfish, bluegills, and yellow perch. The New York State Department of Environmental Conservation ranks the lake's walleye and bass angling as among the best in the country. Annual game fish catches number in the hundreds of thousands and generate considerable economic prosperity.

The lake is home to an impressive quantity and variety of migratory water birds. Common terns, an endangered species, thrive on the islands south of Constantia. Sandpipers, great blue herons, and shore birds feed along Sylvan and Verona Beaches. Gulls, common throughout the lake's basin, feed voraciously on emerald shiners, gizzard shad, and other forage fish. The lake's wetlands support mallards, wood ducks, ospreys, and an occasional pair of bald eagles. Large flocks of Canadian geese, brant, dabbling and diving ducks, and double crested cormorants darken the skies during migration. Bird watchers enjoy Oneida's avian scene and are often spotted on the Sylvan Beach pier, a superb viewing environment.

Oneida Lake has always been one of New York's richest biological blessings.

– Chapter 2 –

"Pictures"

Vivid images blanket Oneida Lake and its environs. These pictures unfold along every shore, in all seasons and times. You can spend time with the lake and delight your senses as the brush strokes of Oneida's panorama's paintings fill the canvasses of your life. Many of you already enjoy rich memories of these scenes. I have been blessed with innumerable opportunities to experience Oneida's artistry. Listen, as my words attempt to walk through a part of Oneida Lake's geography and unveil a tiny section of the gallery of pictures that have rainbowed my life.

January 1, 1972: My first day of research into the lake's history

Snow falls steadily at Sylvan Beach, lending an impressionist's veil to a first walk through the village in winter's early-fading light. Carnival buildings' once-exclaiming red, orange, and yellow clapboards darken with the descending whiteness. Their windows are boarded like an omega to last summer's fun. The buildings beg to tell their stories. Two clowning faces, pasted on an arcade wall, smile broadly and boldly in a not very January grin. The faces question as they laugh at the bundled stranger, ambling in a first day of his first journey into a lifetime's work. Why are we here? How long have we smiled? What happened at this place? Signs and names–Carousel, Midway, Lake Shore, Forest Home, Rollo, The Dog House, Playland, Laffland, Fascination–speak to another time when warmth flowed through this translucent picture. The tall ionic columns of a Greek revival diner, a Puritan-styled chapel, and the gingerbread gothic ornamentation atop a neoned Main Street tavern deepen the statement with antiquity's blessings. Questions arise, memories wait, and the snow falls.

August 2002: Three decades pass and the images continue

Nocturnal pictures hang colorfully in the lake's East Shore gallery. During a midsummer's midnight stroll along Sylvan Beach, a walker enters a night world full of life, light, and sound. The sands are warm from the day's baking and the lake's waters kiss the shore with a comforting, cooling rhythm. Oneida's creatures feed in the shallows in evening. Vast schools of buckeye minnows crowd the shore, dining on the lake's algae and invertebrate life that drifted to the beaches with the day's westerly breezes. The walker's steps scare the buckeyes and whole schools leap from the shallows, their silvery bodies glistening as their sides capture cottage and beach-front lights. Great blue herons patrol the sandy shallows, stalking the minnows. These aristocratic, graceful birds often stand motionless, their long legs acting as spindly trunks supporting their preying bodies. The walker startles a heron, prompting the bird to emit a night-piercing cry that echoes as its great wings glide to the safety of buckeye schools afar.

Other avians thrive on the nocturnal eastern beaches. Mallards dine on plants and algae that have washed into small lagoons, set aside from the lake by shifting, wave-crafted sand bars. Much of the algae are discolored and dying. Their composted odors remind the walker of the lake's incredible life. Gulls rest on the sandbars, secure in their isolation, patiently awaiting the summer dawn. Waves have sculpted these havens into mosaics of geometric forms. Most are abstractly rectangular beaches-in-miniature that parallel the shore, but some sand isles rise from the water in perfect circles and ellipses. Moonlight outlines these unique sanctuaries as its beams dance atop the waves that now, reduced by waning breezes, gently break into acute aquatic angles along the isles' edges. Gulls seem to favor one of the rounder isles and a small flock rests there. Birds post along the circumference, facing outward as they duplicate the isle's symmetry.

Light touches the beach from many angles and, even on the darkest night, visibility presents no problem. Syracuse and its suburbs glow to the west, casting muted oranges and yellows over the lake's horizon. Powerboats' running lights dart atop the water and the green flashers of navigational buoys, anchored about a mile apart through the lake's central channel, display their timed warnings. On clear, still nights, the walker can see the distant lights of Buoy 115, four miles away. Camp and cottage lights, street lamps in the village parking lot, and two restaurants' quiet neons project rays on the lake. The lights penetrate far into the darkness. Amidst this night world, the white crests of breaking waves mirror shore lights, creating a surreal, moving picture, almost resembling a flotilla of elongated canoes that suddenly appear in the blackened lake. Just as quickly they vanish as waves and beach, lake and land, become one. The walker closes his eyes and listens to the waves' gentle, comforting sounds that even in softness drown all other noises in their soothing water music. Content within the scene and with the memories of beach sojourns past and of the generations that came here because of the beach, the lake, and the land, the walker muses and recalls paraphrased words of a traveler from centuries ago.

"We entered Oneida Lake at a splendid time and our sails filled to a light easterly breeze. The lake opened to our view, spreading before us like a sea… its waters gentle, moving, carrying us as they have always carried…."

November 2002: A cooling season, with unique pictures

Autumn is a mercurial time that dramatically alters perspectives along Oneida's periphery. We think of fall in terms of brilliant colors, but other strong pictures can materialize. New York State's Thruway Authority controls Oneida Lake's level and, anticipating spring rains and flooding that might follow, the agency lowers the water every fall. The effects are tremendous. Submerged isles and shoals appear near shore and points elongate far into the lake. Goose Island, a tiny, long-forgotten isle tucked into the southeast corner of Messenger's Bay, emerges and becomes a waterfowl sanctuary once again. As you look westward from Sylvan Beach, the receded waters seemingly elevate Frenchman's and Dunham's Isles. Wantry Island stands at attention south of Constantia, and the entire distant shoreline bisects the horizon.

Oneida's waters along Sylvan and Verona Beaches are shallow and their recession widens these sandy expanses to their pre-Barge Canal stature. Nowhere are the effects of lowering the water more dramatic than here. As the lake recedes, the beaches grow each day until their width exceeds a hundred yards. During summer, little beach remains north and south of the Verona Beach State Park. The lake also submerges the sand north of 24th Avenue in Sylvan Beach. From about mid-November on, however, the East Shore rekindles memories of post card vistas that show vast expanses of sun-bathing utopia. The sands of Sylvan and Verona Beach are on display in their turn-of-the-century heyday, when their aficionados boasted of "five miles of the best bathing beach in the world."

And so, every autumn, the beach returns like a smooth sand carpet spread for someone amidst the scene. This person, walking in a perfect, crisp late fall afternoon, meanders around a labyrinth of tidal-like pools, left by the receding lake. Trapped shiners dart in panic, searching vainly for exits. The walker sees shoe prints…a large pair and a small...avoiding the pools, finding their way along the beach. He envisions a friending couple, enhancing their affinity for the lake and each other.

Nature's wonders adorn the beach environs. Brooks, swelled by autumn's rains, carve crisscrossed patterns. In places these errant rivulets create a beach-long Jackson Pollock painting of the sands as they wind through the maze of pools. The walker meets deer tracks coming from the state park and envisions a buck and doe sneaking to the waterfront for early morn refreshment. Gull and tern footprints form webs on the sand and, in some areas, the beach is a vast checkerboard of imprints and droppings. Hundreds of Canadian Geese rest on the outer sand bars, secure in their distance from shore as they warily eye the walker's every step. A few smaller flocks descend and join the larger goose fraternity. They circle several times, scanning for danger, continually communicating in a cacophonous dialogue with their kin below. Several walleye skins on a fallen, weathered tree trunk remind the walker of evening's anglers who wade along the shore every fall, casting for Oneida's prized fish. Walleyes visit the shallows at night, foraging heavily as winter approaches, terrorizing the schools of minnows that roam there. The walker looks out on Oneida's surface, resting calmly to the west, and imagines the drama of survival that occurs below.

Setting sunlight plays magical games throughout the beachfront panorama. Rays strike downward from darkening western clouds and auras, created as the sun penetrates the graying cover, lend their translucent warmth to an otherwise chilling time. The auras and rays duplicate in the beach pools, dispersing on the ripples, dancing their lighting vitality. Two overturned fishing boats, beached at sand's edge, await winter storage or, better yet, a final trip on Oneida. The walker rests on one of the boats, feeling quiet and at home, perfectly framed within the afternoon's fading beauty.

The lake recedes...its sands change from light tans to deep browns as waters ebb...tracks appear from the now, and from generations past...an ageless sunlight artistry envelops all, as pictures evolve within Oneida's autumn…

The summer of 2003: Nature's warmth embraces Oneida

We call them the "Faulkner trees" and, though William of Mississippi and Yoknapatawpha County never visited Messenger's Bay, he would have rested soundly there, hammocked between the expansive, water-side willows that canopy their summer-quenching shade over lawn and liquid at a blessed, deep southern spot by the bay's shore. Two gatherings of great willow trees, one a family of six, the other eight, replenish life at this spot on the bay as Oneida's waters nourish the trees' twisted, eager roots. The willows soar into Messenger's sky from their massive, adjoining trunks, spreading their webs of limbs and branches as chlorofilled tarpaulins that thrive with a web of bay creatures. Plankton slosh soullessly in the waves that alternately lap, surge against, and pummel the trees. The willows' bases are protected from erosion by large fieldstones, carefully mortared into a kind of flower-potted seawall. Zebra mussels colonize on the stones, cement, and roots. Wave action pushes great quantities of decayed aquatic vegetation ashore, near the trees. This mass of browned organic remnants, almost peat-like in character, coagulates along the shore and, when sprayed on land by heavy seas, attaches everywhere. Invertebrates and tiny frogs find the mire a comfortable habitat. Bait fish such as emerald shiners, gizzard shad, and small perch dimple the water beneath the trees, feeding on insects that fall from overhanging branches. Largemouth bass patrol these shallows, ambushing the baitfish schools from hiding places within dense grass beds. Gulls and terns profit from the bass's misfeeding and, as they dive for crippled prey, their shrill cries give alarming voices to the vital, harsh life-death struggles that fuel Oneida's ecosystem. And, on sweltering summer eves, an orange-red sun seethes into Messenger's gray hazed horizon, backdropping the trees' great drooping branches, suspended in air unmoving, as a Mississippi scene opens night's welcomed cooling time.

The willows oversee a microcosm of Oneida Lake's history. Memories of the lake's nineteenth century logging past live in a small point, beautifully framed by the trees, just to their east. The point, which extends a hundred yards into the lake, rose from stones that early farmers piled atop mammoth foundation rocks that are visible at low water today. Powerful teams of oxen and draft horses, tractors of an agrarian past, muscled the rocks to the lake's shore. As farmers cleared South Shore land, they drew marketable logs to the lake. At the end of the point, loggers lashed the timbers together into what were called "rafts." Steamboats navigated near the point and hitched towing lines to the rafts. Shallow waters that shoaled throughout the length of Messenger's shoreline prevented safe navigation in all other locations. Steamers such as the *Oneida*, *Onondaga*, *Madison*, and *Oswego*, all owned by the Oneida Lake and River Steamboat Company of Brewerton, plied the lake in the mid-nineteenth century. Shallows plagued Oneida's boatmen throughout the lake basin and, to remedy this, people constructed similar points, especially along the North Shore, where logging constituted a more important economic activity.

The willows share Messenger's southern shore with Hamlin's Marina, a unique conglomerate of docks and boat hoists that resembles the kind of facility you might find by the sea. Hamlin's is an "exposed" marina, with no sheltering dikes, and the thirty-some hoists keep boats safe from Oneida's waves. The marina is also a livery and its original fleet consisted of five rugged, wooden "Damon boats," that rented for $2 per day. The family replaced the Damons with heavy, fiberglass Steurys in the 1960s, and now rent Duranautics fishing craft. The Hamlins respect Oneida Lake and believe that people should use the safest possible vessels.

Charlie Hamlin opened the marina in 1950 and operates the business today with his son Charles, Jr. and son-in-law Ron Cook. Born in 1917, Charlie has lived with Messenger's Bay since the Roaring Twenties. Residents speak warmly of "old Charlie" who, they say, "knows the lake like the back of his hand–better than anyone alive." Charlie Hamlin is as genuine an "Oneida Laker" as you can find and his mind holds a mural of memories from eighty-five years on and by the water. Talk with Charlie and the bay's past comes to life. Brushstrokes of conversation paint pictures of his father, Joseph, and uncle, William, who together purchased bayside land in 1907 that included 2,000 feet of lake frontage.

In Charlie's memory lives the Kincaid dairy farm east of the marina, where cows grazed in pastures by the lake until the early 1960s. Through his words we meet Jake Kyser, legendary fish pirate, South Bay hotel owner, and boatman extraordinaire, who bought walleyes from Charlie and his brother, Paul, in the 1930s, and paid the boys the rich Depression price of 20¢ per pound.

We ride the waves with the twenty-five old-timers who fished Messenger's when Charlie arrived, every one of them on the water, every day, before dawn. One of these veterans was Dr. Toyokichi Iyenaga, a retired professor who lived in Sylvan Beach, loved to fish the bay, and devised a way to troll six lines simultaneously.

We walk Messenger's shores with the Geary brothers–Arthur, Emmet, and Robert–who hunted "camp rabbits" that their beagles flushed from beneath cottages on Lewis Point. We learn of Sam Spangler, from the deep South, who could out fish anyone on Oneida Lake and Bill Taylor, the Vernon Downs photographer who perfected a method of "anchor dragging" to attract smallmouth bass.

We chuckle with Ed Denninger, a retired public relations exec for Ringling Brothers who worked at the marina and who, when a customer handed him a $500 bill to pay for a $2.50 boat rental, never batted an eye while opening his wallet and handing the man $497.50 in change. And we experience countless fishing trips, legions of customers, hunting from duck blinds in the wildest weather, and even renting a boat in 1967 to Stan Osterhout and his grandson Jack, who wanted to learn a few of Oneida's secrets.

Messenger's Faulkner trees live with the Hamlins and all the bay's people, framing their movements, reflecting their moods, coloring their seasons. The trees flourish from June's long-lighted solstice days through late August's hazy-sunned hours of impressionist color delight, when hues diffuse from sky and shore to water and waves and children splash and shout on the sand bottomed shallows and teens wave-hop atop their jet skis, laughing with Oneida's high speed fun, and cocktailing campers sip soothing gins and tonics under the trees' protective umbra and anglers troll, drift, and anchor off shore, long-lining, casting, still-fishing within their aquatic realm and kayakers ply slowly, quietly in still mornings' ripples and sailors freshen their glorious genoas and jibs, celebrating the lake's ever-free breezes and a pair of lovers laugh, poke, prod each other as they wade with the bay's creatures, scattering shiners, raising clouds of bottom settled green algae, dragging strands of displaced water weeds around their legs, delighting in an occasional cool feel when their bare feet meet a small spring seeping into the lake, which presses rhythmically wave by wave at them, increasing its grasp as they step deeper to the north as they keep wading, water at their waists, then chests, and the water smells so rich and richer still as the air is saturated with the full, sweet smells of the lake's life and their bodies blend with the weeds, belong with the water now, and the breaking waves becoming gentle rollers as the evening's light lessens, reds to soft pinks, oranges to faint yellows, blues and blue-greens to deep grays as the waters move slower still and the night settles on Messenger's and on the lake's hour and day and season, and the lovers' time, even especially in its beauty, seems to move so fast and terribly fast as they laugh, hug, embrace fleeting joys as the Faulkner trees frame them, the point, the marina, people and all.

And, the next morning, the trees greet another day and the lake and the people…

August 2004: Unveilings abound

Oneida Lake's pictures hang in a fresh, natural gallery that beckons all to walk within. They rest in memories of a friendly, open people for whom the lake means life. The pictures live at Lewis Point in an autumn sunset, the western sun magnificent as its falling rays illuminate brilliant foliage to the east. The pictures evolve on the ice of Big Bay at dawn, the sun emerging over Frenchman's and Dunham's, the dunes of snow appearing like waves frozen at their cresting.

There are pictures in a stretch of shoreline at Bernhard's Bay where forest in its primeval glory meets the water and development has thankfully been forgotten...pictures amidst the grounds of Constantia's Trinity Episcopal Church, its rough-lumbered exterior and weathered graveyard bearing witness to the lake region's early nineteenth century pioneer era...pictures around a boat on the lake on a cool morning in late August, steam rising from every crest and trough over which it glides

There are pictures at the counter of Flo's Diner, near Upper South Bay, with people sipping the famous 10¢ cups of coffee, backgrounded by country and western tunes...underwater in Lakeport Bay, where snorkelers feel the lake flow around their bodies, see droplets of beautifully alive green algae contrast with their pale skin, and find themselves nose to nose with perch, shad, shiners, and bass as they invade weed beds of rain forest density

And there are pictures in discovering Oneida and its people, living with the lake during countless days, sharing it with special friends, and caring for what happens to its uniquely vibrant self.

The gallery of Oneida Lake's pictures awaits you. Enter and feel the lake's boundless life–omnipresent, resplendent, and yours.

– Chapter 3 –

Armies On the Lake

Although General George Pickett and his divisions never charged up North Bay's hill and the flatlands between Lakeport and Bridgeport saw nothing compared to the historic events that transpired on Quebec's Plains of Abraham, the Oneida Lake region witnessed military drama during both the French and Indian Wars and the American Revolution.

Oneida Lake was a part of the great trade and transportation route across New York during the Colonial and Revolutionary Eras. The Fish Creek inlet (now the Barge Canal) at Sylvan Beach and the Oneida River outlet at Brewerton gave the lake military significance because each spot commanded wide views and provided harbors of refuge for bateaux, large flat-bottom boats that were commonly used to transport soldiers. Troops could forage for fish at both places. The Oneida River rifts at Brewerton had been fished by Native Americans since prehistoric times and Fish Creek's salmon "run" provided the Iroquois League's Oneida Nation with abundant sustenance. The British recognized these geographic assets and built the Royal Blockhouse near Fish Creek's mouth in 1758 and Fort Brewerton on the lake's West End in 1759. Part of Fort Brewerton's earthworks exists today and a monument marks the site, on the west side of Route 11 just north of the Oneida River Bridge. A state historic sign, posted on the Barge Canal Bridge at Verona Beach, notes the location of the Royal Blockhouse. The blockhouse was located east of the bridge, where Snug Harbor Marina sits today.

Neither Fort Brewerton nor the Royal Blockhouse approached the size or military importance of Forts Oswego or Stanwix. The Brewerton outpost could comfortably house about one hundred soldiers whereas the blockhouse accommodated around twenty. Other troops often camped near the forts, however, and large numbers passed through both ends of Oneida Lake. Brewerton historian J. Elet Milton was fascinated by military maneuvers that occurred around Oneida Lake and wrote the following synopsis of those events. Milton devoted much of his life to recording Oneida Lake's history. His works are part of the collections of the Brewerton Library and Brewerton Historical Society.

> In French and Indian War times, General Edward Braddock and Massachusetts Governor William Shirley, transferred four companies to Oswego in June 1755. This was followed in July by a New Jersey Regiment, under Colonel Peter Schuyler and, in August, by 1,500 men commanded by Governor Shirley. All of these troops went through the Oneida Lake and River.
>
> In the spring of 1756, Captain Colonel John Bradstreet began transporting supplies and troops in bateaux to Oswego. On one of the return trips from Oswego, the French and Indians surprised his men at what is now called Battle Island, north of Fulton. A lively skirmish occurred.
>
> Colonel Bradstreet and Colonel Marinus Willet, in July of 1758, commanded an army of 3,000 on an expedition through Oneida Lake. The army was en route to attack Fort Frontenac, which is now Kingston, Ontario. The fort was captured.
>
> In June of 1759, Brigadier General John Prideaux and Sir William Johnson, with a force of 2,000 men, set out on bateaux from the head of Oneida Lake (the lake's east end, by Sylvan Beach). Their expedition had two purposes–to capture Fort Niagara and to rebuild Fort Oswego. They passed the Oneida River outlet on June 23 and encamped at Three Rivers.
>
> General Jeffery Amherst commanded an army of 10,000 troops on an expedition against Montreal in 1760. They took the Canadian city. Two very large bateaux were built to ship supplies across the lake. The army returned to Oneida Lake and paused at Fort Brewerton. When it was time to ship the troops across the lake, a large number of New Jersey militia crowded onto one bateaux. During their passage a gale arose. Waves swamped the boat and more than twenty soldiers drowned.

A large force from Colonel Bradstreet's army, on their way to relieve Detroit during Pontiac's War, passed through Oneida Lake in 1764. Later that year, Sir John Johnson led some 550 Indian warriors across the lake.

During the Revolution, British general Barry St. Leger led his army of about 2,100 to attack Fort Stanwix in August of 1777. It is believed that they stopped overnight at Fort Brewerton. A letter, written by St. Leger and sent to General John Burgoyne mentions the "ruined Fort of Brewerton."

On April 20, 1779, a detachment from the Sullivan-Clinton expedition, consisting of about 550 men, crossed Oneida Lake. This expedition's purpose was to destroy the villages and crops of the Iroquois Confederacy, thus limiting the League's military power. They left their boats on the opposite side of the Oneida River from Fort Brewerton. These troops marched to the Onondaga Castle, south of present-day Syracuse, and destroyed the principal Indian villages there. They killed and captured a considerable number of natives. The detachment returned to Fort Brewerton and encamped overnight on Frenchman's Island. The next day they reached Fort Stanwix.

Sir John Johnson led an army of about 1,000 British and Indians over Oneida Lake in his campaign against the Mohawk Valley's settlements in October of 1780. The British also invaded the Mohawk Valley via the lake with some 700 men in 1781.

On the night of February 9, 1783, Colonel Marinus Willet, with 400 men and 120 sleighs, crossed Oneida Lake on the ice. They left their sleighs at old Fort Brewerton and marched along the rivers toward Oswego. The force got disoriented in a large swamp only a short distance from Oswego. They lost the element of surprise and returned to Brewerton. Willet and his soldiers learned, when they reached Fort Stanwix, that the articles of peace with the British had been signed nearly a month previously.

From the foregoing it can be seen that Oneida Lake played no small part in providing a transportation route for large number of troops in the Colonial and Revolutionary Eras. Thus we can see that our lake played a role in shaping the country's early history.

Some notes on the lake's military history merit mentioning:

During the French and Indian Wars, French raiding parties journeyed through Oneida Lake in their campaign of harassment and destruction of British settlements in the Mohawk Valley. While these military actions were minor, compared to army movements, they terrorized the valley's population and put the colonists on continual alert. One of these incidents was cited in *The Papers of Sir William Johnson*. Johnson was the Mohawk Valley land baron and British agent whose diplomatic efforts helped keep most of the Iroquois loyal to the Crown. On October 4, 1758, Major Horatio Gates wrote Johnson, warning him of a French force that had been sighted at North Bay, at the lake's east end. Although Gates does not mention North Bay specifically, his geographic references to "the first bay on the north side of the lake–upon the beach" leave no doubt as to where the French had camped.

To give you the feel of eighteenth-century frontier language, I have not edited the letter. Soldiers were not grammarians and Horatio Gates' writing exhibits an interesting colonial license. "Oineda," for example, meant Oneida.

Oineda Station
4th October 1758

Sir,

I am Commanded by His Excellency Brigadier General Stanwix to acquaint you that Lieu. Tiebout of the New York Regim. is Just return'd from a Scout to the Oineda Lake, and Reports that he Discover'd Yesterday Evening about Five oClock, a Body of about Four Hundred of the Enemy, in ye, the First Bay, upon the North Side of the Oineda Lake, upon the Beach, Marching this way, he is of Oppinion that one Half the Party were Regular troops, as he says he could plainly discover their Uniform. The other Half he takes to be Canadians & Indians. He has further Inform'd the General that the Enemy had not any Packs, or Bagage, from which he concludes them to be either the Advanc'd party of a More Respectable Body, or only A strong Scout Sent to Distress our Working Party's, Cutt off Some of Our Provision Convoys or Some of the Posts or Settlements upon the Mohack River. The General has therefore Commanded me to forward this to you open, that ye Commanding Offrs, at Several Posts and Inhabitants on the Mohawke River, May be prepar'd to give the Enemy a proper Reception.

– Chapter 4 –

Of Feckies, Globules, and an Emetic, Too

Nineteenth century travelers' descriptions of Oneida Lake and its environs provide us with unique images that enhance our understanding of the lake's past. The writings of Francis Adrian Van Der Kemp, DeWitt Clinton, and Alexis de Tocqueville, among others, vividly portray the lake in its wilderness garb, raw and challenging to all who immersed themselves in its richly endowed world. These persons' works received a wide audience and they helped popularize the lake region in an era of settlement and development.

Writings of lesser-known visitors have also contributed to our knowledge of the lake in the 1800s. On January 29, 1811, an Albany newspaper published a letter with a return address "from the interior of the State of New York" at "Three River Point, July 15, 1810." The author had gone through the Oneida Lake region and was eager to communicate his observations.

Our traveler did not have an easy journey and its hardships bothered him. Too low or too high water, fallen trees, stiff winds, bad weather, bears, panthers, mosquitoes, and disease (malaria was common) could make for challenging trips. Turnpikes and canals were still in their infancy in 1810. The writer floated through a canalized portion of Wood Creek near Rome and described the damming method that stored water, which was released to flood the stream and enable boats to navigate its shallows. He makes other interesting comments. The "feckies" he cites were crude torches that Native Americans used for night fishing on Oneida Lake. Whites borrowed the concept and used the torches throughout the nineteenth century, especially for eel spearing, which was primarily a nocturnal endeavor. The author mentions the landlocked Atlantic salmon, once an important Oneida Lake fish that Native Americans and early settlers used for sustenance. Dams on the lake's tributary streams and lumbering practices, that degraded these waters, doomed the salmon. Our writer also states that the lake's fish "are neither very plenty, nor in the greatest state of perfection." He visited Oneida in mid-July, when angling is often poor and summer's warmth causes fish to spoil, if they are not chilled quickly.

Perhaps the letter's most noteworthy comments refer to one of Oneida Lake's famed algae "blooms." The author describes lake water as being "vile," citing the "gelatinous globules" that float on its surface that, if consumed, were "emetic" (something that causes vomiting). Today, many people mistake Oneida's blooms for pollution. Nothing could be farther from the truth. There was certainly no pollution in 1810. The lake's algal celebrations emanate from its bed's natural mineral content, its warm summer temperatures, and the thorough mixing of its waters by wind action. Oneida is relatively shallow for its size (only twenty-two feet deep, on the average) and, situated in its own plain, the lake is vulnerable to strong breezes. The lake's surface can transform from mirrored calm to white capped waves in about fifteen minutes.

That aside, let us now journey from Rome to Three Rivers in the summer of 1810.

> At Rome, after dinner, we entered the locks of Wood Creek. The water from the Mohawk carried us along through, I think, five of them and landed us at dusk, five miles from where we embarked.
>
> I shall say little of the locks. They did their duty well, and their owners may adopt the motto of the bees–sic nos non mater ["thus we, not mother" or "for the good of all"]–the public have been much advantaged, the stockholders little.
>
> The water from the Mohawk was permitted to flow all night, until mounted above the bar gate. And, being overflowing, it was opened and gave water to Wood Creek, without which it would not have been navigable. As it was, we found here and there obstructions, our boat having passed downstream faster

than lock water had flowed. The company had cut through several turns in the creek, by one of which, if I recollect right, we saved seven miles in going through a cut of less than as many chains.

At night we arrived at its mouth, into which flowed the waters of Oneida Lake. The distance we had run during the day was not above sixteen miles, in a straight line. The shore of the lake was low, and the water was shallow to a distance of a mile or more. A family of miserable Indians had drawn their canoe on the beach, and was eating their half-broiled fish, preparatory to their ascending the creek at night, to spear salmon by the light of their feckies. This is a term you are unacquainted with. I will explain it. A hearth is made in the canoe or, which is better, a few old iron hoops are riveted together and fixed on a pole or shaft in the center. They contain pitch pine knots, which are set on fire. The blaze discovers the fish, as the canoe passes up or down the stream, and the spearsman strike them.

The price of salmon in these waters is six pence a pound but, from an Indian, they may be bought at a less price for rum. These fish are from eight to twenty pounds weight. They are not, I think, of the same species with the Connecticut salmon, nor so good. We found an icehouse at this forlorn spot and much better entertainment than, in such a place, could have been expected.

The lake, which is about twenty-one miles long and half as broad, was calm. By sunrise we were on its bosom. The fish, at this season, are neither very plenty nor in the greatest state of perfection. We caught enough, however, to make an excellent chowder, which was eaten at Rotterdam, an establishment belonging to Mr. Scriba of New York, with more pleasure and relish than your friends in New York would of black fish or, those in Philadelphia, sheepshead from Long Branch. Port wine is an excellent ingredient in chowder and equally excellent after eating of it–probatum est ["it's been proven"].

The water of the lake is vile. Its surface is covered with vegetable or animal matter, in the form of gelatinous globules. The boatmen told us that a tumbler of it would prove to be an emetic. We were well and endured the physic. We examined it with a small magnifying glass and we sometimes thought they had life but, whether they were farina, from the trees on the shore, rolled up by the waves into the form of eggs, whether the separated spawn of frogs or fishes or young mosquitoes bursting into life, no man could tell us. Let them float, poor things, till the heat of the sun raises them aloft, or the frost congeals them.

At the outlet of the lake, where a small British fort called Brewerton once reared its mounds against the savages, we arrived at night.

There was bread and milk, and a floor to sleep on. It was as much as could have been expected. The man there was a teacher of a sect. He kept a note book of the defects of his neighbors. Of his own affairs, he kept no account.

There is a rift at the outlet of the lake of some two feet fall. The water is shallow, and the stones might be scraped aside with a turnpike road scraper. The lake would be lowered and, after a few years, the fevers which flit around its present low and swampy shores would cease.

In the first moments, it is true that these light troops of death would be reinforced from the newly drained land, covered with the slime of ages. But thousands of acres might be gained and 'tis better to gain them now, than when the shores are fully populated.

By a winding navigation of eighteen or twenty miles we came to Three River Point. It is a place! Pray heaven I ne'er may see its like again! It was late before we left Fort Brewerton, or we might have arrived at this omnium gatherum ["a gathering of all sorts"] earlier. There was no other house, except at many miles distance and here, in spite of fleas, bugs, filth, and drunken boatmen, we staid all night. This distance of twenty miles by water is lessened to seven by the path on land. I say the path, if path there is, for wagons never rolled their wheels through these impervious woods.

Bill and Janeen Fariel

Levity livens the lakefront at Sylvan Beach, circa 1905.

Ann Hopkins

Writers praised Sylvan Beach's safe, shallow "shelving" beach in nineteenth-century gazeteers. Advertisements characterized it as a beach where "you got tired before you got wet."

Tourists promenade by the Sylvan Beach Midway gate, circa 1900.

Fort Brewerton Historical Society

The Washburn House in Brewerton was a grand inn in the heyday of Oneida Lake tourism. This photo was taken from Denman's Island in the early 1870s.

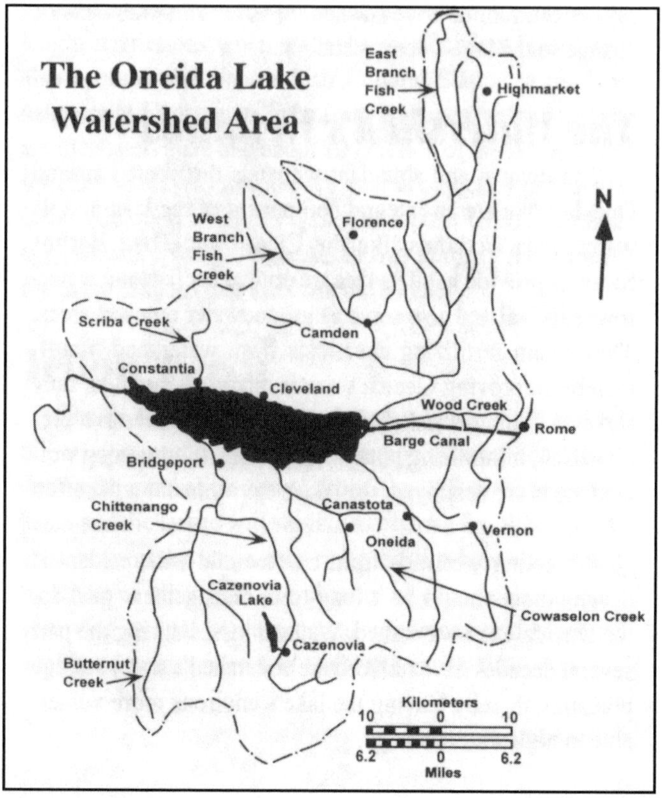

Cornell University

Oneida Lake's watershed reaches north to Tug Hill and south to the Allegheny foothills.

Proud Sylvan Beach anglers pose with their catch of walleyes in the 1880s. This print was restored from a tintype.

Oneida's East Shore beaches in late November – submerged sands and the West End horizon reappear.

Messenger's Bay's Faulkner Trees

Rob Ziegler

A frozen Beach landmark

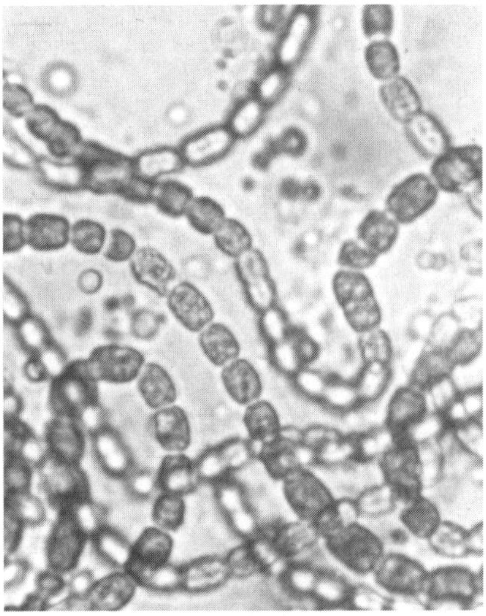

Edward Mills - Cornell University

DeKooning? Picasso? Not quite – a microscopic view of anabaena, a blue green algae common in Oneida Lake.

An algal bloom in Upper South Bay. Oneida Lake's high productivity depends on healthy algal growth at the food web's base.

Roosevelt Wildlife Annals - Cornell University

Emergent vegetation forms "grass islands" in Lower South Bay, around 1925. The isles are vital nurseries for aquatic life. Norcross Point looms in the distance.

– Chapter 5 –

Rafting Logs Across Oneida

Farmers who lived along Oneida Lake's shore during the nineteenth century often needed supplementary income to support their agrarian endeavors. Many of them commercially fished and marketed pike, whitefish, suckers, perch, and eels. Others turned to the forest. Great stands of pine, hemlock, oak, maple, and cherry trees surrounded the lake. Colonial travelers marveled at the potential of the area's primeval forests and the region's early settlers regarded the woods as a lucrative resource.

But getting logs to market proved to be a challenge. Oxen provided power for skidding the timber from the forests to the lake. There, the logs were lashed together into rafts. Steamboats towed the rafts to sawmills. These heavy ships had difficulty navigating close to shore, so farmers and loggers joined to build rock-piled points that extended out fifty yards and more from land. Several of these promontories still exist along the North and South Shores.

Log rafting was a tedious process. Brewerton historian J. Elet Milton explained some of its complexities in this brief history.

> Sawmills were constructed soon after the Oneida Lake country's pioneer settlement. Log rafting, for sawing and for timber, was employed to service those mills near the lake and on the waterways adjacent to it. There were many mills and huge tracts of forest and, as a consequence, the sawmill and rafting businesses became large industries. They were conduct-

ed until the supply of standing timber became very nearly exhausted.

During the earlier days, rafts were poled. Men walked the length of the raft with a long pole held to their shoulder. Many a worker carried a lifetime outline of the callouses that his poles had formed. When the winds were favorable, sails were used to propel the rafts but, as a general rule, rafting was carried on when the waters were still. Later, steamboats were used to tow rafts. This was considerably faster, but by no means rapid. These timber masses offered a tremendous resistance in the water. In the canals' and locks' restricted channels, rafts brought boatmen much annoyance. They were long, heavy, and unwieldy, and non-loggers considered them a nuisance.

The Oneida Lake and River Steamboat Company had four boats, the *Oneida*, *Oswego*, *Madison*, and *Onondaga*. These vessels, the *Teaser*, and other private boats towed many rafts across the lake. The firm of Hopkins and Benson purchased the *Teaser* for this purpose, and for towing canal barges.

Rafts were constructed in this manner. Logs were hauled to the shore, usually in some sheltered cove. Several logs were floated together and two poles were placed across them, one at each end of the raft. Horseshoe-like staples were nailed over the tips of the poles, thus securing the raft and forming a kind of crib. Logs of one specific length were woven into each crib and the rafts were extended to a width of about sixteen feet, which enabled them to fit through the canal system's locks. The cribs were fastened together by means of a "dog and chain," a short piece of chain securely linked with a drive wedge, which was pounded into the logs. These log cribs were sometimes called "bents." On the Saint Lawrence, linked cribs often stretched for one half mile. Oneida Lake's versions were much shorter.

In very still water, it was possible to raft logs within a "boom." This was a series of logs fastened together end to end, forming a huge circle. This enclosure held a jumbled log mass. Calm water was ideal for towing but, if the wind kicked up, the raft was immediately anchored. Waves pushed logs over and under the raft's constraining timbers and loose logs meant lost profit. Anchoring minimized this loss.

Huge log rafts were assembled in Fish Creek, near Sylvan Beach. Many of these were towed east, via the Oneida Lake Canal, to the Erie Canal and nearby sawmills. Oneida Creek was a safe place for raft construction as was Chittenango

Creek, Black Creek, Scriba Creek, and Toad Harbor.

The greatest share of logs were hemlock and pine, as the lakeside forests abounded in these timbers. Hardwoods, however, were often in demand at sawmills. These trees did not float well and their logs were usually placed atop a softwood raft. Sometimes, the hardwood rafts sunk. Rumor has it that one such raft is still lying in the Oneida River bed's mud, about two miles below Brewerton.

Rafts were transported over the lake until well into the 1890s. The last raft that I recall was brought from Constantia to Brewerton and was moored on the Oneida River's north side until it was towed down river by the steamer *Manhattan*. This vessel was originally the Oneida Lake and River Steamboat Company's *Oswego*.

– Chapter 6 –

A Tammany Man at Lower South Bay

The Asa Eastwood Diaries

"I am a Republican. I am for free Territory, free Speech, free Press, freedom in Religion, free everything."
–Asa Eastwood, 1860

When one thinks of the average rural nineteenth century Upstate New Yorker the term "public spirited citizen" may not come to mind. Agricultural toils occupied most people's workdays and rest, neighborly camaraderie, and the occasional church social often dominated what few leisure hours remained. Asa Eastwood, who moved from the New York City area to Lower South Bay in 1817, was a stark contrast to this standard image. Eastwood's interests ranged from national and state political arenas to financial intricacies to world affairs, and from the heated, controversial issues that divided the nation prior to the Civil War to mundane agrarian details. He was elected a delegate to the New York State Constitutional Convention in 1821, representing Onondaga and Oswego Counties. In 1822, his strong Democratic Party leanings earned him the title of "Sagamore" of Tammany Hall, the powerful New York City political organization. National politics brought him into the Republican Party fold in the 1850s. He was elected to the New York State Assembly in November of 1832 and, in addition, broadened his outlook through memberships in the Onondaga County Agricultural Society, the Cicero Temperance Society, and the Salina Literary Society.

His economic life was equally diverse and, besides his farm, he supported his wife, the former Mary Doxsay, and their eleven children, with proceeds from a store in Cicero Corners, from investments in businesses like the Salina Salt Works, and from real estate dealings. Eastwood was a remarkably fit person who enjoyed excellent health. On October 28, 1858, he wrote, "I walked 4 miles to Cicero Corners to attend a Republican meeting." He was then seventy-seven years old.

The Asa Eastwood "Memorandum Books," in the collection of the Syracuse University Library, contain four diary-like journals. Written in a broken, yet easily understood, vernacular, the diaries reflect Eastwood's multiple dimensions. Through his words we view him as a loving family man, an attendee to business's minute transactions, a philosopher, a politician and political analyst, an observer of national and world events, a social commentator and, most importantly from this book's perspective, a chronicler of nineteenth century life in the Oneida Lake region.

With the exceptions of placing commas to separate phrases, and adding comments in brackets, I have not edited the Eastman journals. What follows are a few selected entries that reveal the man and his worlds.

> **1830**–the Snow came about the middle of Jany and from that time till the first of March we had fine sleighing. Weather cold tho not severe some heavy winds which drifted the snow much.
>
> *April 8th*–The Ice cleared out of the Oneida Lake. We have had dry weather for about two weeks, The Ground is drier than it has been before in many years at this time of year.
>
> **1836**–On the 27 Nov last a Small Steamer Came from Baldwinsville into the Oneida Lake went to Roterdam [now called Constantia] and the next day returned and left the Lake. She came up the Oneida River. This was the first Steam Boat that was ever in the Oneida Lake, One is about being Built by a company at Utica to navagate the Lake next Season and most likely more will be on hereafter and at a time not far distant.
>
> Side cut–a canal was finished last fall at the head of the Oneida Lake [at the east end] connecting to it with the Erie Canal so they can now go with Boats from any part of the Lake

to the Erie Canal. [The Side Cut, the first Oneida Lake Canal, linked the Erie Canal at Higginsville with Fish Creek, about one mile east of that river's mouth at what is now Sylvan Beach.]

1842–*March 3*–this day Martin Travers oxen broke into the [Oneida] Lake through the Ice between My House and the upper Island [Dunham's Island], the Ice was about 6 inches thick and Somewhat honey comed, the day was pleasent and warm and they were soon got out without injury

April 1–myself Benjamin & Nelson took into a Common Sised Skiff forty odd bushels of apples & Oats to Carry to E.J. Dennis, when we started the Lake was very Still but when we got about half way a cross the wind began to blow and continued to increase till we got to the Shore, the waves Roled into the boat So She was one eighth full and Soon as we Struck the Shore She nearly filed, if we had have had a short distance further to go we Should have had to through over board our Load or part of it

1847–The Ice cleared out of the Oneida Lake as follows: 1824, March forepart; 1834, 1 April; 1835, 12 April; 1836, 27 April; 1837, 16 April; 1841, 25 April; 1842, 25 March; 1843, 27 April; 1844, 15 April; 1845, 2 April; 1846, 8th April; 1847, 23 April; 1848, 31 March; 1849, 4 April...[Eastman kept this log until 1869, the year prior to his death. That year the ice left on April 20.]

1849–Steam Boat–a steam Boat to tow on the Oneida River was Launched at Brewerton on the first day of November. I was present, She went off very nice. And on the 5th day of Nov an other Steam was launched at the same place, Much larger to tow on the Oneida Lake. She also went off very nice. [These boats belonged to the Oneida Lake and River Steamboat Company, which operated four towing/passenger steamers on the lake–the *Oneida*, *Madison*, *Onondaga*, and *Oswego*.]

1850–I went to Brewerton this morning to go on the Steam Boat, Oneida, to the head of the Lake. we left Brewerton about 9 oC in the Morning went to Rotterdam took in tow there and at Barnards Bay & Cleaveland five Boats loaded with Lumber to Fish Creek at the head of the Lake, where the Side Cut Canal terminates. at this place we broke our rudder, took three hours to mend it. Near Sun down took four Boats in tow for Rotterdam. Stayed there over night. at 7 next morning went without tow to head of Lake. took 4 Boats in tow for Brewerton 2 of them the old Oswego regular line.

1857–*Feb. 20*–This day I enter on my 77th year. I do not recollect of ever being laid up, or confined to the House a day with Sickness in my life, my appetite has always been good, I never had a taste for intoxicating drink, but used some in my younger days for fashion sake, always drank a good deal of tea & coffee, but very weak

May 22–Went to the Island [Frenchman's Island] on Board the *Queen of the Lake*, Capt Norcross, being the first Trip She ever made. She goes at the rate of about 14 miles an hour

1859–*Augt. 27*–They had a Steam Boat Excurtion and Picknick Party Started from South Bay to Cleveland, there was about 200 they had a Band of Music they went a mile from Cleveland to a Grove where they took dinner and returned to the Boat, John & Wife, Nelson and family Lucinda & I went, the Weather was too cool and the wind too heavy to make it realy Pleasant, but they had a pretty good time of it.

Sept. 8–This day I went with a Picknick Party to the [Frenchman's] Island, in the *Oneida* Capt Crandall, We left the Picknick Party at the Island and some of us went in the *Oneida* to the Town fair at Constancia, then returned to the Island took on Board the Party, went to Brewerton down the River a Short distance, then back round the Islands to South Bay, I see Neal and Eben Dennis at the Fair, We had on Board 200 persons including School Children, a fine Band of Music, Good Singing, the day was Beautiful, the Roads good but very durty, there was at the South Bay House 50 Carraiges.

1861–War. On the 12 April the Seceding States Took Fort Sumpere, Major Anderson evacuated it, and they took Possession, the President has caled out 75000 Militia & they are Now 23 April on their way to Washington, they refuse to let them pass through Baltimore, and some Blood wil be shed

April 29–Syracuse, I went Syracuse with Saml, Wife Barb & Nate Van Antwerp, The Flags of Stars & Stripes are flying from Buildings all over the City, the drum & fife is playing, and thousands are on the move towards Washington, which is expected to be attacked by the States that ceded from the Union

May 20–While writing I look out of the window upon that Beautiful sheet of water the Oneida Lake so well supplied with fishes of various kinds suitable for the food of man, when I first saw this Lake more than forty five years ago the scene was Beautiful but never more so that at the present time, while writing the little Birds are warbling on and they sing most Beautiful, Seemingly for my entertainment, they come within a few feet of my elbow, while writing one seemed to say write on old man your time is short, yes but how long is your time, oh this is our heaven we remain here, Just long as we live we have no trouble about a hereafter yet we know Just as much about that thing as you do, we gave a lay down and took a nap first repeating those four little lines which our Mother taught us in our infantile days, and which we never omited to repeat on going to Bed from the time we were three years to the present day, when wheather on the Briny Ocean, in the Battle field or in our own quiet and peceful Rural domicil,

"Now I lay me down to Sleep
I pray the Lord my Soul to keep
If I should die before I wake
I pray the Lord my Soul to take"

Sept 13–Dead we have. Just learned that my grand Son Geo Eastwood was killed in a Battle near Richmond

1863–*July 4*–This day was Celebrated in its usual Style, the weather was nice some of the time a little over cast and drisly it Injured none, lay the dust and made the day Pleasant. The company at the South Bay House and Island was large and quiet, three Steam boats were Plying from Brewerton South Bay and Constantia, I partook of the Pleasures of the day though not without reflections and sadness. I felt as though I was company for no one, a tresspasser in the world far beyond the time alloted to man, while my country is in such trouble and suffering humanity crying for help there will be but little comfort for me this side of the Grave, altho every Body treats me very respectful & kindly

Sept 16–Cranberries, yesterday Saml Nelson and families, also N. Whiting, G. Whiting their families and others went to the Cicero Swamp Cranberying. they are very plenty, they got

10 or 12 Quarts cash, fine day, th 82 degrees

1864–Parralysis on the 24 Dec. last, I had a Stroke of this disease on my right Side which impaired my Speech and I Still talk imperfect and feel stiff in my Joints, But no pain or loss of appetite, But my jaws being weak its difficult to masticate food, I improve very slow

June 18–This day I Sold my Store at Cicero village to Hamilton & Coonley for $800, they $50 down, and are to pay $300 the first of April, then 4 anul instalments, the Contract was down M Sweet and left with him

1865–*April 3*–Richmond was taken this morning

April 14–Went to Syracuse Good Friday, went Thays Meeting, Fulman & Lee Spoke, sat to Liverpool, staid Tus. Back to Syracuse, Staid till Fri, the to Enos, Sat. home, President Lincoln had been Shot dead in the Theatre, at Washingon the Night of the 14 inst, there a Sham funeral in all the Pricipal Cities in the U.S. on Wen 19, all the Buildings in city was draped in morning, a large funeral Prosession, Business all Suspended &c in Syracuse, the murderer is well known to be Booth, a commedian, a Reward of $30,000 for his apprehensuion, afterwards the Reward was increased to $100,000, and Booth was taken but he was Shot dead before taken

May 15–Jeff Davis the Rebbles President has been Captured in Georgia while trying to make his escape, a Reward of one hundred thousand dollars was offered for him, he was taken in female attire in disguise, The Rebellion is now at an End but we Shall keep quite a large Army on duty for Some time to Come

July 4–This day was celebrated in more than its usual good Style, But the doings at Syracuse and elsewhere took many from South Bay and the Island, So there was comparetively but few at those places, I stayed home till after dinner then I took a lonely strol to the Island, the dinner at the Bay and Island was one dollar, my whole expence was 20 cts., much like than in by-gone days when I was good company for every Body, But now a stiff old man left to take Care of myself, But thank God I can do that yet, and the will to do it

1866–*20 Feb*–went to Town meeting, good Sleighing, not very full meeting, the Republican ticket Elected, my Birthday, 85

1 Sept–Picknick, Yesterday I went with a Shool Picknick

party from Deyos dock [In Maple Bay, west of Bridgeport.] in the Steamer *J.W. Norcross*, we went to the [Frenchman's] Island, had an exelent dinner, a Splendid day, fine agreeable company composed of the Children and Inhabitants of the district with a few outsiders of invited guests like myself, in the company there was over twenty of the Eastwood nation, the Company numbers about 115 old and young

1868–*1 June*–Sat by the fire all day

8 July–State Convention at Syracuse very large, Republicans for Grant & Clofax, I was present

10 Augt–Went to Cleveland in Steamer *Henrietta*, Capt Noss, staid all next day, see the work on the Midland Rail Road little Back of village, in the afternon got a Ride to Constantia, looked at large tanery, the village Midland Rail Road little Back of village

1869–*26 March*–We have had 4 month snow and sleighing without any intermision, Sleighing is good on the Land & Lake, the Ice is very black and Solid, 18 inches thick

July–As I am now in my 89th year I don't think that I Shall ever attend an other Excursion Party [to the lake] of any kind, if so this is the last and one of the most pleasant and agreeable ones I ever attended in my life

1870–*15 Feb.*–I went to Town Meeting, being the fifty third one I have attended in this Town unless temporaly absent, I have not the least but I thot it is the last I Shall Ever attend for I am failing quite fast and Shall soon be releived from the troubles of this World of which I have a large Share, I am not aware that I have an ennemy in the World to leave behind

20 Feb–I am 89 to day never been confined to the House with Sickness a day in my life, but for 3 month past I have failed more than in several years before, I am on the down hill of life, I am prepared for the Event, I have seen trouble enough in this world and feel quite sure of a better place in the next life

The last note in Eastwood's diary, penned by one of his children in 1870, stated, "Father died 1/2 past 9 o'clock 25 February, in the morning."

– Chapter 7 –

Captains, Pirates, and Maidens

A Lower South Bay Fantasy

On July 17, 1854, the Syracuse *Daily Standard* published a marvelously descriptive, light-hearted account of a visit to Lower South Bay, a lakeside community that was just beginning to blossom as a fine summer alternative to urban life. The author rejoiced in his Oneida experience, drinking freely from the lake's overflowing cup of imagery, while interspersing his travelogue with jest, exaggeration, and fantasy. He had great fun describing the mid-nineteenth century celebration scene at Lower South Bay. For example, he spoke warmly of the "Humbug Grape Club's" sailboat. This loosely organized South Bay fraternity enjoyed picnics flavored with wines that had been fermented from local grapes, many of which were picked from vines that thrived on Frenchman's and Dunham's Islands. The paper's reporter likened the purple hues of a fading sunset to the effects of Valhalla's gods on a celestial "bender," a unique way of capturing a dramatic lake image. His concluding Ave Santissima is a Latin phrase that translates to "Hail to the sacraments" and we can speculate, with some certainty, that he savored a most unholy form of communion.

> *South Bay, July 13, 1854*–We have just returned from a sail on the *Syracusean*, whose crew and commander consisted of the redoubtable Captain Terpenny. The lake lies calm before me and the sun, just sunk, has left his glittering crown in the west.

The islands look cool and soft through the lingering light, and the musical chime of waves that break leisurely on the beach soothes the soul to a dream-like quiet. Flowing like billows over my heart come memories of other days.

Our friend said to us last night, "How can you endure staying here? What do you find to amuse you in this lonely place?" Why, we have every variety of character around us... histories enough to fill a book as lengthy as any of Dickens, even when he receives a "stipulation" for every extra page. We have a commander whose reputation is worldwide...king of the seas and commander of the goodly fleet that lies spread out before us. Captains and adventurers without numbers daily leave our port, boldly daring wind and wave in search of bass and pleasure. Sturdy and sunburnt sailors gaily sing while washing down the decks of frigates and pleasure boats that crowd our harbor and women, gentle and lovely (in poetry), are not wanting to crown with a star-like radiance the human scenery around us. Even now, across the waters, I catch the glimpse of innumerable white sunbonnets, and angelic notes float on the breeze, informing us in dulcet tones that "The bears came over from Georgetown to see what they could see." Her tender care was visible in the six well-covered baskets that left for the island with the picnic party this afternoon and it was beautiful to mark how four swains, doubtless rude and warlike in their natural state, subsided into the meek docility of youthful kittens while walking each with an arm about the waist of his beloved.

In the fading light I see two graceful forms, clad respectively in red and green, descend to the beach, unmoor a skiff and, with the boldness of hardy mariners, turn their prow to the open sea. A woman's hand is on the oar, yet how unerringly the little boat darts through the waves. Perchance it is sweet Ellen Douglas who guides the bark and she is returning to her island home with the dame beside, rescued from the loneliness of mountain wilds. The fragrant heather will be spread, and the two will sit beneath the star-decked heavens, listening with rapt souls to the weird and thrilling music of the hoary Harper. Or, it may be she has heard her Graham's bugle and therefore it is that for which her skiff bounds over the lake. Ah, there will be a meeting under the whispering boughs, the stars will look down unreprovingly on two loving hearts, and the rapture of sinless souls will mingle with the ceaseless music that gushes up from nature's heart.

But I am aroused by loud and angry cries...away, to the right, two vessels are darting over the waves. One seems to be pursuing the other and every sail is spread to the wind. How eagerly the flying vessel bounds and quivers in her efforts to escape, while her enemy with sportive malice darts now on this side and now on that, in careless security of her victim. It must be a band of bloody pirates who, thus, dare the strength of Uncle Sam's retributive arm! My spirit rises indignantly. What! Shall not a crew of noble men unfurl their sail to the breeze, but these human hawks become their masters–possess their little store, and doom them to a life of sin or an alternative of death? And there may be women, delicately reared, whose friends will mourn for their return. I shuddered. With nervous impatience, I seize a telescope when, to my joy and somewhat to my mortification also, I discover my mistake. The devoted vessel is neither more nor less than the noble *Syracusean*, and Terpenny is flying from rudder to sail and from sail to rudder, with the velocity of a torpedo, his face glowing, his hair streaming to the breeze, his eyes in fine frenzy rolling, in short his whole person bearing indubitable proof of his deliberate and unalterable determination to "go it while he's young." The vessel in his rear is the swift and graceful boat said, by the way, to belong to the "Humbug Grape Club," and it curvets and dances around its more staid *compagnon de voyage* like a young and gay coquette around some bachelor of sixty with a "pocket full of rocks."

By aid of this lens I also discover that my "Lady of the Lake," with her gentle companion would, in all probability, resemble the elegant Dulcinea del Toboso in being accompanied, from culinary associations, by the delicate, yet pungent, aroma of onions.

The shades fall deeper. The islands grow more shadow-like and, in the west, the fiery and crimson hues have faded and the horizon is flecked and streaked with purple. Methinks it is the mighty walls of Valhalla, and the gods have been on a "bender," dashing their celestial wine over pavement, ceiling, and dome. I humbly ask their pardon if my mythology is at fault for, according to my own notions those staunch old Northern Immortals should never have got "elevated" upon anything less than Beserk's ale.

Still closer settle the beautiful shadows over the earth. The west puts on her vesper robe, and the soft breeze sings with the harmonious waves, "Ave Santissima."

– Chapter 8 –

Dinosaurs From the Depths

It was springtime for the Brewerton fishermen, a late April of migrating fish teeming through the creeks, the river, and the lake in their annual spawning rite. It was time for people to emerge from winter's rest and join life's resurgence within Oneida's waterscape. It was net-setting time, when trap, fyke, and gill nets were placed in the traditional fishing spots where the suckers had always run, the pike blanketed the bottom, and the catfish and bullheads awakened from seasonal slumber. It was the spring of 1856 and fish meant survival, income, even a chance to buy luxury for the men of this tough river town, and for the women who partnered with them in their angling. The people knew there would be fish this spring for the smokehouse, salt barrel, stove, and marketplace. After a seemingly eternal winter, the Brewerton folk gave thanks that the season of renewed warmth had finally arrived.

The nets had been set after ice-out on April 20. The fishermen placed them in the shallows of Muskrat and Big Bays and near the mouths of the tiny brooks that fed the lake and whose churning, warmer waters attracted fish. Many nets were lodged where the Oneida River leaves the lake, on the gentle rifts that had been fished by whites and their Native American predecessors for generations. The men hauled their nets each morning, stripped them of fish, patched openings that snapping turtles had ripped in the mesh, and reset the nets. Occasionally an overnight downpour freshened the current and moved the nets slightly but, aside from that, the operation flowed with customary precision. Thirteen hundred pounds of fish were caught during the opening days, a good sign, the fishermen thought, of a record harvest upcoming. Everything progressed smoothly, fishing day after fishing day, until Saturday morning when the men came to the river to check their nets. They paused, puzzled and amazed when they saw that the largest net, originally set in the rifts north of Denman's Island, was now fifty yards upstream. Its red marking buoys, that once stretched across the river, each ten feet from the next, now formed two lines, parallel to the current and barely three feet apart. The net's shore anchor line had vanished. Two men rowed a boat to mid-river and found the errant cord. Tying it to their vessel's stern, they loudly cursed the young hooligans whom they concluded had played cruel games with their net.

Returning toward shore, the men took up the rope's slack. When the line pulled taut, however, the net would not move. The men oared with renewed vigor, but they could not draw that net. In the past, nets had fouled on bottom or in submerged logs, but this one didn't feel snagged. Rather, it seemed to be slowly surging like some bizarre, unknown undertow. What was happening, what was wrong, the men thought.

Quickly adapting, they shouted for another rope. A partner rowed out and they spliced a long, heavy twine to the net line and the boats came ashore. Six men in tandem pulled and strained and slowly the net moved. When it was in the shallows, about thirty feet away, the river water seethed, almost boiled, as the fish surfaced, her body slowly flexing from side to side. The men stopped pulling. They stared in awe and fifteen minutes passed like one. "My God, my God–what a creature!," was all they could say.

The fish was a lake sturgeon. She was six feet eleven inches and weighed 104 pounds. Strange in appearance, powerful in every way.

Lake sturgeons resemble relics from the dinosaurs' era. Adults' rough skins are colored battleship gray, but juveniles are a lighter gray, enlivened by some brown and greenish hues. Unlike most fish, sturgeons' sides are covered with plates, not scales, and these resemble miniature versions of the best a stegosaurus could model. Ten to fourteen plates adorn the fish's top, or dorsal, section and between eight and eleven armor the bottom, or ventral, part. Around twenty-eight plates extend along each of the fish's sides. Sturgeons' eyes seem tiny and threatening and the four food-sensing barbels, which protrude near the mouth, add to their primitive mystique. A powerful, suctioning mouth and a blunt snout enhance the fish's ancient aura. When people, especially children, first view sturgeon in hatchery tanks, their reaction usually ranges from shock to awe.

Sturgeons can be monstrous fish. The largest lake sturgeon ever recorded was subdued in Lake Superior in 1922 and weighed 310 pounds! A sturgeon's longevity is equally impressive. The oldest fish on record, taken from Lake of the Woods, Minnesota, was 154. Many sturgeons live for more than fifty years.

Lake sturgeons feed on the bottom. C. Lavett Smith's *The Inland Fishes of New York State* describes the sturgeons' preferred menu as featuring delicacies such as "mayflies and midge larvae, and other benthic invertebrates including snails, clams, amphipods, and crayfish." To this bill of fare might be added fish eggs, leeches, mollusks, a few plants, and zebra mussels, a 1990s newcomer to New York waters. Sturgeon will, on occasion, spice this diet with small fish such as gizzard shad and sticklebacks, but their suction-designed mouth makes it hard to pursue baitfish.

Because its numbers have dwindled, the lake sturgeon is classified as "endangered" in New York State and anglers must now release any that they catch. Throughout history, ignorance and avarice marred fishermen's attitudes toward sturgeons and this helped precipitate their decline. In *The Freshwater Fishes of Canada*, W.B. Scott and E.J. Crossman discussed reasons for the sturgeons' collapse. "The lake sturgeon was once looked upon with scorn by fishermen," they wrote, "as a worthless nuisance that destroyed gear set for 'valuable fish'... Before 1860 this species, taken incidental to catches of other fishes, was killed and dumped back in the lake, piled up on shore to dry and be burned, fed to pigs, or dug into the earth as fertilizer. It was even stacked like cordwood on the wood dock at Amherstburg, Ontario, and used to fire the boilers of steamboats plying the Detroit River."

When Americans acquired a taste for sturgeon, the fish's marketability soared and an intense commercial fishery blossomed. Sturgeon flesh was smoked or made into delicious fish chowders. Its eggs became prized caviar and tanning transformed its tough skin into a kind of leather. In addition, the fish's swim bladder contained a gelatin-like substance that could be used in the textile, pottery, brewing, and winemaking industries.

When lake sturgeons became valuable, commercial fishermen ravaged them. At one time the annual catch from Lake Erie alone exceeded 5,000,000 pounds. Less than a decade of commercial fishing reduced populations in some lakes by 90%. Lake sturgeons grow and reproduce very slowly. It can take from twelve to thirty-three years for a fish to reach sexual maturity and it only spawns once every four to nine years. The sturgeons that avoided angler harvests could not produce enough young to replenish their kind.

Many biologists believe that Oneida Lake's sturgeons were merely itinerant visitors from Lake Ontario. There is evidence, however, that a small, perhaps non-reproducing, population existed. Oneida Lake offers sturgeons ideal habitat. These fish are bottom feeders and the invertebrate and bivalve smorgasbord that thrives on the lake's bed provides excellent nutrition. Sturgeons prefer to spawn along the shore of rocky islands or in fast running water. Stones form the base for all of Oneida's major islands, the lake contains numerous rock-covered shoals, and the Fish, Chittenango, and Scriba Creek tributaries have rapids.

Stories of incredible fish that towed boats, snapped stout tackle, and inspired classic yarns color the lake's history. In some cases, these fish weren't positively identified as sturgeons. One old-timer told me about an instance when, using heavy, braided line (at least fifty pound test), a steel fishing rod, and a large, rugged bait-casting reel, he hooked a fish near Wantry Island that he couldn't move off the bottom. The behemoth swam toward the lake's channel, slowly pulling fisherman, boat and all. After half an hour, the fish rose to the surface and the angler couldn't believe what he saw. In fact, he didn't know what he saw! He described the fish as appearing "prehistoric," like something you'd see in a "science book." It had a pointed nose, a rough looking hide, and a tail that reminded him of a shark. The fish rolled on the line and broke it. "When it sank back in the lake," recalled the angler, "I felt like I was watching something from another world swim away." He guessed that the fish was over six feet long.

Occasionally, Oneida's anglers emerged victorious in their battles with sturgeons. Listen to this account by Rod Hunter in the Syracuse *Post-Standard* on May 18, 1973:

> Charlie Bronner, of Lakeshore Road, Cicero, is still getting over all the aches and pains of the Oneida Lake catch that he made last Friday and all the attention that he later aroused.
>
> He was merely looking for a nice mess of walleyes, but he ended up with a sturgeon. It was four feet long and its weight was estimated at forty pounds.

The veteran Oneida Lake angler was trolling a Mirro-lure deep in the channel, off Frenchman's Island, when the lure hung up. Then, it moved–slowly. This occurred at about 1 P.M. Two hours later, he finally got the fish off the bottom.

Until then, he figured that he had hooked up with one of Oneida's heavy channel catfish. He couldn't put too much pressure on it because his walleye rig contained only twelve-pound test monofilament line.

When the big fish finally tired and came alongside the boat, Charlie suggested that his fishing buddy net it. The buddy took one look at the prehistoric sturgeon and came up with a couple of suggestions of his own.

They finally subdued the monster and found that the Mirro-lure was hooked around its mouth. Charlie still isn't certain, however, that it really struck at it.

Once ashore, excitement boiled over. Everybody who saw the head of that sturgeon hanging over the side of Bronner's truck wanted to hear all about it. He said that he turned around in Martino's parking area and a traffic jam developed along Lakeshore Road. "People chased me down the road all the way home," he said.

The lucky, or unlucky, angler thinks that maybe the sturgeon came up from Lake Ontario last summer, when all the locks on the canal were opened to get rid of the water raised by Tropical Storm Agnes. It's an academic question for the sturgeon. He already has been smoked by the Bronners and set aside for future feasts.

William R. Daly, of Sherrill, wrote me a letter in 1997 that contained documentation of Oneida Lake's sturgeon population. After serving in the Navy during World War II, Daly returned home and met Dwight Chapman, an Oneida Lake "old timer" who lived on the South Shore. They became angling partners and Chapman, then in his seventies, entertained his new friend with fishing stories from the early twentieth century. Daly's letter narrated one of those fascinating tales.

Dwight was a carpenter, plumber, electrician, dowser, and a "jack-of-all-trades." He had the brains and I had the back, so we made a good team. Dwight originated somewhere around the Messenger's Bay–Lakeport area and he knew a great deal about the lake and its people.

> Dwight used to say that many of the farms along the South Shore were paid for from fish caught at spawning time. The farmers would hitch their teams and tie huge nets to them and then sweep the shore.After drawing the nets, they would put the fish in "democrat" wagons, pack them in ice, and head for the market in Syracuse.
>
> Dwight said that this was an all-day affair. They would leave early in the morning and come home in the dark. He said that they usually got about 10¢ per pound for the fish.
>
> One day they caught a sturgeon that he said was native to Oneida Lake. Dwight said that he had seen a few caught when he was a boy, but they were rare. He said that the sturgeon weighed between forty and fifty pounds. The farmers kept the fish alive and fed in a pen in the lake. One of them went to the Madison Hotel in Oneida and made a deal with the owner. The hotel's proprietor bought the sturgeon and then had a huge viewing tank constructed to show the big fish off to the public.
>
> Apparently the newspaper picked the story up and the day the fish was delivered there was a large crowd gathered at the hotel. Dwight said that several men carefully lifted the fish out of a fishing boat and carried in the back of a wagon.
>
> Several men lifted the docile sturgeon into the barroom and gently lowered it into the glass tank. Dwight recalled that the tank was furnished with running water. The sturgeon seemed to enjoy its new home for a short time. Then all hell broke loose. The fish got agitated and, with one gigantic swat of its tail, "adios amigo" went the tank. Gallons of water, lots of glass, and fifty pounds of fish landed on the barroom floor. This was too much for the owner and he dispatched the sturgeon. It ended up on the hotel's menu.

A few sturgeon populations survived overfishing's ravages. Some even flourished. Wisconsin has an open season for the fish and several Canadian lakes support enough sturgeons to justify commercial fishing. The Saint Lawrence River also contains lake sturgeons. This source provided the biological fuel for New York State's sturgeon restoration program, centered at the Oneida Lake Fish Cultural Station at Constantia. The program was inaugurated on May 11, 1995 when a shipment of 100,000 fertilized sturgeon eggs from Canadian sources on the Saint Lawrence arrived in Constantia. Richard Colesante, former Director of the Station, described his facility's methodology for raising sturgeons:

> Seven days after the eggs were received, tiny sturgeons emerged, resembling white tadpoles. The fish lived off their yolk sacs for about two weeks before beginning to feed. On May 26, approximately 40,000 sturgeon larvae, each one-quarter inch long, were stocked along the North Shore of Oneida Lake, in Frederick and Scriba Creeks. The remaining larvae were kept at the hatchery and fed brine shrimp at five-minute intervals for twenty-four hours per day, using automatic feeders.
>
> When the sturgeon fingerlings were about three inches long, in late June, they were weaned from a brine shrimp diet to a formulated diet, like that fed to trout. As they grew, they were fed this artificial food at the same frequency as brine shrimp, though in greater amounts. The Oneida Hatchery sturgeon grew faster than anyone could have imagined. By September, the fingerlings were ten inches long. Five thousand were stocked into Oneida Lake at that point.

Positive results from Oneida's sturgeon stocking program are already surfacing. Every summer, researchers from Cornell University's Shackelton Point Field Station net fish as a part of their aquatic census program. Anthony Van De Valk, a Station biologist, reported that fifty-one sturgeons were netted in 1998, ninety-nine in 2000, and forty-eight in 2001. The largest fish recorded in 2001 measured forty inches and weighed twenty-two pounds! The number of sturgeons examined in 2000 was higher because researchers set more nets during that year. All fish were returned unharmed to the lake. These are excellent returns, exceeding many expectations. In addition, anglers have been catching sturgeons. A forty pound, fifty-two inch fish was boated and released by Cornell University Biologist Tom Brooking and fishing charter Captain Ray Brown during the spring of 2003.

Today, zebra mussels infest Oneida Lake. They feed on algae, and this feeding has brought instability to the lake's ecosystem. Sturgeons are proven zebra connoisseurs and, hopefully, their renaissance may help control this troublesome bivalve. Whatever the fish's effects, its Oneida Lake rebirth is a heartening event. In this era of environmental problems, it's encouraging to know that a species that once hovered on the brink of extinction can again become a viable part of a thriving New York State fishery.

And perhaps, in another fifty years, storytellers will revel in superlative tales of anglers' memorable encounters with Oneida Lake's "dinosaurs from the depths."

– Chapter 9 –

Cleveland Style Patriotism

Though the American Civil War (1861–1865) was fought primarily in the distant South, its events profoundly influenced the Oneida Lake region. Recruits from lakeside communities swelled the Union's ranks and some, like David and James Johnston of Toad Harbor, both of whom fought with Company H of the 147th New York Volunteers, made the supreme sacrifice for the Northern cause.

After the war, veterans of the Grand Army of the Republic (the official name for the Union Army) organized "posts" in lakeside communities. Forty-three ex-Northern soldiers started the H.L. Farmer Post 16 G.A.R., in Cleveland in 1880, and forty-five former Constantia bluecoats began the D.B. Lewis Post that same year. Many Grand Army of the Republic veterans are buried in cemeteries near the lake. Thomas Deans, the last member of the Cleveland G.A.R. Post who was a carpenter, undertaker, and storekeeper in that village, passed away in 1935.

Political demonstrations provided local citizenry with a chance to flaunt their patriotism during the war. One such event was held in Cleveland in June of 1861, two months after the Confederate army's bombardment of Fort Sumter in Charleston, South Carolina, ignited the conflict. The community's vibrant nationalism, which reflected Northern zeal for the "noble cause" in the war's early stages, was articulated in this lively account from a local paper, authored by a person who used the pseudonym "Constitution."

Cleveland, Oswego County, June 29, 1861

Sirs–I hasten to inform you that we had a grand Union flag raising in our village today. In accordance with previous arrangements, the Union men of the Town of Constantia and the village of Cleveland, met here today and raised a fine Union Liberty Pole nearly one hundred feet in length, and on which now most majestically floats a grand National flag, thirty feet long and 20 feet wide. The mere display of a national flag of the above dimensions is, of course at this time, of no unusual occurrence, but when I inform you that this same flag is at least fifty years old, and was used by Union-loving men in the War of 1812 (when our country was invaded by a foreign foe) to cheer the Union men and supporters of democratic liberty in that successful struggle for National rights and personal protection, then assailed by the strongest military government in Europe, you must admit that we have just cause to feel patriotic over this ancient relic of the past, and most appropriate object of the present. Though half a century has transpired since this revered flag first greeted the vision of the early pioneers of Oswego County, the colors of this flag remain almost as perfect as when first it appeared in its original hues.

George Scriba, the great land proprietor of Oswego County fifty years ago, purchased this flag at a cost of $100, and unfurled to the breeze this time-honored ensign at Constantia, on the North Shore of Oneida Lake, and by which he then pledged himself, in union with his friends, to stand by and defend it in honor of this country, the land of his adoption and home of his choice. Thanks go to his time-honored lineal descendants, who kept this honored memento of the past, a sort of heirloom of the Scriba family, and again dedicated to the service of Constitutional liberty and civil equality by the citizens of Constantia and Cleveland. Much credit is due to those individuals who, by their untiring efforts, have succeeded in gracing our lakeshore village with this emblem of a previous generation, and which they honored and defended. Much praise is justly due to our worthy townsman Israel Morse, through whose influence this appropriated flag was obtained.

After the stars and stripes were seen to wave from the masthead of this magnificent pole, a National Salute was given. Henry Garber, Esq., was then loudly called for and he came forward and addressed the citizens assembled in an appropriate and patriotic speech. He forcibly and most conclusively showed the great necessity of sustaining the Constitution and the laws of our country, and in aiding the Lincoln administration in supporting our government in all Constitutional acts. He urged them to stand by and defend the honor of our National flag, the polar star of democratic liberty, adopted in this last great experiment of self-government in the western hemisphere.

The whole civilized world had looked at us in bewildered astonishment, at our wonderful success as a nation, while we were united and happy, under the administration of a Washington, an Adams, a Jefferson, a Jackson, and others, and the nations of Europe, now struggling for popular liberty, are watching us with burning anxiety, eager to know if we intend to allow the lawless politician, the political demagogue and disunionist, to arrest from our possession the great experiment of Republican institutions, and blot from the list of nations this world-respected Republic. Dishonest politicians, political demagogues, and Southern fire-eaters had now run our National Ship upon those breakers pointed out to us by Washington in his farewell address, and our craft is now boarded by Southern pirates and Northern robbers, and already ten states are thrown overboard.

Mr. Garber said he trusted that there were conservative elements enough in our country to yet save it from the vortex to which it was fast drifting, but it required immediate and energetic action by all the friends of law and order. We must let rebels and disorganizers of national laws, and constitutional rights, know that the law, which governs and protects us, must govern and shall protect them, and will also mete out to them the rewards to the disobedient and disloyal, that disloyalty merits. Mr. Garber differed, he said, with the lamented Stephen A. Douglas, in one particular. Douglas said he was for his country, right or wrong. Mr. Garber said he was for his country only in the right, for he knew she never could be wrong. Politicians may be wrong, and political demagogues are always so, but this country never could be otherwise than right.

He said he never could willingly consent to allow the stars of our Confederacy to be any less, or see the flag of our country insulted without making an effort to avenge the insult. Our country's flag had, impressed upon its folds the principles of equality, equal rights to every citizen, equal rights to every state, and equal protection to all without discrimination of

> interests. Constitutional liberty for free men, free speech, and free press, and the noble equality of citizenship, with all its concomitant privileges, ought never to be abridged. Palsied be the hand, and cursed be the soul of him that attempts to curtail this noble right, this God-given blessing, secured and purchased by the blood and treasure of the founders of this once-happy and prosperous nation, and most carefully intended to be guarded by constitutional enactments and guarantees. Mr. Garber closed his remarks after saying that but one object should now be the desire of every friend of humanity in our common country, that was to make the defense of the Constitution and laws a common cause, and to stand by the honor of our flag. In quoting the following lines of appropriate poetry, he recited:
>
> *Our Flag*
>
> In battle storms, its triumphs wave,
> It cheers our sons, and nerves the brave,
> Our country's emblem, a freeman's choice,
> And entitles all to equal voice.
>
> Then stand by your flag, of varied hue,
> Defend its stars, encased in blue,
> Protect this flag, that waves so high,
> Fight for its rights until you die.
>
> Mr. John Vandenburg, Esq., followed Mr. Garber in an able and effective speech, doing ample justice to the subject and the occasion.
>
> The meeting then adjourned with three soul-stirring cheers–for the flag, our country, and the speakers.

A touch of irony tints the Scriba family's flag contribution to this patriotic spectacle. George Scriba purchased over half a million acres of land, roughly between the North Shore of Oneida Lake and Lake Ontario, in the 1790s. He invested his life's fortune in that territory, speculating that an early nineteenth century land boom would bring him prosperity. This never occurred. A variety of factors kept sales down. The War of 1812, that Scriba so strongly backed, was one of them. His land was on the New York frontier and British military activity discouraged major settlement. Scriba was a fervent patriot, but the war he so strongly supported helped engender his economic failure.

Fort Brewerton Historical Society

The *Oswego* was one of four log-towing steamers operated by the Oneida Lake and River Steamboat Company. Captain Henry Shafer, on the far right of the upper deck, piloted the ship.

Ann Hopkins

A Constantia sawmill around 1900. The teams of horses towed logs from the lake (in the background) to the factory.

Fort Brewerton Historical Society

The Asa Eastwood house in the latter 1800s. Sylvester Eastwood, Asa's grandson, lived there when this photo was taken. The home's right wing was built in 1817.

Asa Eastwood's house still stands on Lakeshore Road in the Town of Cicero. This historic structure is currently being restored.

Fort Brewerton Historical Society

William Dunham built the Anglers' Club, Lower South Bay's grandest hotel, in 1901. This magnificent inn burned in 1908.

Henry Crownhart's Hotel, located on Lower South Bay's east shore, was a popular destination throughout the 1910s.

Oneida Lake Association

Duck hunters stand proudly in their sailboat in Lower South Bay, 1898. The bass drum in the vessel to the rear was used to call waterfowl.

Onondaga Historical Association

Successful anglers sort their catch on a Lower South Bay dock, 1889. Frenchman's Island backdrops the scene.

Captain Ray Brown

Oneida Lake's sturgeon restoration project has been extremely successful. Cornell biologist Tom Brooking hefts a fifty-one-inch, forty-pound fish that he caught in Messenger's Bay in June 2003. Lake sturgeons are protected and the fish was released unharmed.

Ann Hopkins

Patriotism on parade in Cleveland. Army veterans march down Main Street, around 1908.

The Deans building, made of corrugated iron, was used as Cleveland's village hall for years. Thomas Deans, who built the structure, was a businessman and justice of the peace. He was a charter member of Cleveland's H.L. Farmer Post, Grand Army of the Republic (G.A.R.).

Corky Winn

North Shore G.A.R. veterans prospered after the war. George Clough, pictured by his Federal style home east of Constantia, was a Lieutenant in the 5th New York Volunteer Cavalry. The Clough home later became Bishop's Restaurant.

– Chapter 10 –

Perfectionists in Paradise

America's nineteenth century industrial revolution brought dramatic changes to the country's social, political, and moral fabrics. Urbanization accelerated at a breakneck pace, trusts and monopolies wielded vast governmental clout, and societal upheavals inspired philosophers, economists, and even religious theorists to pose alternatives to capitalism's creations. In Indiana, Robert Owen created his "New Harmony" model of utopian socialism. Marxism, imported from Europe, found followings among radical labor groups. And, amidst a bucolic setting near Sherrill in western Oneida County, John Humphrey Noyes and his followers created the "Oneida Community," an experiment in living based on Noyes' concepts of "perfectionism" and "Bible communism."

The Oneida Community was started in 1849 and lasted until outside pressures and internal dissent caused its dissolution in 1879. The group's unconventional ideas (for example, marriages didn't exist, couples wanting to have children had to have the approval of Community elders, and babies were raised in a common nursery) alienated many of its Upstate neighbors and helped bring about its demise. Economically, however, the community's silver plating and animal trap manufacturing businesses thrived. After Oneida disbanded, some Community leaders founded Oneida Limited, Inc., a company that became a pillar of the region's economy and one of America's leading makers of silverware.

Community people were a bright, sensitive, life-loving folk who actively pursued intellectual enrichment. One of their greatest joys was visiting the Sylvan Beach area, where they built a small retreat cottage called "Joppa" in 1873. Oneida Lake's East Shore was then largely undeveloped. Vast groves of stately oaks and pines rose from the sandy soil. Waterfowl and fish abounded to such a degree that conservation was largely ignored. The Oswego-Midland Railroad (later called the Ontario and Western) operated a station at "Fish Creek," a hamlet located about one mile east of contemporary Sylvan Beach (This settlement was sometimes referred to by the railroading label "Sylvan Junction."). Community members could board Midland trains at the Oneida Castle Station and, after arriving at the Fish Creek depot, enjoy a leisurely cruise or pastoral stroll to their Walden.

To history's benefit, some Oneida Community members loved to write and wrote with a descriptive flair that vividly captured images of life along Oneida Lake's East Shore in the days just prior to the area's initial development. The following stories, originally published in the Oneida Community *Circular*, exemplify the joie de vivre that characterized Community prose.

Our first story, "A Summer Jaunt," details an outdoor sporting experience shared by four Community members. The "Mr. S." cited by the author was James D. Spencer, Sylvan Beach's founder. Spencer was a multi-faceted businessperson–real estate, sand marketing, store keeping, and hotel management (he owned the "Spencer House" mentioned in the article) were among his interests. He sold the Joppa property to the Community and became the perfectionists' close friend.

A SUMMER JAUNT
August 16, 1872
Fish Creek Station

Dear Circular–Fish Creek is a station on the Midland near the head of Oneida Lake, and makes a convenient stopping-place for persons intending to recreate at the largest of New York's inland lakes. Here, in the cozy sitting room of the Spencer House, is seated your correspondent (one of a party of four), just in from a few days of sport with the fishing rod and fowling piece. Our party, by the way, includes several old contributors to your columns, and among them "Woodcraft," who may gather from his experience here material for a new series of his sketches. In the mean time, a short account of our trip may be acceptable.

We purposed setting out for the lake on the morning of Tuesday the 13th instead, but the unpropitious aspect of the weather, with other reasons, had almost induced us to postpone the expedition when, fortunately at the eleventh hour, the clouds broke away and everything seemed favorable. Our kit was soon packed and, at half-past 10 A.M., we were off. A half hour's ride through the flat country bordering on the lake brought us to Fish Creek, where we left the cars. A walk of a mile and we stood on the lakeshore.

To one who does not live near the sea or a large body of water, a fresh sight of it always brings a thrill. As we gazed over the wide expanse extending in one direction farther than the eye could reach, we realized how easily one could learn to love the "bright, blue sea."

Procuring a boat of Mr. S., we crossed the mouth of Fish Creek and, rowing down the beach a quarter of a mile, selected a site for our camp, a shady grass plot near the water. Our tent was soon pitched and everything in order. We had scarcely got well encamped when a shower came up but, snug in our tent, we suffered no serious inconvenience from the rain. In a short time the clouds broke away and, in the afternoon, three of us went up the creek in our boat with a view of trying our luck at "trolling." A word in regard to this art. In fishing by means of a troll, the hook is left bare, an artificial bait called a "spoon" being arranged above the hook. A great length of line, one hundred feet or more, is used, which is allowed to run out to stern. The boat is kept in motion, which serves to keep the hook near the surface. By the initiated, "trolling" is considered as a very fascinating and successful mode of fishing.

But our efforts in this line were not very encouraging. It is possible our apparatus was at fault. We did not for a moment entertain the idea that our lack of success resulted from want of skill on our part. As we floated quietly down stream on our return, H. shot at and wounded a bittern, a bird nearly the size of a crane, but it escaped into the bushes that lined the bank. It was quite dark ere we got back to camp and our supper was cooked by the ruddy glow of the campfire.

On the following morning our three Nimrods rose bright and early, on the alert for game. C., in particular, who was very anxious to get a shot at an eagle, would watch by the hour beneath some "eagle tree" to get a chance at one. These eagle trees are dead trees on the beach frequented by these birds, who live upon fish. Here they watch for prey, and here return when their booty is secured. The sand beneath is covered with fish bones, the debris of their banquets. C.'s patience was at length rewarded. After wounding one or two, he finally dropped one fine fellow. Unfortunately, the bird lodged high up in the branches of a pine and could not be secured. We were quite surprised to find this inland lake frequented by eagles in such numbers. We had heretofore supposed this "emblematic bird" to be confined mainly to his home "by the wild waves foam," but we not infrequently saw three or four of these bald eagles at once, winging their way o'er lake and shore. Much to the discredit of this "glorious bird," it is said that he obtains his living for the most part by dishonorable means. That, instead of securing fish himself, he will watch until a crane or other bird who lives upon fish, has seized and is bearing off its prey. Then he gives chase. His superior might soon enables him to overtake his victim who, closely pressed, drops its booty. His object attained, the eagle descends with a swoop, seizes the fish ere it reaches the water, and bears it off in ignominious triumph.

On the ensuing forenoon we tried our luck at fishing in the lake. Lake fishing is somewhat complicated by the fact that the fish which abound there, the perch, run in schools. If you do not happen to strike one of these schools you may fish for hours without a nibble. It was not our luck to hit upon a school and, after a few hours of well-nigh fruitless labor, we returned to camp. In the evening, as we were snugly ensconced and ready for sleep, a storm came upon us which put our canvas tent to a severer test than it had yet experienced. In fact, we soon found it was no protection at all against the fury of the rain. Our prospects for a night's rest seemed for the moment somewhat dubious, but the storm soon passed over. A dry blanket was spread down and the night was passed with no serious discomfort.

At noon the next day B. was obliged to return home, but the down train brought us J., with additional supplies and a fine enthusiasm for fishing. Kindled by his zeal and example, we returned to fishing with renewed ardor and, thereafter, our table at least was well supplied. In the afternoon, the wind freshened, rolling in the waves in fine style, and we enjoyed an exhilarating bath in the surf. On the following morning, though, it did not rain and there was a peculiar hush in the atmosphere, which denoted an approaching storm. We had decided to return home that night and, as at noon rain was evidently close at hand, we concluded to break up camp immediately, return to the depot, and there await the train due about 7 p.m. Accordingly, one of S.'s fine teams was engaged to carry us and our traps to the station where we arrived, just in time to escape the storm.

Our trip is done, and if our little experience in thus living close to primitive Nature has had no other effect it has, at least, increased our appreciation of the vicissitudes and hardships of a woodman's life. To us there seems to be a kind of heroism appertaining to those hardy sons of the forest whose lives are devoted to settling and subduing the wilderness and, thus, making room for the advance of civilization.

But now the shrill whistle announces the train at hand. Good-bye ye denizens of the lake and shore. In one short hour we shall be among the well-known scenes and surrounded by familiar faces of home.

Contemporary ice fishing, with its fish finders, graphite jigging rods, power augers, and ATV-snowmobile transportation, presents a stark contrast to nineteenth century methodology. Primitive, home-crafted tip-ups, baited with minnows, were the primary means for catching fish through Oneida's icecap then. Holes were laboriously axed through the ice and anglers trudged through snowdrifts to reach the fishing grounds. James D. Spencer introduced John Humphrey Noyes and several other Community members to this winter pastime in December of 1873. The *Circular* dutifully recorded their adventure.

The Tip-Up Races

One of our fishing enthusiasts, writing on December 14, said:

Last week was the great time of the tip-up races and I assure you that horse racing, donkey racing, steeple racing, hurdle racing, and all other popular methods of running man or beast, are not to be compared for fun and excitement with a good lively tip-up race. But I must first tell you what a tip-up is.

Take a strip of a long shingle an inch or two wide with a notch at one end and a half-inch hole near the middle. Hitch a line with hook and sinker to the notch and run a willow rod two feet long through the hole, and you have all the essentials of a tip-top tip-up. With this machine go out on the ice till, by sounding here and there, you find water eighteen feet deep.

There, make a hole six or eight inches in diameter, bait your hook with a minnow, *i.e.* a small live fish, and drop him down the hole nearly to the bottom. Place the tip-up so that the end of the shingle from which the line is suspended will be over the hole. The shingle should be nearly balanced on its willow axis, but the free end should outweigh the line-end just enough to keep down on the ice so long as there is no extra weight on the hook. Then, when a fish down below takes the bait, up goes the free end, and either stands perpendicular or bobs about, thus giving notice as far as it can be seen that a fish is ready to be hauled up. The bob-end should be painted black, so as to contrast with the snow and ice and, thus, more surely attract attention.

Suppose now that we have fifty such tip-ups set at as many holes, arranged in two parallel lines, with a distance of two rods from hole to hole, making the double line fifty rods long.

Now for a specimen of actual racing.

Last Thursday morning, at the first glimmer of daylight, five of us started for the fishing station already equipped with tip-ups, half a mile out on the lake, west of our lodge at Joppa. We took along plenty of live bait in pails and a hand sled to bring home fish. On reaching the lines, our first business was to re-bait the hooks. At the first glance along the rows of tip-ups we discovered that two of them had their black tails sticking up. These we took in hand at once and, on raising the lines, we hauled out on one of them a two-pound pike, and on the other a three pound lawyer. The "lawyer" is the name lake people give, for what reason I cannot say, to a fish that is very ill looking and generally rejected as worthless, though some folks eat it and speak well of it. In shape it is a great polliwog, and its color is dappled brown and white, like that of a frog or lizard. We caught a good many of them, first and last, and left them on the ice as nuisances. They finally found a customer. A man who liked them drew off a sled load and salted them down for family use.

After raising all the hooks and putting fresh bait on those that needed it, we took our stations at equal distances along the lines and the sport began. Bear in mind that, whenever a tip-up began to bob and stick up its tail, we were all under the greatest inducement to get to it as soon as possible, not only from natural eagerness for the sport of hauling out fish, but because there was danger of losing the chance by delay, as the fish generally got away with the bait if left alone for a minute or two.

In order to give any idea of the fun, I must here abandon systematic writing and proceed in a helter-skelter style.

All hands watching. First bob on the extreme right. Spencer from the extreme left shouts, "Tip-up behind you, Wood!" Wood turns and runs. Pitt at the center shouts back, "Tip-up behind you, Spencer!" Spencer turns and runs but, casting an eye backward, he shouts, "Two tip-ups to your left, Pitt!" Pitt whirls and makes a dash at the first. Noyes rushes in for the second. Bradley takes a long run down the line for a tip-up that he discovers bobbing on Pitt's beat. Pike, perch, and lawyers are flopping on the ice. Hooks baited again in a hurry! Eyes meanwhile darting hither and yon. Tip-ups bobbing in all directions! All hands shouting and all hands running. Bradley's heels fly up and he comes down easy. Noyes hauls a big pike half out of the water and then sees him disappear. So we go on hour after hour, watching, shouting, running, hauling, and baiting, with all variations of luck and disaster and infinite laughter. I, for one, got so tired running on the slippery ice that, after the first hour, I wouldn't go out of a walk for all the fish in the lake–because I couldn't.

At the close of our forenoon's work we had a fine sled full of fish–about sixty pounds of pike and half as many of perch, leaving a good supply of lawyers for our friend who is fond of them.

After a day or two of this fun came warm weather and rain, weakening the ice and threatening to break it up.

The Oneida Community's Joppa adventures ended when the group dissolved in 1879. It is doubtful, however, that Community adherents would have visited the Sylvan Beach area much longer. In the late 1870s more and more Upstaters discovered Oneida Lake's East Shore's charms. James D. Spencer started selling Sylvan Beach cottage lots and his son Lyman built the "Forest Home," the village's first commercial hotel. Soon, thousands would come to frequent the Midway's Carnival Park, to frolic with train loads of hop growers at their annual picnic, and to stroll along what was billed as being "four miles of the best bathing beach in the world." The days of blissful perfectionist isolation, of eagle hunts, tip-up races, experiments with trolling, and of an almost child-like blending with a yet-unspoiled scene, were gone forever.

– Chapter 11 –

Tales From the North Shore

Joni Hines was President of the Cleveland Historical Society when she sent me copies of several "war stories" that local residents had submitted to her organization. These brief tales captured the experiences of Oneida Lake's people on both the military and home fronts during our nation's conflicts. Laurence Cottet was the society's source for the account that follows. A renowned storyteller, Cottet was Cleveland's unofficial historian for many years. He operated the Como Candle Company in the village prior to entering the service during World War II. After his discharge, he worked for Revere Copper and Brass in Rome. Locals regularly sought his answers to questions about North Shore history and his fascinating tales enriched many a meeting and conversation.

Laurence Cottet's family remembered how he told the following story and they shared it with Ms. Hines and the historical society.

The Joys of Armistice

November 11, 1918. A little after 11 o'clock, in the old Cleveland School, the principal suddenly entered our room and, laughing and crying simultaneously, threw her arms around our teacher and danced around the room. We children looked up, completely amazed. What was going on? Teachers and principals in those days never showed emotion. They were prim and proper, unsmiling and strict. Then the principal told us that World War I had ended and that the Germans had surrendered. We were sent home and told to return to the schoolyard at 2:00 p.m. It was a sunny, warm day, so unusual for November.

Promptly at two, all 300 students and teachers assembled. A number of old Civil War soldiers joined us. We formed a parade. Mr. Thomas Deans, most vigorous of the veterans, led the parade. I think it made those old soldiers feel very important. They were needed again and their service was being recognized. When Mr. Deans passed away in 1935, he was the last member of Cleveland's Grand Army of the Republic veterans' post.

The parade was very regimented. We were sharply reprimanded if we got out of step or line. Slowly, we wound our way around the village's streets.

An amazing thing happened. As we passed each house, the residents came out and joined the parade. Even aged grandparents got in step. Our line was a mile long. There were no spectators because everyone in the village was marching!

It was a solemn occasion. No bells were rung. No one shouted. A very tired group of marchers assembled at the village dock when the parade ended.

A team of horses drew a piano to the dock. We sang all the patriotic war songs, and we sang with spirit. It was such a rich, good feeling. Father J.B. Mertens, a priest at Saint Mary's Church for twenty-five years, spoke. He was a native of Belgium and he told how his homeland was now free. He spoke for an hour and it was a very emotional speech.

The big event occurred after Father Mertens ended. A huge bonfire was lit and an effigy of the German Kaiser was thrown into the blaze. We all cheered and shouted! We returned home believing that this was the last war. Peace had come and would reign forever.

An article about Constantia, published in the *Syracuse Herald* on April 6, 1919, contained these entertaining pieces that captured some of that village's early twentieth century flair. We can view a small community of industrious, yet entertaining, people, through the author's prose. Post-World War I Constantia reflected national trends, such as prohibition and the dominance of the Republican Party.

The Anchoring Wager

John Barnett conducts Constantia's new Vanderbilt Hotel, where once stood the famous King Tavern. Mr. Barnett is contemplating managing the Pontiac in Oswego. Constantia folks dread to see him go. But there is one in this place, who has not committed himself, but who it is rumored would just as soon have John go as to remain. That is Garry Pickett, the ex-constable and famous Oneida Lake boatman. The villagers relate that Mr. Barnett took $10 from Mr. Pickett by unfair means.

A large anchor rests on Vanderbilt's lawn. One summer afternoon, a few years ago, the "boys" were seated on the hotel steps, visiting. Mr. Barnett offered to bet $10 that he could place the anchor on his shoulder, carry it to the icehouse, and throw it upon the roof. Mr. Pickett who loves to wager, lost no time covering the bet. Garry knew the anchor weighed 500 pounds, for he used it on a steamboat years ago. Mr. Barnett was to perform this act at 9 p.m. on July 4.

The story goes that, in the meantime, Mr. Barnett and the village cabinetmaker, A.A. Beardsley, made an anchor, using basswood, identical to the iron anchor. It is said that, during the night of the third of July, Barnett and Beardsley removed the iron anchor to the hotel's barn and placed it under lock and key. Then, they substituted the basswood anchor.

On the Fourth of July's evening, a large crowd congregated at the hotel to witness the feat. Garry explained what Mr. Barnett was to do and, if he accomplished the feat, the stakeholder, Supervisor W.A. Beebe, was to pay him the $10 and no questions would be asked. John seconded Mr. Pickett's remarks. Then, John took hold of the anchor. At this moment, Mrs. Barnett appeared on the scene and pleaded with her husband not to attempt the impossible. Mr. Barnett, of course, would not listen to her entreaties.

John made several attempts to raise the anchor, but to no avail. Garry laughed. John got his second wind, took hold of the anchor, and slowly placed it upon his shoulder. The crowd cheered. He walked to the icehouse, his knees bending. The crowd followed. When he reached the icehouse, Mr. Barnett placed the anchor on the ground, rested a minute, took hold of it, and hurled it to the roof of the building.

Then something unexpected happened. The anchor broke and a piece of it fell to the ground! Garry picked it up and cried,

"Fake! Fake!"

The stakeholder paid Mr. Barnett his winnings. He kept the $10 for several weeks and then gave it to Mr. Pickett, telling him that he was certainly no judge of anchors. Some time after that, John gave Garry the anchor. It was repaired and placed in the Scriba Masonic Lodge. Mr. Pickett has been active in that lodge for years.

Villagers say that it cost Mr. Barnett $15 to build the basswood anchor–a somewhat expensive, but worthwhile, joke.

A Few Constantia Notables

Many interesting people call Constantia "home." Allow me to introduce you to some of them.

Arthur Coleman, better known in Constantia as "Cottontop," is the town's champion frog catcher. In frog season Mr. Coleman supplies the hotels and boarding houses and ships, and sends his surplus to New York. In June, when the season opens, Mr. Coleman starts out with a pail strapped over his shoulder, and a long stick in his hand. He can be seen in the swales, along the creeks, and in the meadows and, when that stick strikes the ground, a frog passes on to the next world.

Not only is Mr. Coleman the champion frog catcher, but he is a trapper and gets more skunks and muskrats than any other trapper in town.

Jeff Getman avers that Mr. Coleman has made a life study of fur bearing animals and, from that knowledge, he can predict the weather as accurately as Doe of Ogdensburg, King of Oswego, or Foster of Washington. Mr. Getman states that, last November, Mr. Coleman was examining a skunk pelt he had just secured and he remarked, "Jeff, we are going to have an open winter. There will be little snow and it will be warm." Mr. Getman claims that he asked Cottontop to explain his prediction and Mr. Coleman replied, "The skunk proves it to me. The hair is thin...there is not much of it. If the winter was to be cold the fur would be thick and matted to protect the animal." Mr. Coleman's prediction came true.

Rufus Dobson is one of the old Constantia boys. There are few men living that know Oneida Lake any better than Mr. Dobson. He does not profess to be a prognosticator, but he is a statistician. Should you want to know how many cows there are on the Rowe farm, ask Rufus. He will answer, "Seventeen cows, five calves, and ten pigs. And, on the Scoville farm are thirty cows, three horses, eleven calves, fifty hens, and four hogs." An impressive memory.

Edward Vanderwerker is the Constantia cart man. He draws the freight for the merchants and does many odd jobs about the village. Constantia people say that he is the most accommodating man they ever knew. They say that, one afternoon last summer, Mr. Vanderwerker was passing the post office and met a small girl who was wheeling a baby carriage. The child asked him to hold the carriage while she went into the post office. He granted her request and the little miss disappeared. Ed wheeled the carriage back and forth in front of the post office for fifteen minutes. The girl appeared, thanked him, took hold of the handles, and was about to depart when Mr. Vanderwerker asked to see the baby. The girl pulled down the covers and showed Ed a large wax doll.

Constantia folks tell many stories about Mr. Vanderwerker. They say that, one afternoon a few weeks ago, he delivered several boxes to Bristol & Marcellus's store and saw a kettle with a yellow substance in it. He asked Mr. Bristol what was in the kettle and was informed that it was a new type of axle grease for wagons. Mr. Bristol, who is also known as a joker, advised Mr. Vanderwerker to try it. Ed carried the kettle to the street, removed one wheel of his wagon and greased the axles. Mr. Bristol stood near and advised him to put it on thick. The axles oiled, Mr. Vanderwerker departed. People claim that, an hour later, the wheels squeaked so loudly that they could be heard for several blocks. Mr. Vanderwerker returned to the store and, in a roundabout way, learned that the kettle contained glue, not axle grease.

Miss Aura Cole is the superintendent of schools here. She has the schools in the Towns of Schroeppel, Hastings, West Monroe, Constantia, and Amboy to supervise and fills the position with entire satisfaction to the taxpayers. Miss Cole has the habit of walking into a school unannounced, just to see how things are progressing and, if she has suggestions, she makes them. She is working to place the schools of this district second to none in the state.

Edgar G. Blankman, who has made maps of Oswego, Jefferson, St. Lawrence, Lewis, Franklin, and other counties, has returned to Constantia and is principal of the village school. Mr. Blankman is the author of *Deacon Babbit*, a novel about early life around here. Besides teaching and cartography, Mr. Blankman is raising a hen, which he terms the "perpetual layer."

Fred A. Beebe conducts a general store on Main Street. Constantia is a G.O.P. town, with a large Republican majority. Mr. Beebe stands out as the Democratic politician of the area.

H.F. Tallcott is the Constantia postmaster. When Mr. Tallcott is not stamping letters, reading postcards, answering questions, and distributing mail, he is compounding drugs, selling hair dyes and corn plasters. Everyone likes this versatile postmaster and says that he is efficient.

Mrs. Daniel Dunn carries the mail between the post office and the New York, Ontario and Western Railroad Depot. Four times a day, six days in the week, she can be seen with her express wagon, heaped high with mailbags. No mail pouch has been found too heavy for Mrs. Dunn to handle and she throws the bags into the mail cars as if they were pound packages. Mrs. Dunn has carried the mail for several years and says that she likes the work.

Constantia has a volunteer fire company, organized in 1913. The boys have a good outfit and are well-drilled and ever ready to answer a fire alarm. William L. Bristol, whose practical joke fooled Mr. Vanderwerker, is chief and they say that he makes an ideal official. When there is a fire meeting, the members all attend because, if they don't, they know they will receive a calling from the chief. Mr. Bristol is a leading businessman and his firm, Bristol and Marcellus Grocers, feeds Constantia. The volunteer firemen congregate at the store.

Constantia is dry. Prohibition has had its effects here. The Dobson House, for years one of the leading hostelries in town, closed its doors last October. Frank Orlando still keeps his hotel open at the depot. A sign on the door offers the property for sale.

Dr. J.A. Wood treats all diseases within a radius of six miles of Constantia. Irving L. Livingston is Constantia's undertaker. Mr. Livingston makes the day price and night price for dying the same.

While Constantia is a summer resort, the people do not rely on what they make off summer boarders to carry them through the winter. The village has a state fish hatchery, where a number of men are employed year around. Daniel Miller is the superintendent. Every year, millions of pike eggs are hatched and pike fry are shipped to all parts of the state.

Years ago, Constantia had an iron furnace and a brick kiln.

The village's tanneries were running, and Oneida Lake had real steamboats, some known as side-wheelers. The village turned out more Erie canalers than any other place on the lake's shore. Nearly one hundred canal boats were tied up at Constantia's docks for the winter. Captains and drivers and steersmen wintered here and told their stories of the rough rides on Oneida Lake's tempestuous seas.

The village is still a very healthy place in which to reside. Whether Oneida Lake's breezes affect the villagers' health and cause them to live to ripe old ages has not been determined, but numbers point that way. Mrs. E. Andrews is active at 89 years and Mrs. M. Batchelor is 82. Mrs. Minerva Marcellus is 83, the wagering Garry Pickett 80, Abram Marcellus 88, and Andrew Daffler 89.

Life certainly flows with vigor and longevity on Oneida Lake's North Shore.

Constantia's African-American Heritage

Relatively few African-Americans lived in Upstate New York in the nineteenth century, but Constantia Township had two that received newspaper coverage. Ned Sherman moved to Cleveland in 1851 and, in 1879, was elected "President" of that village. Sherman was certainly one of the first African-Americans elected to public office in New York State.

Joni Hines sent me an interesting obituary from a local paper, dated September 13, 1874. The obituary highlighted the life Constantian Peter P. Feeler, described as "an old colored citizen who died at his home at the age of seventy-seven years, two months, and twenty-three days." Feeler's obituary indicates that he was an exceptional person and also contained a poignant example of the suffering that African-Americans endured throughout the nineteenth century.

> Peter was one of the pioneers of the Reed Tract, north of Cleveland, in the Town of Constantia. He was born on June 10, 1797, in Dutchess County, New York, a slave to Jacob Schermerhorn, who gave him his freedom. He married a beautiful Negress named Jane Knapp, a slave to Andrew Whitbeck. Mr. Whitbeck also settled in our town. Jane's freedom was purchased by her father for $100.
>
> In 1834, Peter bought a lot of wild land, sixty-eight acres in

the Reed Tract, owned by Roswell Reed of Coxsackie. He moved up immediately, taking his small family into the wilderness. He remained in residence here until the time of his death.

For many years he made it a part of his special business to go down in early spring to the Hudson River to catch shad. He owned and kept all the necessary fishing equipment on the river. For the last eight or ten years, however, his advanced age and family requirements kept him at home. He was a good neighbor, always ready to assist and advise all newcomers. He had many friends, among who he counted the Hon. Gerritt Smith, who never failed to respond financially if called on. Peter was also a man of good mind and strong argumentative power, quick in retort and comprehension, though not of much education.

In 1845, he appeared as counsel for his son-in-law Ed Wilson, before Abner H. Allen, Esq. Isaac Drought had sued Ed for killing his pig. The evidence was that the pig had got into Edward's garden and had been driven out on a very hot day. It was found dead, just outside the fence, with many black and bruised places.

Peter's opponent counsel said that the pig was whipped to death. Peter, though, in summing up, explained that the black places on the pig were produced by the dampness of the ground. The opposite counsel countered that the spots were on the pig's upper side. Peter replied that it must have been that the sun had greater power, and had produced the spots. Many local people attended this trial. Peter Feeler gained the victory in the case, amidst great applause.

Jane Ann, his accomplished daughter, remains on the homestead and has the care of her aged mother, who has been an invalid for many years. Feeler's oldest son, Peter, went to sea as a sailor some years ago, but unfortunately got kidnapped somewhere in the southern waters. He was sold into slavery some twenty years ago and has not been heard from since the war.

The Death of a "Favorite Oarsman"

The archives of the Onondaga Historical Association in Syracuse contain treasures of Oneida Lake lore. One of these gems is an obituary for Zinah M. Fuller, included in the *Syracuse Standard* of November 11, 1878. In the tradition of individuals like Valentine Dunham, Jake Kyser, Jack Rogers, and Clarence App,

Fuller was an old-time, vintage "Oneida Laker" who lived with the water throughout most of his life. You should enjoy meeting him below.

> Zinah M. Fuller, an oarsman well known to hundreds of people who visit Oneida Lake, died suddenly last Saturday of apoplexy, at North Bay.
>
> Mr. Fuller had lived at North Bay for many years and was quite a character, such as one seldom meets. The *Utica Herald* speaks of him as a "second Neptune" who spent most of his life on or in the water. Local inhabitants gave him the nickname of "Pollywog." He would land a party in shallow water and, stepping over the side of the boat, shoulder the occupants and carry them ashore, one after the other. In going out after a sailboat at anchor, he never took the trouble to go in a skiff but, summer or winter, waded out until the boat was reached.
>
> The water was his element and he was considered an authority on all that related to boating and fishing. In taking out a party, he did his work not as a task, but entered into the spirit of the occasion with the keen zest of an amateur sportsman, being always ready to go to any point, no matter how distant. He ventured on the roughest of water and remained out as late as the latest.
>
> He was strictly temperate, though given to exaggeration like all those of his class. The stories with which he regaled his visitors were enjoyable for the vein of humor that pervaded them, as well as their remarkable statements.
>
> He was obliging, even to a fault. On one occasion two prominent lawyers, one an ex-district attorney of Oneida County, the other a Roman [from Rome, New York], crossed the lake in "Zine's" boat. When shallow water was reached Zine prepared to wade ashore, carrying the men. The district attorney, wishing to have a joke on his friend, slipped a bill into Zine's hand and whispered that perhaps he might fall while carrying the Roman. The Roman was shouldered and carried some distance but, just before reaching shore, the oarsman stumbled and fell into the water with his load.
>
> The Utican had a good laugh at the Roman's expense, but his triumph was short. After stopping at South Bay for a time, the parties returned and the Roman, thinking it a poor rule which would not work both ways, gave the oarsman a bill and remarked that it would be a singular coincidence if he should

stumble again. The Roman was carried to the boat in safety but on the second trip the bottom became treacherous. The oarsman stumbled and the Utican fell headlong. Zine rather enjoyed the wetting and, while his passengers had a laugh on each other, he could laugh at both.

His cheerful disposition and kind heart made him a general favorite and visitors at North Bay will miss him.

Wild and Crazy Foxes

The *Brookfield Courier*, once the official newspaper in that southeastern Madison County township, contained an amusing article in its March 30, 1892 edition. The piece, entitled "A Modern Fox Chase," recounts a Constantia man's wild ride across Oneida Lake's ice.

> A Constantia farmer one night recently was driving across Oneida Lake on his return home from Syracuse when, as the story goes, he was set upon by a pack of foxes. Being alarmed by the boldness of the animals, he whipped up his horses, but the fierce brutes became more ferocious than ever and snapped at his horses' heels and jumped upon the sleigh. His wife was with him and his sleigh was loaded with numerous packages and a dressed hog.
>
> As the situation became more alarming, a happy thought came to the farmer and, acting upon it, he tossed the carcass of the hog overboard, whereupon the hungry pack stopped to devour it, allowing the escape of the farmer and his wife. If the chase had been resumed, it is probable that the good wife would have next gone by the board, as there were no more hogs in the cargo.
>
> The public safety demands that these foxy highwaymen be brought to justice and, perhaps, a round up, participated in by all the inhabitants of that section, would have the desired effect. They might meet with success equal to the three thousand hunters up in Dakota who, after an all day's drive, cornered two wolves in a swamp and then allowed one to get away.

Ann Hopkins

The Oneida Community's impressive "Mansion House" in Kenwood, Sherrill, 1901

Fort Brewerton Historical Society

Community members rode trains from Sherrill to the Fish Creek Station of the Oswego-Midland (later, Ontario and Western) Railroad. They either walked or took a launch, like the one pictured here, one mile west to their "Joppa" cottage by Oneida Lake. They navigated a waterway called "Wood River," formed by the union of Fish and Wood Creeks. Wood River flowed into the lake at Sylvan Beach.

Onondaga Historical Association

Stoddard and Garvin of Oneida constructed the Algonquin Hotel in Sylvan Beach in 1884. It was located near the site of the Oneida Community's "Joppa" cottage (near today's Canal View Restaurant). Ferries, like the one moored to the hotel's dock, were needed to carry tourists across Wood River since the first bridge wasn't built until 1889. The Barge Canal channelized Wood River in 1917, leaving several oxbow bends, like the Snug Harbor Resort in Verona Beach today.

Ann Hopkins

Oneida Lake's North Shore is very rocky and stone-covered points, like this one at North Bay in 1900, are common. Many of the points were built to create landing access for steamboats.

Ann Hopkins

Stylishly dressed Clevelanders pose by their horse and carriage during that village's prosperous glass-making era, circa 1900.

Corky Winn

The Ontario and Western Railroad served North Shore communities throughout the late nineteenth and early twentieth centuries. This photo shows the Constantia station, located on Mill Street, circa 1910.

Ann Hopkins

Andrew Young stands by his houseboat, dry docked at North Bay in 1914. Young was a true "Oneida Laker" whose living depended on the water – Zinah Fuller's latter-day counterpart.

Corky Winn

Cleveland's historic St. James' Episcopal Church, designed from a plan by famed architect Richard Upjohn, and its neighboring millpond created a scene fit for any poet's pen. The church is being restored.

Ann Hopkins

Cleveland's glass factory, circa 1900

Ann Hopkins

A beach, a boat, and bountiful bathing attire made for a fine day along Oneida's East Shore, circa 1900.

Jeff Gursky

The ornate Cleveland Methodist Church radiated the good feelings of that village's glass-making era.

Ann Hopkins

Early Sylvan Beach was often referred to as a "retreat" from life's stresses.

– Chapter 12 –

Eloping On the Waves

Popular nineteenth century literature often focused on romance, intrigue, and adventure, stimulating material that piqued the imagination. Entertainment offerings were limited and people read for excitement and fun. When real events intersected fantasy's realm, the press was quick to report them because sensationalism sold papers. The following tale, set in Beacon Beach (Sylvan Beach) and Upper South Bay in the early 1880s, met all the requirements for news marketing and appeared in the *New York Morning Journal*.

> SHE WAS THE CAPTAIN'S DAUGHTER
> *A sea yarn, that is not a fish story, told about Oneida Lake*
>
> Beacon Beach, Oneida Lake, New York–August 19–What Coney Island is to New York, Brooklyn, and Jersey, the snowy sands of Lake Oneida's southern shore are to the cities of Syracuse, Oneida, and to the people of the many pretty villages along the Ontario and Western railroad.
>
> Lucy Barnes is the fairest of Oneida's daughters and, despite her modest and uncoquettish nature, she is the heroine of the latest sensation in this rural society. Her age is not yet twenty and her plump, graceful form, her clustering curls of chestnut bronze, her dreamy hazel eyes and cherry lips have successively enslaved the hearts of all the rural gallants. But, guarded by a jealous and muscular father, Lucy has until recently been

worshipped from afar. Captain Barnes owns and pilots the largest screw steamer on Lake Oneida and is in every sense of the word the autocrat of this beautiful sheet of water. Next to his daughter, his steamer is the pride of his heart and, because he came very near losing both only yesterday, the gossips of Oneida Lake have a racy story to tell.

The stranger to these "blue Alsatian mountains" who caused all this trouble was a young New York journalist on his summer vacation. Fate brought him face to face with the lovely Lucy just as he stepped from the train. He took passage for South Bay on her father's steamer and, having providentially rescued Lucy's hat from a watery grave, he struck up an acquaintance that resulted in an attempted elopement.

Having registered at the Elberon House, kept by Erhardt Wirth at South Bay, the infatuated young New Yorker set himself to his perilous task of making secret love to the Captain's daughter. She lived just across the road and it was not for several days that their moonlight meetings and boat rides on the lake reached the ears of the terrible Captain Barnes. He laid in wait for the presumptuous suitor of his daughter and there was a stormy interview on the hotel pier late one night. The fair Lucy had just landed after a moonlight sail with her Bohemian sweetheart and, as she fled in tears to her home, she heard her father's infuriated words:

"If I catch you fooling around my daughter again, I'll drown you in the lake!"

The young journalist met this rebuff with professional intrepidity and, having assured the irate Captain of his honorable intentions, withdrew rapidly to his hotel, brandishing a heavy oar by way of emphasis.

The next evening, when Mr. Wirth's private steam yacht left the hotel pier to connect with the New York express train on the Ontario and Western road at Beacon Beach, there were two passengers, and Lucy Barnes was one of them. Scarcely had the steamer left the pier when there was great commotion in the Barnes mansion. The Captain missed his daughter and quickly acted upon his suspicion. His own vessel had steam up and, in five minutes, her screw was churning the blue waves in hot pursuit of the *Erhardt Wirth*. Both are fast boats and such a race had never been known on Lake Oneida. The boat bearing the fugitives had a start of about half a mile and the distance to Beacon Beach was three miles. The progress of the two vessels

> was watched from the veranda of the Elberon Hotel and sympathy was generally divided. Captain Barnes grasped the wheel and shouted to his engineer to put on every pound of steam. The engineer of the *Erhardt Wirth* caught the spirit of the race and did likewise, and the relative position of the boats was scarcely changed when the first one glided along the wharf at Beacon Beach.
>
> The eloping couple leaped ashore and hastened to the depot, but the train was behind time! There was a moment of terrible suspense. Then there was a deafening uproar! The safety valve of the pursuing steamer had blown off just as the Captain ran her high and dry upon the beach, in his eagerness to save the time of landing. The train thundered into the depot and Lucy and her companion boarded the cars. Captain Barnes, with gigantic strides, dashed over the sands and yelled for the train to hold on. To the dismay of the trembling fugitives, the train waited. Captain Barnes leaped on board and flew through the cars. Realizing that all was lost, Lucy's companion gave her one passionate kiss and sought refuge in the baggage car. Lucy herself was seized by the Captain and dragged shrieking upon the depot platform, just as the train rolled slowly away.

Our tale requires a few notes. Oneida's sandy beaches are located on the lake's eastern, not southern, shore. The distance between Upper South Bay and Sylvan Beach is about two miles, not three. Other steamboat races occurred in the lake's history and, while all attracted press attention, no other boilers got fired because of romance.

Lucy Barnes eventually married Will Spire, of Brewerton, and enjoyed a fine life within that community. The fate of our young journalist remains a mystery, however. Let us hope that his dramatic Oneida Lake adventure heralded a long, headline-filled career.

– Chapter 13 –

A Constantia Visit, Anyone?

Late nineteenth century journalists found the Oneida Lake scene to be a fertile source of news for seasonal feature articles. In villages like Lower South Bay, Brewerton, Constantia, Cleveland, and Sylvan Beach a vibrant, pluralistic population of craftspersons, factory workers, farmers, fishermen and, of course, summer tourists thrived. Their colorful lives often made for great copy.

The *Syracuse Journal* published an article about Constantia entitled "A Summer Holiday" on August 17, 1881. The two-part travelogue described the community, cited its history, and also placed that settlement within the context of the Oneida Lake region. Some fine lake imagery and Constantia village lore highlight this section. In the second half of the story, the author ventured inside the "Scriba Mansion." George Frederick William Augustus Scriba was a nineteenth century Constantia land developer who, although unlucky in his business transactions, left a lasting mark on his town. The writer's words convey a unique, detailed portrait of that home and its grand lady, Mrs. Frederick W. Scriba, George Scriba's daughter-in-law.

A SUMMER HOLIDAY–THE ATTRACTIONS OF ONEIDA LAKE

An Ancient Village Bits of History–A Great Landed Proprietor–Beauties of the Lake, Its Islands and Shores–An Enjoyable Resort–Notable Families and Pleasant Memories

When this little village was founded, nearly a century ago, great expectations were entertained of its future prospects. Its site was included in the famous Scriba's Patent, of more than half a million acres, and its projector laid out a road from New Rotterdam (as he christened this embryo city) to the mouth of Salmon Creek on Lake Ontario. This road Mr. Scriba expected would become the main route of trade between the lakes. The settlement was visited at an early day by several distinguished foreigners, among them being the Duke de la Rouchefoucault-Liancourt, a French nobleman, who traveled in this country in 1795-97 and the Baron DeZeng, a German nobleman, who resided at Rome after serving in our revolutionary army.

The lake at this point is seen to excellent advantage. To the westward lie Dunham's and Frenchman's Islands, with their forests of fine old trees while, in the offing, rise half a dozen smaller islands, or reefs, covered with a growth of tall, coarse grass, which forms an admirable retreat for cranes, wild ducks, and a variety of waterfowl. Almost any evening cranes, in pairs or singly, can be seen flying, with long flapping wings and outstretched legs, from or towards these reefs. And, if the visitor is so disposed, he need not be an unusually expert shot to bring down a specimen. Flocks of snipe abound on the pebbly shores and, a few nights ago, four black ducks darted off with a whirr as we rowed near a reef. It is not lawful to shoot duck now, of course, and the birds were not molested.

To the eastward the lake stretches away until it is lost in the horizon, and it is not difficult to imagine the miniature sea to be a bay of the ocean, leading out to the great unknown beyond. When provoked by the wind, it is a turbulent little body and the waves roll and the white caps dash over the ends of the reefs and on the shores, as if fretting and chafing at their own limits. It is a shallow sheet of water, the greatest depth being, it is said, but thirty feet. This, doubtless, accounts for its occasional tempestuousness. No finer sport need be desired than a row across its ambitious waves or scudding with a sail before a stiff breeze to and from one of the islands. If a longer pull or sail is desired, it is but three miles to Frenchman's Island, with its historic associations, or five miles across the lake to South Bay. Then there are Bernhard's Bay, Cleveland, West Vienna where there is a Roman Catholic school, and North Bay, on this, the north side of the lake. Messengers, Lakeport, and Bridgeport are on the opposite shore.

Constantia claims a population of seven hundred souls. To the casual visitor, this figure seems magnified, but one magnanimously gives the census the benefit of the doubt. The village was laid out liberally and the streets are pleasant, the chief drawback being the lack of proper sidewalks. It is a sleepy old town and only needs an infusion of genuine Yankee enterprise to make it a popular and prosperous watering place. The Episcopal Church occupies the highest point of land, a most beautiful location. Both the building itself, the lot upon which it stands, and the adjoining property, to the extent of perhaps two or three acres, are the gift of the original proprietor, Scriba. The fine lot on the west of the church was designed for the rector's use, but the rectory remains unbuilt. The church has not been opened for service for two years, death and removals having so reduced the numbers of the attendants that those remaining are unable to support a clergyman.

In the rear of the church is a small burying ground, in which lies the body of George Frederick William Augustus Scriba, whose grave is marked by a tall, flat marble slab, bearing the inscription, "Sacred to the memory of George Scriba, who departed this life, Aug. 14, 1836, in the 84th year of his age." After coming to the wilds of Oswego County, the rich New York merchant dropped his three middle names, probably as being too pretentious and unwieldy a cognomen for his new surroundings and stirring business life.

In the central part of the village stands the Lake View House, the one hotel of the place, which is large enough to accommodate a small army of guests. It has three full stories, containing forty or more large rooms, with that necessary adjunct to modern hostelries–a ballroom above. It is owned by Mrs. Waggoner, of Syracuse, who lately has put it in first class order, painting the building and extending a broad two-story veranda across the entire front overlooking the lake. Here, hammocks are swung, easy chairs are brought, and light literature is blown about by the breezes that are wafted constantly from the lake. Perhaps the present lessee is not able always to "entertain angels unawares." Those who are entertained here find the house well kept, free from the lounging and disorder of most country taverns, everything in neatest style, and the table liberally spread with well cooked and well served viands. Charges are very moderate and a more healthful or attractive place to spend a quiet vacation need not be sought.

The shore of the lake here is gently sloping, running into a succession of curves and small bays. One of the latter has an abundant growth of pond lilies, whose delicate blossoms float gracefully on the water. Some of the plants have been left stranded on the shore and are at the mercy of those who like to experiment with planting them in a tub of sand and soil, with a liberal supply of water. Vast quantities of tan bark have accumulated along the shore, the washings from a large tannery half a mile up Scriba Creek. The tannery has, for many years, done a large business, but now is run only occasionally and in a small way. This tan bark, which long was regarded as a nuisance, has come to be prized for its land making value...something on the "first pity, then endure, then embrace" principle. Owners of the waterfront now will not allow a single load to be removed. Constantia is the center of an extensive lumber traffic and 800,000 feet of timber have been shipped from here this year. Two canal boats are now in the process of construction at different points on the shore, the oak and pine of which they are made being taken from the neighboring forests. This was the early home of the Hon. E.B. Judson, of Syracuse, who still owns much property here, including a large saw mill in active operation.

Any sketch of Constantia without mention of Mr. Robert Black, the village blacksmith, would be incomplete. A fair-haired, blue-eyed, strong-armed Scotchman, with the good sense, intelligence, and thrift characteristic of his nationality, he is at once the worthy citizen and excellent companion, having the esteem of the community. It is the height of enjoyment after the day's work is done, to be rowed by his strong arms out upon the lake, and across the tossing white caps. There is scarcely less pleasure in having for a companion his son, a fine lad of eighteen, who aspires to beat his father at the oar. And you are not quite sure but that he can do it, too. He certainly can when tubs are substituted for skiffs. Already he has taken one prize in a tub race and probably will take another at Brewerton on Saturday next. If you call at the house a hearty welcome will be extended by Mrs. Black and, perhaps, her younger daughter will play upon the organ and, with her sister, will sing for you.

All these things, and many more, make a Constantia holiday delightful to remember.

Inside the Scriba Mansion

Of the famous Scriba, the sole survivors are the widow of Frederick W. Scriba and her son. Frederick was the only son of George Scriba. The son, Mr. George Frederick Scriba, is a young bachelor and lives with his mother [Mrs. Frederick W.] in the old family mansion in this village. The house is situated upon rising ground near Scriba Creek and, doubtless when built, commanded a wide view of the lake, now partially obstructed by shade and fruit trees and buildings. It is a large, old-fashioned structure with a broad hall in the center, branching off at the end in opposite directions. On each side in front are large, square rooms, with generous open fireplaces that yawn to glow with cordiality. The windows are provided with close, wooden shutters which, like the clapboards, once were painted yellow, but long ago lost all color save that which time and storms bring. The house contains some valuable specimens of antique furniture and bric-a-brac. A very handsome tall clock in the hall, showing the movements of the moon and other celestial bodies, attracts attention. The sitting room has sideboards of dark wood built into the wall on each side of the great chimney and quaint mirrors, surmounted by gilded ornaments, hang on the walls of this and the drawing room.

Over the fireplace in the latter apartment is a curious picture in wax, emblematic of the nation's grief over the death of Washington. It is a work of a German artist named J.C. Rauschner and was made in 1800, the date appearing in wax. The mantel supports a pair of large and elegant vases, a hundred years old, handsome enough to drive a curio hunter wild with delight. In the hall hangs a rare old map of the State of New York, made in 1802, by "Simeon DeWitt, Surveyor General."

All these things and many others shown are noteworthy. Interest in them is greatly enhanced by the presence of the gentle lady who still presides over the old mansion. The daughter of an English gentleman named Lander, she came to Constantia as the wife of Frederick William Scriba, some thirty years ago. Favored with superior personal attractions, and fitted by education for and accustomed to the best society, Mrs. Scriba previously had traveled extensively in France, Italy, and other parts of Europe, and spent two years at Malta, where her uncle, an officer in the British army, was stationed. There, social life was very gay and brilliant, and time flew by on golden wings.

Mrs. Scriba receives her visitors with old time stately grace and courtesy, beautiful to see, and they at once are charmed and put at ease by her cordial and sympathetic manner and intelligent conversation. With her slight figure and spirituelle face, which yet retains a delicate beauty, one looks upon her in her present surroundings as upon a slender lily in a rude and neglected garden. Her abundant dark hair, silvering with years, is done up in a high roll upon the top of her head, in a becoming style, that gives her the appearance of just having stepped from some antique portrait frame. By special request, Mrs. Scriba permitted us to see her collection of rich and curious jewels, laces, fans, etc. These are mementoes of "auld lang syne." Some of them she wears on occasion. She sits at her sweet toned, ancient piano, and plays the melodies of fifty years ago with the skill of youth. For the enjoyment of a young lady guest a collection of duets, gems from the operas, is brought out, upon the performance of which the twain enter with equal enthusiasm. Mrs. Scriba's husband has been dead these twenty years or more. His grave is in the little churchyard on the hill, near that of his father.

Of the latter, Mrs. Scriba has two miniature portraits, done in wax, with natural hair ingeniously woven into a queue and powdered in one, and in the other, a later picture, worn short. The face has a fine, aristocratic mould, showing culture and character. It seems a pity that the immediate descendants of a man who once owned more than half a million acres (the exact number was 525,063) in this and adjoining counties, including twenty-four entire townships and who was ruined financially by his liberality, enterprise, and public spirit in developing the country, should be left with but a little tract of thirty acres and the old house. People in the village say that at one time Mr. Scriba had a store, opposite the hotel, in which he carried a stock of goods valued at $100,000. He also had a large store on Lake Ontario, which was managed by an agent. By choice he made his home at Constantia, then called Rotterdam, which was the first post office in Oswego County. A township in this county, adjoining Oswego City, justly perpetuates the name of Scriba.

– Chapter 14 –

The Lakeport Philosopher

The *Madison County Times* reported the news in that county's northernmost communities in the nineteenth century. Published in Chittenango, the paper had correspondents in Bridgeport, Lakeport, and Messenger's Bay (more commonly referred to as "Oneida Lake," the name of the local post office). These writers kept the *Times'* readers abreast of events that occurred on Oneida Lake's South Shore. Lakeport resident Welcome Otway Spencer, known by the pseudonyms "White Wave" and "Ivanhoe," was by far the most prolific and accomplished of these correspondents.

Spencer was a Lakeport farmer who owned land located along the main South Shore highway (now Route 31), just west of the village. Part of his acreage included the great Lakeport field, a beautiful expanse of cropland that stretched from Route 31 one half mile northward to the lake. The field is currently being developed into townhouses and businesses. Welcome first worked as a farm hand for his father, Jacob, and eventually inherited the elder Spencer's holdings. He was married twice and had one daughter, Edith.

Welcome Spencer was unique for an upstate nineteenth century farmer. He might have been labeled a "plowman musing of Plato" or an "Aristotelian agrarian." His death notice in the *Oneida Democrat Union* stated that "he was a man of much intellectual ability–well educated, his knowledge comprising both the works of science and the classics. He was a Latin and Greek scholar, was familiar with nature in all her varied moods and, in historical subjects, was especially well versed." Spencer's work received praise in his January 12, 1894, obituary, published in the Madison County Times. The eulogist wrote, "His name was known in every newspaper office of the county because, to every paper in the county at some time, he had contributed, either in poetry or verse. He was a man of considerable intelligence and had devoted much of his time to reading and study, even to the injury of his financial matters, and was well posted in ancient and modern history. His delight was verse, and he was proud that some of his writings had been published by the New York Sun and other New York dailies, and by some of the best magazines of the country...He had his views and expressed them. Particularly this was true of death and the hereafter, and of God and his goodness. He could not be said to be much of a believer in the Bible, but liked to study it and wondered about its most serious and mysterious teachings."

Spencer's Lakeport was a small, homespun community whose economy centered on farming and tourism. The village clustered around Lakeport Bay (Spencer calls it "Fogger's Bay," a name that comes from an early settler). All homes were built along the South Shore highway or by the road that led south, through the Great Swamp, to Chittenango. Two hotels, the Larkin House and the Avon House, catered to tourists and served as meeting places for the village's literary and social clubs. Cultural events were common in Lakeport and Spencer probably encouraged these. The settlement had a school and a general store. Dr. Lyman H. Wilson lived just east of town, by the point that bears his name today. Spencer was often in ill health and may have been one of the doctor's patients.

Several cheese factories clustered around Lakeport. One of these, owned by E. Stanbury, was located across the street from Spencer's home. Since keeping milk fresh was a problem, many farmers had their product made into cheese. Bridgeport was but a short drive to the west and Lakeport's agrarians probably patronized that village's numerous businesses and mills. Farmers with last names like Chapman, Bushnell, Hubbard, and Billington, names associated with the lake's landmarks, lived in close proximity to Lakeport and were an integral part of the community's social and economic fabric.

A pensive, direct style with an undisguised editorial bite distinguished Welcome Spencer from the average local news reporter. While he could capably detail Lakeport's mundane activities, he often digressed into beautiful imagery, informative tangents, and commentaries that captured other aspects of that community's nineteenth century life. What follows are a selected series of Spencer columns that illustrate the man's flair.

Lakeport, May 6, 1876–The lake has been clear from ice since the 21st of last month, and its blue rippling surface once more invites the boatmen and excursionists.

The lake is the pride of the people of this locality. Some people talk of the hills, some of the valleys, others of rivers and wandering streams, but give me a lake like our own Oneida and the other people may have all the rest.

Lakeport, June 22, 1878–I confess that, for some little time past, I have been tardy in keeping the readers of our valuable home journal supplied with the news from this stirring and wide-awake little town. Perhaps I deserve to be scolded, and certainly I know that I deserve all the little rebukes and insinuations that have been given me so kindly by my friend, "Rambler," of Chittenango Station [another *Times* correspondent.] I must now wake up from my long nap and report for duty. Perhaps now, that our town has grown so large, and its business and commercial interests become so great, that I shall not be able to fill the responsible position of correspondent from this place in a manner acceptable to the readers of so influential a public journal as the *Times*.

If I should fail, it would be the easiest thing in the world to fall back into retirement and let some younger enthusiast spring forward to take my place. When my mission is filled, and the full extent of my influence thrown out upon society and the world for good or ill, and I hope for good, I believe I shall have the good sense to know it, and not lag "superfluous on the stage." It is a good thing to know enough to know when to retire before the foot lights.

As a citizen of Lakeport, I have tried to have some pride, and certainly have been ambitious to have it built up, and see that its affairs are conducted in a reputable manner so that, when a little distance abroad, I could hear its name spoken without a blush being forced to my cheek.

Along this lakeshore, from Bridgeport to Messenger's, a distance of eight miles, we have as handsome a farming country as there is under the sun. Its extensive and thrifty meadows, its beautiful and luxuriant fields of waving wheat, are the surprises and envy of persons less favorably situated. It is the garden of Madison County, and situated upon the shore of the loveliest inland lake in the Empire State. Half way between the above mentioned places, situated upon Fogger's Bay, Lakeport claims the attention of the tourist, and is the objective point of many a weary beast and traveler.

Lakeport, September 3, 1878–The busy season at this celebrated watering place is now nearly over, and we shall soon again begin to breathe without some new sensation to distract our minds, just as we thought ourselves ready to set down to a quiet meal. Our rustic ways and stubborn proclivities are hard to yield to the innovations of foreign style and manners, but we think we learn something as we go along and, at the end of the season, we expect to feel that the pleasant summer days, now past, have not been spent here in vain.

Miss Ida V. Gilbert, of Syracuse, has acquitted herself in a very creditable manner. She is a young lady of fine accomplishments and has the faculty of making everybody her friend. As a teacher, she wins the affections of her scholars, and consequently has great influence over them. Her school closed Monday September 2d. The good people of school district No. 15 held a picnic in Larkin's grove the Saturday previous and the children enjoyed themselves hugely. The declamation was good, the music fine, the dinner excellent, and the general social feeling exuberant and delightful. Miss Gilbert, who by the way is an excellent artist, gave each of her scholars a fine drawing, the work of her own hands. May they long remember the fair giver.

"Still other stars added to the bright blue sky.
Still other remembrances of days gone by."

Lakeport, August 26, 1879–The cool days of the fall have come, and the farmers are busy plowing for wheat sowing.

Now is the time for picnics, and everybody seems to be improving it, by water and by land. Parties are constantly going for rest and recreation after their hard summer's work, and the practice of these social reunions has been brought up to a fine art. The numerous groves and sylvan retreats to be found around our lake are being made valuable as places for picnics and resorts, and our fathers would be astonished at the numberless ways we have for enjoyments, when they had to content themselves with the rough work of pioneer life.

"Blackberrying across the lake" is one of the things our citizens indulge in occasionally, and a book could be written upon the country and inhabitants of that section of creation distinguished for rocks, sand, and bushes, and situated from two to three miles north of the north side of Oneida Lake. The natives of that country form an interesting study of themselves, and many valuable statistics can be gathered there in relation to a business that has become one of no inconsiderable importance.

Oneida Lake, after all, is to furnish the finest watering place this side of Albany. At Wood Creek Ferry [a name for Sylvan Beach in the 1870's] it can be found and seen. There can be seen the lake, mingling with the sky in the distance. There is the fine road on the sandy beach for driving, and glimpses of the lake through the opening vistas of as fine a grove as the Divine Hand ever caused to grow. Already the railroad has found this beautiful place, and it is fashionable to go to Wood Creek Ferry.

Lakeport, August 14, 1880–The Avon House has been reopened for the season. Mr. Reuben Cross comes to the business without any experience but, so far, he has made an admirable landlord. He has plenty of good boats and tackle and the "Avon table" is said to be up to the highest standard of excellence.

Lakeport, April 18, 1882–The soft purple hue of the atmosphere, the flitting shadows, and summer-like temperatures of today signify to such as yearn for the return of spring, that they will not have to wait long. In a little while birds and blossoms will come to reign, and the meadows will again appear in their glory. Most heartily we say, "Welcome spring!" Once more, our enraptured vision shall feed upon the glories of earth and sky, and upon field and wood. When spring reigns we are peasants all.

Lakeport, May 26, 1885–During the past few days the fields and meadows have changed their appearance in such a wonderful manner that it would seem as if some great magician had strode over the world and wakened to life and beauty flower and foliage, and thrown down with wanton hands the green carpet that everywhere beautifies the earth. Imagination now lags behind, or folds its wings. Everywhere there is beauty in bud and blossom, and the sickly ideality of poets is poor in comparison with the glory of the external world.

Lakeport, April 9, 1886–The ice is entirely out of the lake. A strong south wind that blew on April first carried it bodily to the North Shore and, at night or before, the whole surface was as free from ice as in midsummer. Our oldest inhabitant does not remember the time when the lake was cleared so nicely and quickly as this spring. I am reminded of the lines:

> "O, there's a sweet look in the golden sun,
> And tressy wave of light upon the fields,
> Make for hills and valleys their carpet green,
> And give their luster to the bright wide world.
> From capricorn to summer's north-west bounds,
> Great floods of light come moving from afar,
> And beautiful again shall be our hills,
> The glory of the sun is in our land."

– Chapter 15 –

Blizzard!

One of my favorite Oneida Lake authors is a writer called "Bertrande," a columnist for the Syracuse newspapers during the 1930s and 1940s. Bertrande spent much of his late nineteenth century childhood in the North Shore community of Jewell and his memories of that era, especially of the times shared with his uncle, Noel Gardiner, are warm, instructive tales of a distant lakeside lifestyle. In 1947, he wrote about the famous Blizzard of 1888s effect on Jewell and on the rugged, independent folk who called that hamlet home.

> The Blizzard of 1888 was one of those convulsions of nature that live long in the memory, especially in that of a little boy who enjoyed every moment of it!
>
> My Uncle Noel stood at the door of his little carpenter shop in the back yard on the afternoon of March 10, 1888. He gazed out across Oneida Lake with critical eye as he reached for his red bandanna and blew his nose with a resounding clarion call which, but for the wind, could easily have been heard through the confines of the little hamlet of Jewell (also called West Vienna), where we lived.
>
> I had come over from our home, next door, to get a bag of shavings, which dad liked to use as kindling for the early morning start of the kitchen fire.
>
> Yep, we always had an all-night fire in the house during the

winter, but not in the kitchen range. The big chunk stove, strategically placed to heat both the huge kitchen and the still larger "settin' room," was always going full blast during the cold weather. With the proper draft adjustments, a couple of hard maple chunks would keep the old round-oak functioning all night.

As Uncle stood spraddle-legged against the wind and completed his survey of the conditions, his ruddy, eighty-year old features broke into a wide grin and he remarked, as if this were a thing greatly to be desired:

"She's goin' to be a sockdolager, Bertie. Th' signs all p'int to it. An' if this here don't turn out to be th' wust storm in twenty years–then my name ain't Noel Gardiner!"

A steadily increasing wind blew from the northwest and the unchecked tumble of the big white flakes increased in volume as we watched. Our normal three feet of hard-packed snow was being swiftly increased. As we entered Uncle's kitchen, I looked back through the afternoon's early-waning light and saw that our tracks from the shop had already been obliterated!

I helped Uncle fill the wood box with a dozen huge chunks from the woodshed, ate a small saucer of jelly and a bare half-dozen of Aunt Cyrena's sugar cookies (each with a large raisin in its exact center), and scurried across the yard, with the snow to my knees–heading home for supper!

Next morning, there was no sky, no earth, no lake, no nothing–just a shifting curtain of white, obliterating the entire landscape and making a little boy feel that he was marooned, isolated, and most happily abandoned in the middle of a vast ocean of snow. Boy, it was glorious!

The adjacent houses and buildings had become totally invisible and, even when the wind lulled a bit, all that could be seen of them was a darker shadow on the white screen of falling snow. Our kitchen windows were darkened by drifts up to and above the top of the lower sash. I recall that I had to stand on a chair to look outside.

After a breakfast of oatmeal, pancakes, sausage, fried potatoes, maple syrup and coffee, dad and I started to shovel a path to the barn, which stood about sixty feet from the back door of our woodshed. Between the two buildings the wind had enjoyed full sweep all night, and the result was a drift of snow, almost to the top of the barn door. So, we tunneled. Right through the snow we bored our laborious way and, when the path was roughly finished, there was a fifteen-foot span near the center that had a snow roof at least five feet high.

We finally reached the barn, which at this time sheltered only Mary, the old white mare, and a few chickens. They greeted our arrival with proper acclaim and we attended to their wants. Dad had been out, shoveling a pathway to the pump, before I was awake that morning. So, now, we were all set and, in the accepted mode of the times, we went back into the house and proceeded to "let 'er snow"–which it sure did. For twenty-four hours the stuff came down without hindrance until, when the skies finally cleared a little, we boasted a snow blanket of more than five feet on the level, with drifts in many places too high to even estimate!

During the course of the storm we had received from time to time desultory visits from our nearest neighbors, Uncle Noel, Charley Wright, and Leroy Page. Plowing through the drifts, they stamped in, laughing, cheerful, and seemingly unoppressed by this splurge of nature. The general attitude seemed to be, "Here it is–we might as well enjoy it!"

You see, folks, it is a fact that, in those days, we ruralities lived closer to nature and we depended more upon our neighbors and ourselves than we did upon science. Our room corners were enveloped in dark shadow at night, but our hearts were lighter. Our manner of living was, perhaps, crude and our rounds of pleasure more restricted, but we lived happier and we died easier than the moderns. Our lamp chimneys smoked and our "shower baths" were all taken outdoors, but we had more time to praise God and pass the cider.

As the big storm died away and we began to note a pale sun behind the clouds, my Uncle Noel stamped his snow-laden boots on our woodshed floor and entered the kitchen, bearing a huge chicken pie, cloth-covered and steaming-fresh from Aunt Cyrena's oven. Baked in a milk pan it was–and its aroma filled the kitchen.

"We baked two of 'em," apologized Uncle, "th' oven had to be hot, anyways, an' it don't take no more heat fer to bake two pies than it does one!"

Then he turned to me, with an expression of grave concern, and condoled:

"Bertie, I'm afeared she's lettin'up an' our fun's pretty nigh over for this time. But don't you worry, none. We'll prob'ly have a dang sight wuss one next winter."

This cheering prophecy comforted me, to no end–and time

proved that Uncle was right.

"Mary," continued Uncle, "put that there pie into th' warmin' oven an' let it gather flavor a-settin' an' a-simmerin'. You folks waller back home with me an' help us eat 'tother one."

So we all plodded over to the next house and spent the evening in pleasant converse and an almost continual round of eating.

At intervals, after supper, neighbors dropped in–Cousin Art Leete and his mother (she was the station agent), Dick Bevan the blacksmith, carpenter Ben Tripp, postmaster Zene White, and others. Uncle descended to the cellar and drew a gallon pitcher of his famous grape wine, which the elders drank with due appreciation, while Art and I regaled ourselves with some of auntie's root beer. There was popcorn, there were apples–pound sweets, spies, gilliflowers, and there were hickory nuts but most of all there was fellowship, jollity, and an atmosphere of content and well being.

About 10 o'clock, Uncle suddenly interrupted himself in the middle of a heated debate with dad as to the oratory of Bob Ingersoll. He rose to his feet, yawned, and announced:

"Neighbors, I'm a-goin to bed. Fur as I'm concerned, ye kin set here all night, or ye kin trot along home, jest as ye please. In any case, God bless ye all and have ye in His holy keepin'. Good night, folks–an' dry yer feet good afore ye go to bed."

Jake Kyser's hotel was a prominent structure on Upper South Bay's Main Street, around 1920. The inn was located approximately where the Oneida Lake Marina is today.

Ann Hopkins

Lucy Barnes and the stranger may have eloped from Coppernoll's Pier, a popular steamboat dock in Upper South Bay. The photo was dated 1908.

Clarence Bitz

The "Scriba Mansion" was built by George Scriba, Constantia's late eighteenth–early nineteenth century land developer, in 1795. Located on the north side of Route 49, just east of the fish hatchery, the home has been nicely restored.

Corky Winn

The Vanderbilt was Constantia's grandest hotel. The inn was called the "Lakeside House" when it opened in 1849. When John Barnett bought it in 1913, he renamed it "The Vanderbilt," after a Syracuse hotel.

Corky Winn

Constantia's Main Street (now Route 49) was named George Street, for George Scriba. The post office building is the large structure directly left of the horse and buggy. The Vanderbilt Hotel lies to the right of the post office. The Coble House is beyond the flagpole, on the photo's right.

Corky Winn

Constantia's Coble House sported spacious verandas where patrons could enjoy Oneida Lake's cooling breezes. The hotel, located where a convenience store sits today, burned in 1911 and was rebuilt and renamed the Dobson House.

A section of the Town of Sullivan from an 1870s map shows Lakeport. Welcome Spencer's property is slightly left of center, below number 109. He is cited as "W.O. Spencer."

The great Lakeport hay meadow stretched north from Route 31 to Oneida's shore. Spencer's farm included part of this land. It was the last piece of working agricultural property that bordered the lake. The meadow is now being developed.

Mike Wameling

Winter's depths swallow the Sylvan Beach boardwalk, around 1910.

Fort Brewerton Historical Society

Ambitious Brewertonites dig out from a major storm. The taller building in the background was the Washburn House, the village's largest hotel. Chuck and Millard Rogers' Brewerton Bait Shop occupied the structure to the left of the Washburn from 1946 through 1974.

– Chapter 16 –

Messages

If you sat on the Forest Home veranda at Sylvan Beach in the summer of 1908, you might have overheard this conversation:

> "You know, Mabel, I've been thinkin'. We've been at Sylvan Beach for nearly a week, and there's another seven days to go in our vacation. We haven't had any contact with the folks back home. They're bound to think somethin's ailin' us. Don't want 'em to worry none."
>
> "You're right, Arthur. They're surely frettin' by now. Better send 'em some of them fancy-colored postcards we saw at Louie Serby's Department Store. You know, the ones with the hotels, the trains, the beach, and that excitin' toboggan slide on them. No bathin' beauties, though. They might think you're up to somethin'"
>
> "Sounds great, sweetie, but what do we say on the back of the cards?"
>
> "I don't know. We'll just send 'em a message. Any message. That'll do just fine."

There have been thousands of Mabels and Arthurs, and tens of thousands of postcards in Sylvan Beach history. The cards are vintage documents of the village's visual past. Their messages capture the spirit of their times, as well as entertaining hints at their senders' characters.

The Beach is fortunate to have a notable collection of historical photos and cards on permanent display at the Canal View Restaurant, located on the Barge Canal near the lake. The restaurant might easily be called the "Sylvan Smithsonian" because of its marvelous exhibits of historical memorabilia. Fred and Marge Testa opened the business in 1977 in the remodeled home of Emory and Ruth Sauve, former owners of the Sylvan Beach Midway. Their endeavor prospered and, aided by their children, the Testas expanded and developed a sizable clientele. Marge's daughter and son-in-law, Jean and John Kowalski, purchased the restaurant in 1990. When Jean and John opened, Fred and Marge gave the Kowalskis a sign from an old Sylvan Beach photo studio that read, "Pictures Taken–Any Place on the Beach–on Short Notice." Jean liked the antique poster and it made her think, "Why not start a collection of Sylvan Beach photos and artifacts and use history as the restaurant's theme?" She began that day.

Visit the restaurant and you enter the world of Sylvan Beach's past. Tastefully arranged displays of photos and post cards bring images of a turn-of-the century Beach with its crowds of picnickers, carnival delights, beautiful groves of tall trees, and wide, immaculate sandy expanses to the restaurant's lucky patrons. You can view the Rowe Brothers Bath House stretching into Oneida's waves and the famous toboggan slide, with scores of swimmers lined up for an unforgettable fifteen cents thrill. In other prints a St. Charles Hotel coachman discharges his passengers at the inn's elegant entrance, vacationers relax on the porches of the Forest Home and Algonquin Hotels, and Ontario and Western Railroad trains rumble down Main Street, that was called "Railroad Avenue" until autos replaced the great excursion trains. You can smile with loving couples posing for pictures, you can mingle with multitudes in the Midway, and you can sit back, relax, and savor an impressive diversity of Sylvan scenes. A great wooden sign projects the memory of "Head's Store" and wall cases display vintage souvenirs. Jean and John Kowalski have done their village a great service by preserving and sharing rich visual expressions of its fun-loving past.

The post cards and photos in the following section are organized like this. Captions under each visual describe its content. Messages that I copied separate the pictures. Unfortunately, I didn't find Arthur's and Mabel's messages but, if I examine a few hundred more cards, I may succeed.

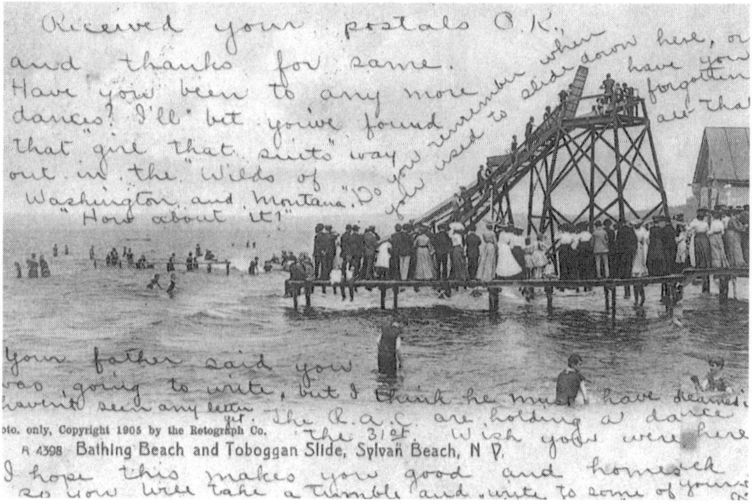

Bill and Janeen Fariel

Tourists often squeezed their messages into unusual spaces.

***"The fishing is fine, the bathing sublime.
To Sylvan the crowds are all going."***

Vacationers model their beach fashion finest on a chilly summer day, around 1920.

Bill and Janeen Fariel

Crowds line the bridge and riverbanks during a Hop Growers' Picnic, around 1900. The building in the distance was "Black Bill" Dunn's Riverside Hotel.

"Nothing gives you a better appetite than dieting."

-I. Kent Diet

This was a common postcard backdrop at Sylvan Beach during the early 1900s.

"When in the world are you people coming here? Take pity on us soon! PLEASE!"

Bill and Janeen Fariel

Bell's Block, now Labella's Pancake House, projected its Greek Revival splendor onto Main Street in the 1920s.

Bill and Janeen Fariel

Steamers await their passengers along the Beach's waterfront. The Forest Home is on the right.

"You will be surprised to hear from me at Sylvan Beach."

-Mosquitoes Point Hotel

Jean Kowalski

Picnickers stroll along the park promenade, next to the O.&W. Railroad tracks. The building on the left housed Isaiah and Minnie Head's General Store for decades.

Bill and Janeen Fariel

The Hotel Royal, now "Yesterday's Royal," in its heyday

"Well, my dear, this is where I am at. I can swim like a fish and am learning to roller skate. It's great!"

Mike Wameling

The lady high-diver attracted large crowds to the Beach's Midway.

Mike Wameling

The Windsor Hotel's staff pose with their fleet of rugged Oneida Lake rowboats, 1907. The hotel was located near today's Pfhol's Beach House.

***"Come on in, the water's fine.
Am having a dandy, sandy time."***

The toboggan slide and Rowe Brothers' Bath House from another angle. The building with "hotel" on the roof in the background is the Eagle Hotel. This card was printed around 1900.

Jean Kowalski

The St. Charles' private carriage deposits patrons at the elegant hotel's Park Avenue entrance. The inn, built by Louis Chesebrough of Vaseline fame in 1899, added an aristocratic flair to the beach scene until fire destroyed it in 1914.

"The next time sign your name. I studied ten hours to discover who your card was from. I should have known from the message. Don't you ever come to the Beach?"

-Frustrated in Camden

Ann Hopkins

Sylvan picnic groves were a major attraction at the Beach since James D. Spencer and sons established the first one in the 1870s. This photo was taken in the park, in back of the O.&W. Station.

Jean Kowalski

Luna Park and Carnival Park were the Beach's two amusement areas in the late nineteenth-early twentieth centuries. Luna was located along the Barge Canal, east of the bridge.

"We are enjoying ourselves great good-bye."

Mike Wameling

This photo shows Carnival Park's interior. The postcard company altered reality by transposing people into the scene.

Jean Kowalski

Bell's Post Office, prior to the addition of the Greek columns, highlights this scene. Three buildings to the left of the post office is the gingerbread-trimmed McAndrew cottage and just left of that is St. Mary's Roman Catholic Church. Gothic revival architecture spiced many Sylvan Beach structures.

"How is the shirt waist girl getting along? It is very pleasant out here and I am having a good time."

The Arcade building has been a Midway mainstay since it was erected around 1900.

Bill and Janeen Fariel

Sylvan Beach's first municipal building was located in the park between today's troopers' barracks and the Midway.

"Be sure and bring an old dress or something so you can go in. We'll meet you at the train, which gets here at 10:20."

Jean Kowalski

Trains were the Beach's economic aorta during the village's early twentieth-century heyday.

The old Barge Canal bridge had a long incline leading into the Beach. The Forest Home is on the left.

"Hi, Pal. Can't wait until Pals' day."

-Your Pal

Mike Wameling

Winter's grasp locked Sylvan Beach doors for several months. These ice slabs rest in front of the St. Charles Hotel.

– Chapter 17 –

The First Oneida Lake Hatchery

Today's Oneida Lake Hatchery, located in Constantia, is a far cry from its predecessors. This high tech facility, officially named the Oneida Fish Cultural Station, opened in 1993 and raises not only walleyes, but also diverse freshwater fish like lake sturgeons and paddlefish. In addition to its technologically superior facilities, the station boasts a fascinating visitors' center that educates the public in Oneida Lake ichthyology. Hatchery tours are especially popular during walleyes' spawning time, usually in early April, when these fish are netted and stripped of their eggs and milt. The hatchery's staff is composed of friendly, informative people who give visitors warm welcomes. Large viewing tanks, in which major Oneida Lake species are on display, delight thousands annually.

The first Constantia hatchery was built across the street from the present Fish Cultural Station. It was used until 1942, when another structure arose on the site of today's lab. *The Oswego Daily Palladium* published plans for the first hatchery on April 12, 1897. Constantia was then the site of a makeshift hatchery operation and local authorities were lobbying to make the village the home of a permanent, more efficient facility. The paper recounted this story.

> LOCATING A PIKE HATCHERY
> *Fish Commissioners Visit To Constantia Saturday*
>
> A party of distinguished men visited the little village of

Constantia, Oswego County, on Saturday and their coming to that place was of much importance, as at least part of their number have within their power the authority to locate an interesting and highly valuable industry there.

Several weeks ago it was announced that Assemblyman Bonds, of Onondaga County, had introduced a bill appropriating $6,000 for the erection and proper equipment of a modern hatchery for pike, on one of the interior lakes or the streams tributary thereto. As this bill is now well on its way to passage, and as there was established at Constantia four years ago a small hatchery, the members of the State Fish, Game, and Forestry Commission decided to visit the place on Saturday and look over sites for the proposed building, so that when the money is available there may be no delay in building the new structure for the propagation of fish life.

When the State Commission decided to visit the small hatchery, the N.Y. Ontario & Western Railroad Company kindly offered a special train for the conveyance of the members of the party from Fulton to Constantia.

Assistant Chief Game Protector M.C. Woris, of this city, invited a number of Oswegonians to join the commission on its visit. Constantia was reached about one o'clock and the party immediately repaired to the hatchery, which is situated on Scriba Creek near the railroad station. The present hatchery is merely a small, temporary shed. The building was erected to be used while experiments in pike hatching were being made.

The hatching is now in full operation and the mode of extracting the spawn, and the subsequent handling and hatching of it, was a revelation not only to the party of guests, but to the Commissioners as well. Pike begin to run ashore and up creeks to spawn about the first of April and, until about the fifteenth, there is a continual immigration of the fish to the spawning beds in the shoal water. Scriba Creek is the favorite spawning place for the pike and, during the season of fifteen days, about twelve men are kept at work catching and stripping the fish.

The fish are first caught in large nets, sometimes as many as 250 being taken at a dip. They are taken to the hatchery, where a man "strips" them. That is, he squeezes the spawn from the fish into bowls. In nature only about ten per cent of the eggs are ever matured, while by the artificial means ninety-five percent are hatched out. The liquid in the bowls is gently stirred and "loam water" (water in which there is sand) is added. This loam water is used in order to separate the eggs from each other, for if they are left clinging together as they are when taken from the females, they will never hatch.

When the loam water and spawn have been thoroughly stirred, they are placed in large tanks, which have a perforated bottom through which water continually percolates. The sand in the mixture drops through the holes in the bottom, while the running water keeps the eggs separated and slowly moving. The few in which life becomes extinct rise to the top and are taken off. The water in the tanks is kept at from thirty-five to forty-five degrees. After about a day the eggs are placed in large cans and shipped to the Caledonia and Clayton hatcheries, where there are facilities for bringing them into a state of fishhood. Twelve days suffices to hatch the eggs and, by the fall following, they are "fingerlings" or small fish and are ready to be placed in the lakes and streams to "paddle their own canoes."

As there are countless millions of pike in Oneida Lake, and as a good share of them run up Scriba Creek during the spawning season, the gentlemen in the party saw more fish than they ever did before. But not one could be taken, as the law protects them until May 1st. The stripping of the fish does not injure them, and they are placed back in the creek to return to the lake.

The number of fish thus stripped and the number of eggs obtained at Constantia during the time the hatchery is open, between the 1st and 15th of April, is beyond all compensation. No other fish are hatched there, and so the hatchery lies idle the greater part of the year. The men employed work night and day, as the greatest number of fish is obtained at night. They cannot be stripped as fast as they are brought in, so they are kept in five large troughs until needed.

Other places on Oneida and the interior lakes will be visited and the most available and advantageous location selected. The hatchery, if the bill appropriating the money passes, will be built this fall, in readiness for the next season's work. When the place is built it will be large enough to take care of the spawn from the time it is extracted until it is matured, so that it can be placed in lakes and streams. This will obviate the necessity for shipping the eggs to larger hatcheries for proper treatment.

The eggs must be shipped to these larger establishments, as they hatch very quickly in warm weather and, should it become mild quickly, there is not room to take care of them at Constantia, and they would hatch and die.

– Chapter 18 –

The Cottagers' Life

Sylvan and Verona Beach experienced their initial major growth during the 1880s. One of the families attracted to these "retreat communities" (as they were then advertised) were the Tuttles, from Oneida. John Forbes Tuttle and his wife, Cornelia "Nellie" Dyer Tuttle, rented camps at the Beach during that decade. The Tuttle children loved the lakeside environs and, in 1890, the family constructed "Seven Oaks," one of Verona Beach's first lakefront cottages. The practice of naming a summer cottage was common and many dwellings along Sylvan Beach's Park Avenue and Verona Beach's waterfront proudly wore titles like "The Eagle's Nest," "Seasands Edge," and "Sylvaneida."

The Tuttles were very accomplished. John was graduated from Hamilton College and subsequently earned a law degree from Yale. He first practiced in Oneida, but later moved to Syracuse. He and Nellie raised six children. Annie Tuttle Rush graduated from Smith College, became a teacher, and lived in Westfield, New Jersey. Bertha Tuttle Bowe, who was also a Smith College alumna, resided in Syracuse. Jack Tuttle, a Yale graduate, became president of Crouse-Hinds Corporation in Syracuse. Howard Tuttle also received a Yale education and became president of the National Casket Company, Boston. Burton Tuttle, another Yale man, moved to San Francisco. Maurice Tuttle was attracted to agriculture and owned a successful dairy farm in the Canastota area.

The Tuttle family enjoyed Seven Oaks until it was sold in the mid-1970s. Sadly, the dwelling deteriorated into a state of disrepair. It was razed and another home built on the site.

Annie Tuttle Rush wrote a beautiful memoir of the family's Oneida Lake years to commemorate Seven Oaks' diamond jubilee anniversary in 1965. The story, supplemented with information from Cornelia Tuttle Bowe, Bertha's daughter and a free-lance writer in Summit, New Jersey, provides a unique documentation of some of the joys that families experienced at Oneida Lake during the late nineteenth and early twentieth centuries.

The Early Years

Along in the 1880s, early in the spring, Howard would begin his plea,"Whenerwegoint'th'lake?" After a while the square trunk, with its domed lid, would be brought down from the attic to pack "things for the lake." In would go dolls, cookie forms for sand pies, jack knives, etc., until we gradually filled it. Then we waited and longed for our "ten weeks vacation." When the day finally arrived, trunks, boxes of food, cradles, and toys were loaded on to the "democrat wagon" and Grandfather William Dyer would drive the load from our home in Oneida to the cottage.

The family would sometimes travel by train from Oneida to Fish Creek and then would take a small steamer down to Sylvan Beach. There was no bridge across the creek, but there was a choice of two ferries, one a small scow-shaped raft with a fence guard on it and the other a larger scow for teams and wagons. We preferred the larger ferry, ostensibly because we liked horses, but the small one was frail and wobbly. The ferryman and passengers pulled these ferries across. People grasped the dribbling, slimy rope that ran along the ferry's rail. The rope was tied to both shores. They got the ferry across the creek by pulling together. Teamwork was essential. We children wanted to help, but were not allowed to do so.

At the first sight of the lake, all the children would whoop for joy and rush into the water, thoroughly drenching their clothing and shoes. They returned to the house and cried for bathing suits. Thus began that glorious, exciting "ten weeks vacation."

Long summers at the lake gave the children the opportunity to swim and to handle boats. A St. Lawrence Sailing Skiff, anchored in shallow water, was their training ship. There were also canoes, rowboats, catboats and, eventually, Lightening Sailboats. Shortly after 1901, Howard had a gaff-rigged sloop whose draft necessitated its being moored to a buoy some distance from shore. He named it *Boola*. The vessel's crew and passengers were transported from our dock by rowboats. Guests often were rowed while dressed in their city clothes. Proper ladies' costuming for rowing, sailing, or for a ride in one of our series of naphtha launches was a dress to the ankles, a hat, shoes and, on sunny days, a parasol. Our bathing suits, with skirts attached, came to our knees and, below that, we wore black stockings. The men's suits covered their bodies from neck to ankle. Every cottage had its own dock and, after dusk, lighted kerosene lanterns were hung on the mooring posts that extended well out from shore.

One day Betty Babcock, a teenage neighbor, lost her [hat] pin overboard just as she was transferring from the *Boola* to a rowboat. After she left, the boys began to dive for Betty's "bauble," a pin about ten inches long with an ornamental gold bead. That night the whole gang had dinner at the old Syracuse Yacht Club, on Onondaga Lake. Corn-on-the-cob was served and, to the great surprise and amusement of all, the ear served to Betty had her hatpin stuck through it.

As we grew older, we liked to walk over to Sylvan Beach to ride the roller coaster or the merry-go-round and to munch freshly fried potato chips as we sat on the porch of the Forest Home Hotel. The Algonquin Hotel, nearer to the lake, was a most fashionable and glamorous place, where the young people from nearby towns gathered for the Saturday evening dances. After these galas, we used oil lanterns to light our way as we walked home through the woods.

This was a happy, carefree time. Days were spent bathing and boating. Evenings centered around a bonfire on the beach or playing hilarious children's games around the large dining room table. Then, there was no smoking, no drinking, no bridge playing, and no "twosing."

The biggest crowd of the year gathered at Sylvan Beach for the Hop Growers' Picnic. Early in the morning we would see farmers, their wagons filled with families, coming along the beach road that stretched from Oneida to Fish Creek. All day they would pass, not bumper to bumper, but horse head to tailgate. On the return trip, that night, the men would be roaring happily or nodding with sleep after a most exciting day.

SEVEN OAKS

For the first five summers our family rented cottages, one of which was the Fox Cottage at Sylvan Beach. The Fox family owned the manor house in Durhamville, a large brick house surrounded by an ornamental iron fence. Durhamville was, at one time, an important Erie Canal port. A dripping aqueduct can still be viewed there, but the mule teams on the towpaths are only a memory. After one summer in the Fox's place, we rented the Dwight Chapin Cottage for several seasons. Mr. Chapin and his bride took a unique wedding trip in 1870–on a canal boat from Durhamville to Utica. Next to the Chapin structure was the Downing's camp, called "The Eagle's Nest" because there was a nest nearby. Next to Downing's was a lot on which grew seven oak trees.

In 1890, mother commissioned the construction of "Seven Oaks," our family's own cottage, on that property. I believe that this was the fifth such structure on Verona Beach. Later, the Klock and Beal cottages were built.

Fortunately for later generations, our cottage was designed to accommodate a large family. In addition to our parents, four children, two maids, visiting relatives, and other guests often stayed there at the same time. There was no gas or plumbing. A wood burning stove in the kitchen provided hot water and a pump brought drinking water from the lake, purified by its flow through the sand. The lake also served as our bathtub. Pails were used to carry lake water to the house for washing. Washstands were built into each room to hold a bowl, pitcher, and tooth mug. Slop pails rested nearby. There was a path to the outhouse behind the barn. Later, water was piped from North Bay and the maids' room was converted into a bathroom. The kitchen and "powder room" were also equipped. Around 1931 the cottage acquired the nickname, "Rattlebox," and a wooden nameplate was nailed to the back porch.

Those were happy days. The house was always full of people. We never knew how many would show up for weekends. Bananas were bought by the stem and hung in the barn. Household employees saved mothers the burden of cooking (the Brennan sisters worked for us for many years). Occasionally, when we were without a cook, we walked half a mile up the beach to Mrs. Breitenstein's Boarding House. She would lean on the high shelf that separated the kitchen from the dining room and joke with her patrons, who sat at long, bare tables. The price of a well-cooked Sunday dinner of meat, vegetables, and homemade pie was twenty-five cents.

At that time there was one small store at Sylvan Beach. We kept our own ice supply. Three families together built an icehouse, which later became the Brewer garage. Every winter, ice would be cut from the lake and packed in sawdust for use the following summer. It was a chore each day to climb the outside ladder to the high opening to the ice supply, brush away the sawdust, get out the large blocks, hose them clean, and carry them to the "ice box." This was literally a box with half its space reserved for the huge chunks. For fresh vegetables we depended on the farmers who sold their produce from door to door. The milkman came every day, in a little buggy just big enough for himself and two large milk cans. He would dip his quart measure with its long, upright handle, into the cans and pour the milk into our milk pitchers. No bottles. No pasteurizing. No ice.

Under these conditions, one might expect typhoid fever to strike. The milk supply finally brought this dreaded disease. Three little children in our Verona Beach colony became ill. They were Nellie Downing, Eunice Klock, and Howard Tuttle. To transport these children to Oneida, the Elmira, Cortland, and Northern Railroad (afterwards known as the Lehigh Valley Railroad) arranged to send a combination coach and baggage car to our little station at Verona Beach. A Mr. Ralph, of Utica, had built this small station on the rear of his property and somehow contrived to get the trains to stop there. The children were carried on cots, umbrellas held over them to shield them from rain, and were placed in the baggage section of their train, while their families rode in the coach. Special permission had been obtained to switch over to the Ontario and Western tracks and ride directly to Oneida. There, the children were taken in hacks (horse-drawn coaches) to their homes.

In the late 1890s there were a dozen cottages along Verona Beach, all belonging to our Oneida friends. A footpath ran from one front porch to the next, along the line, and in back a road meandered between the houses and their barns, in farm style. The beach, about a hundred feet wide, sloped right up to the porches; no lawns needed to be cut. The sandy roadway that ran along the shore remained usable even after autos appeared. Often cars became stuck in the dry sand and boys, sitting in wait, would rush out five or six strong to give a mighty push. As the lake gradually lowered during the summer, the beach widened and islands would form off shore, providing an ideal playground for children. It became necessary to put in a sea wall when the Barge Canal was built.

Building the Barge Canal

Masons and dredgers worked hard on this project from 1903 to 1918. The Algonquin Hotel was razed, probably to make room for the lighthouse at Fish Creek's mouth. Concrete restraining walls along the creek and Sylvan Beach's long pier were constructed to shelter and stabilize the village's harbor. These structures' builders were unaware that, years before, there had been a stone pier that jutted out from the south side of Fish Creek, into the lake. In the 1890s rowers had to be careful to avoid that pier, which was submerged under the high water line and extended some distance from shore.

Plans called for a lighthouse along the Verona Beach front but, by that time, all lakeside lots had been developed. Providence provided the one piece of property needed when the Klock family cottage was struck by lightening. Neighbors, using wet blankets and the "bucket brigade" technique, tried to extinguish the fire, but the building burned to the ground.

Summer after summer we endured the construction's noise and soot, but enjoyed watching the project's progress. Our interest increased when the canal opened and the barges and oilers arrived. Tugs would sometimes tow a line of six wooden barges and, several times, storms tore the vessels loose and they drifted ashore on the beach. One time, wave action washed scores of hay bales in front of our cottage. News of this quickly spread and farmers came to gather the bounty. Another time, tons of grain were scattered along the sand. Once, a canal boat housing a family broke loose and drifted near shore. The frightened people kept crying for help, but were calmed by children who, playing on the beach, splashed out to the stranded boat and called, cheerily, "You can walk ashore."

We could not only watch the canal's traffic, but also the races sponsored by the yacht club at Lewis Point. One year they scheduled a race involving Lightening Sailboats. Nine vessels entered. The weather looked threatening and several crews dropped out and returned to the point. But the steady, strong wind encouraged five boats to continue. When they reached the middle of the lake, a gale struck. Three craft quickly capsized. The other two, moments prior, had lowered their sails to ride out the storm. Nine people bobbed in the water, one mile from shore. Two boys, watching the race from our cottage, rushed to Sylvan Beach, where an excursion boat was discharging its passengers. The steamer's captain took the two volunteers on a rescue mission. Oneida Lake was terrifically rough. The little boat puffed valiantly and reached the racers in half an hour. The drenched sailors were brought back to our cottage, where they were warmed inside and out.

Another rescue comes to mind. This example shows how fast storms rise on Oneida Lake. One sunny morning, a number of us were returning from church, wearing our "Sunday bests." As we unloaded from the cars, the wind hit and, by the time we could push ourselves around to the front of the cottage, we saw that our sailboat had broken its anchorage and was rocking rapidly toward the canal. Several of the boys jumped in after her, white flannels and all, and just managed to catch the boat before she crashed into the breakwater.

Union Chapel

On Sundays we rowed or paddled to Sylvan Beach's Union Chapel, stacked our oars in a corner, and took the front pews to help the choir. The James D. Spencer family, pioneers of Verona and Sylvan Beach, were among the chapel's founders and the sanctuary was constructed three years prior to our cottage in 1887. The building was designed with an imaginative foresight that accommodated future crowds. All the sidewalls opened and overflowing congregations could relax on the lawn. In the early days, benches were placed outdoors and some of the sides were vented. It was a pleasant, cool place to sit. Unfortunately, this situation had some serious drawbacks. The Ontario and Western trains discharged hundreds of jovial picnickers at the station in the village park. Lunchroom proprietors, bar tenders, and concessionaires rang bells and blew horns. The poor preacher could only despair.

Sunday night hymn singing at our cottage was a revered tradition. Mother led the grandchildren, using hymnbooks borrowed from the chapel and the vocalists arranged themselves along the sea wall or around a bonfire on the beach. These devotions were timed to coincide with the lake's magnificent sunsets. On one occasion, a visiting minister's young son volunteered to sing a solo and piped out "Davy Crockett." Bowing to the applause at the performance's conclusion, he murmured, "It's the only song I know." After catching a disapproving glance from his father he added, after a long pause, "Besides 'Jesus Loves Me.'"

On August 1, 1965, the day that followed our cottage's diamond jubilee celebration, there was a cross dedication service at Union Chapel in honor of my parents. The gold cross, which had been given in their memory to Park Central Presbyterian Church in Syracuse, was no longer used by that congregation and was reconsecrated at the chapel. This service rekindled warm and fond memories.

Parting Thoughts

Celebrating Independence Day, with an especially large bonfire and a marshmallow roast, was a time-honored family tradition. Later, the holiday became an occasion for family gatherings, flavored by a barbecue and buffet. Now, in the 1960s, the bonfire idea has spread and the lake sometimes wears a sparking necklace, a reflection of many blazes that ring the shoreline all the way from North to South Bay.

Oneida Lake's bird life has changed. Eagles have disappeared and great blue herons are far less common. In their place we now view more seagulls and shore-loving sandpipers. The lake's abundant fish and insect populations provide nourishment for these birds.

The Barge Canal's business traffic has greatly diminished, but motorboats and private yacht usage have increased. Trains no longer bring the vast crowds, who now arrive by automobile. The railroad beds of the Ontario and Western and the Elmira, Cortland, and Northern have now, in part, become highways. A few abandoned railroad ties, a reminder of the trains' former importance, can still be found near Fish Creek Landing.

Seven Oaks is now the oldest Verona Beach cottage still owned by descendents of the area's pioneer vacationers. Our parents, John and Nellie Tuttle, left us with more than a dwelling. We will always feel a deep affinity for this place and for the rich memories of our childhood paradise.

– Chapter 19 –

Beacons in Triplicate

The Story of Oneida Lake's Lighthouses

Three identical lighthouses–at Brewerton, Verona Beach, and Frenchman's Island–have guided Oneida Lake's navigators since the Barge Canal opened in 1917. Bill Orzell, a director of the Canal Society of New York State, wrote a fine story about these beacons' history and I am honored to include it here.

> Lighthouses have a charm all their own. Whether their glow provides a warning signal to mariners, a sightseeing stop to auto-bound tourists, or a special character to a waterfront, every lighthouse has a distinctive quality.
>
> The New York State Barge Canal System, that amazing and complex network of man-made structures and natural waterways, includes three unique lighthouses, all on Oneida Lake. The canal's engineers designed today's system to be used by motorized vessels, breaking with the traditional draft animal towage of the original nineteenth century canals. This allowed the Barge Canal to take full advantage of our state's abundant large lakes and rivers. Thus Oneida Lake, the largest body of water located entirely within the state's boundaries, was incorporated into the canal system.
>
> Oneida's twenty-one miles of open, shallow water are notorious for blowing up into a ferocious boil of wind and waves. To provide a safer passage on this potentially hazardous lake, the state constructed three large lighthouses.

One of the lighthouses stands in Verona Beach, on the lake's eastern end, across the canal from the popular resort of Sylvan Beach. A second lighthouse is on Frenchman's Island, near the western end. The location of this large and historic isle is an excellent point on which to fix one's position when navigating the big lake. The third is situated on the lake's extreme western end, at Brewerton. Its strategic location on the north side of the canal allows its beacon, in combination with another light on the Route 11 bridge, to provide an illuminated range. Navigators line up these lights, one atop the other, and are guided safely into Brewerton harbor.

These three lighthouses are identical in design. They were constructed of reinforced concrete, using the same forms at each location. From large square bases, which provide foundations as well as entry areas and fuel storage spaces, the towers rise some eighty feet. The round towers taper gracefully to support large lanterns and maintenance platforms at the pinnacles. Wrought iron-latticed railings ring the upper platforms.

The lantern platforms are reached by climbing five separate stairways, contained within the tower, illuminated by slender rectangular windows. The lower windows have, sadly, been used by vandals to gain access. These malicious acts necessitate that canal authorities block off the openings with steel plates.

Despite periodic damages, the Barge Canal Lighthouses have proven to be remarkably durable. They have stood since 1917, when they were erected by the Lupfer & Remick Company, of Buffalo, and have been in constant service ever since. Their solid construction has withstood Oneida Lake's often tempestuous spirit.

Some additional modifications have been made at each lighthouse site. A steel frame tower was added to the platform of the Frenchman's Island structure to lift the beacon above the surrounding trees. The Brewerton lighthouse was originally equipped with a red light, since it is on the canal's north bank, which is marked by other navigational aids that are painted red. Mariners remind themselves that "Red is right, returning from the sea." This was modified to white light and combined with the previously cited light on the Route 11 bridge to form a complete range. The Brewerton and Verona Beach lighthouses were update from self-contained gas cylinder fuel systems to electric power in the 1920s.

> To casual observers, the lighthouses resemble large candlesticks, an image consistent with their purpose. As Barge Canal features, they have often been overshadowed by the more familiar locks and lift bridges. Nonetheless, they possess a special, functional beauty, not only as beacons to mariners, but also as romantic elements of our state's unique canal system.

A Syracuse paper published an article on September 28, 1917, heralding the Oneida Lake lighthouses' advent. The piece contained data that expands on the Orzell story.

> Lighthouses and tower lamps, which spell "safety" for night navigation on the Barge Canal, have been completed and are in operation on Oneida and Onondaga Lakes.
>
> The lighthouses are 80-foot concrete structures, erected at a cost of about $10,000 each. They are situated at Frenchman's Island, Brewerton, and Sylvan Beach and are equipped with gas lamps estimated at $2,400 in cost. The lamp at Frenchman's Island sends out rays of light in all directions, while the other two have reflectors and project their beams only toward the lake. They are mantle gas lamps, supplied by fuel that is stored in large tanks under pressure.
>
> Floating buoys have been anchored between the lighthouses and are filled with gas at 100 atmospheres, which tests to a pressure of 4,000 pounds per square inch. This supply enables the lights to burn constantly for nine months without refilling the chambers. [These numbered, navigational buoys still mark the lake's channel.]
>
> When the lake freezes over, the buoys will be taken up by a derrick boat and placed on the banks until after the spring thaw. An inspection trip will be made by motorboat to the lighthouses and buoys at regular intervals, at which time any defect will be remedied.

Oneida Lake's lighthouses continue to guide. Brewerton's and Frenchman's flashing lights direct night navigators on the lake's West End while the Verona Beach lighthouse, in addition to its nocturnal use, is easily spotted from afar and shows the way to Sylvan–Verona Beach harbor. The beacons, and the grounds surrounding them, exist in vividly contrasting locales.

To reach the Brewerton light, drive north on Route 11 and cross the Oneida River bridge. Take your first left, on Oswego County

Route 37 (labeled CORT 37 on the road sign). You'll see the lighthouse, about a quarter mile down the road, on your left about a hundred yards off the highway. Trees obscure the view and the overgrown grounds make for difficult walking. A visit during spring, when vegetation is at a minimum, would be preferable. The lighthouse is best viewed from the Oneida River's south bank. To reach a good vantage point, turn left on Library Street, prior to reaching the river's Route 11 Bridge. Follow that street to its end and you'll arrive at the Brewerton Boatyards, a marina owned by the Carroll family. Be sure to ask for sightseeing permission at the marina office. You'll view the lighthouse across the river, nestled just west of the railroad bridge. It's a fitting, somewhat symbolic scene, with railroad and canal structures side by side–two transportation means that sparked growth in the Oneida Lake region.

You can easily see the Frenchman's Island lighthouse by motoring your boat along the isle's north side, where the Barge Canal's navigational channel passes the island. If you want a closer encounter with the island's light, a difficult, but interesting, journey awaits.

Drive your boat to the isle's south side. You'll note a large pier. This dockage facility is in poor condition, but it's the best way to land on Frenchman's, unless you want to anchor in the shallows and wade. The pier is high and ramshackle, so be careful. After you leave the pier, you'll see a pathway leading into the woods. To find the lighthouse, take that trail and bear to the left. Stay on the trail as much as possible–poison oak and poison ivy thrive on Frenchman's. You'll probably have to step over discarded beer cans and other party refuse. New York State owns Frenchman's and the isle serves a variety of "public" functions.

Any inconveniences encountered are worth the effort expended because, on Frenchman's Island today, images of the 1790s thrive. Litter aside, you can imagine the isle in the wilderness when the Frenchman and his family lived there. Great maples, beeches, and oaks soar skyward in primeval majesty, their expansive circumferences bearing witness to antiquity. The beeches are noteworthy because, on the "mainland," blight has devastated thousands of these trees. Amidst the island's sequestered environment they flourish in arboreal splendor. Omnipresent hanging vines connect the great trees, shading the island floor like rain-forested umbrellas. Thick, prickly berry patches, growing where sunlight penetrates, infringe on the pathway, almost saying that this isle is nature's place and you'd best watch where you tread. Frenchman's

Island is an amazing, beautiful, isolated locale. The lighthouse stands proudly, sentinel within its deciduous jungle. Vines reach for its tower and branches brush its concrete sides with every Oneida Lake breeze.

The Verona Beach lighthouse is the easiest to visit and the best preserved of all three beacons. To get there, take Route 13 north from its junction with Route 31 (at South Bay). Pass the entrance for the Verona Beach State Park and make your next left onto Lake Shore Road. Drive down Lake Shore for about a half-mile and turn left onto Forest Avenue. The lighthouse is located about one hundred yards down the road, on the left, slightly away from the highway. You can't miss it.

The Verona Beach light stands amidst a scene as close to "Oneida Lake in 1900" as exists today. Several old-time gothic cottages surround the lighthouse and, though devoid of their original gingerbread ornamentation, the dwellings are exceptionally well maintained. History seeps from every clapboard. Screened porches, stretched hammocks, moss-covered shingles, Adirondack style chairs, delicate curtains, and comforting shade trees enhance the cottages' style. A narrow beach, punctuated by scattered driftwood and grass, leads from the lighthouse to the lake. The property commands a panoramic view of Sylvan Beach harbor, framed by its rock piled jetty and weather-beaten concrete pier. This is a private locale, so beautiful that the visitor almost feels like he's intruding. The lighthouse's walls are clean and you can still read "Lupher & Remick, Engineers & Contractors" on the padlocked, cast iron door. Don't visit for long, however. It's only fair to respect the residents who maintain this gem of a living space.

The first Constantia hatchery consisted of several small buildings, like the one pictured here by Scriba Creek.

Ann Hopkins

A worker poses with walleye propagation apparatus. Holding tanks occupy the foreground. The overturned pans were used for mixing eggs and milt. Fertilized eggs were held in the tube-shaped jars behind the fisheries technician.

Ann Hopkins

A steam launch enters Scriba Creek, circa 1910. Hatchery nets dry above the docks that line the stream. The old cast iron bridge in the background was replaced in 1932.

Corky Winn

Jean Kowalski

Bucolic scenes such as this view of National Lake, east of Vienna Road, adorned the Sylvan Beach tapestry that the Tuttles enjoyed.

Cornelia Tuttle Bowe

The Tuttles' "Seven Oaks" cottage was a gorgeous gothic revival structure. The Sylvan-Verona Beach community contained many gothic cottages in the early twentieth century.

Mike Wameling

The Tuttles sailed across Wood River's mouth to get from their cottage to Sylvan Beach. This photo was taken prior to the Barge Canal's construction in the 1910s.

Fort Brewerton Historical Society

The Barge Canal dramatically transformed the Sylvan Beach area. This photo shows Wood Creek entering the canal near the present Cove Road bridge at Fish Creek hamlet, east of the Beach.

The Verona Beach lighthouse guides Oneida Lake navigators.

Mammoth maple and beech trees thrive amidst Frenchman's Island's dense deciduous forest.

– Chapter 20 –

Murphy's Cows Stayed In the Barn

The 18th Amendment to the Constitution was ratified in 1918 and the United States became legally dry. Temperance societies and teetotalers rejoiced as the amendment, and the Volstead Act that accompanied it, outlawed production and consumption of "demon rum," "John Barleycorn," and virtually any other alcoholic beverage. This attempt at legislating morality sparked more civil disobedience than any law in American history. Speakeasies, places where alcoholic drinks could be purchased, sprang up all over the country. Bootleggers did a land office business. Smuggling beer and other alcoholic beverages from Canada, where production was legal, became widespread. Organized crime got involved in the booze business and conflicts like the famous Elliott Ness–Al Capone rivalry ensued. Women gained suffrage and some became "Flappers," who defied norms by wearing slacks and smoking cigarettes. Jazz revolutionized the music world, autos enhanced personal mobility and altered residential patterns, professional sports gained popularity, and the economy, for many groups, "roared." A conservative movement like prohibition, which lasted through the '20s until its repeal in 1933, didn't stand a chance amidst the prevailing national spirit.

William "Buddy" McCarthy was a young lad at Sylvan Beach during the prohibition era. His life and times echoed major events in the Beach's early history. He was born in 1917 at the Cavana Sanitarium, located on the corner of Park and 13th Avenues, and was delivered by Dr. Martin Cavana, who was Sylvan Beach's leader during its initial heyday (the "Gay 1890s" through the "Golden 1920s"). Buddy's family was friendly with the Cavanas and, on occasion, the doctor invited the McCarthys over to listen to his radio, which had superb reception from the high antennae on the sanitarium's roof. Sunday afternoon religious broadcasts were especially popular during these social gatherings. Buddy's grandfather, William T. McCarthy, first came to Sylvan Beach on assignment for the Buffalo Amusement Company, but liked the village and stayed. "William T.," as many knew him, got involved in the Beach's Midway. He built and operated the roller coaster, roller skating rink, and "Figure 8" ride. He also built several homes in the village. McCarthy's construction talents were multi-faceted and, when New York State's Barge Canal project threatened to engulf Sylvan Beach's important Algonquin Hotel, he directed the efforts that moved and saved the building. Buddy's parents, William "Bill" and Theresa Cook McCarthy, were also Beach entrepreneurs. Bill purchased the Forest Home Hotel and operated it for decades. He and Theresa also owned the Elk Restaurant, across the street from the Forest. Bill McCarthy was a close friend of the Spencers, the Beach's founding family and, through this association, became chairman of the village park's board of directors. In 1934, Chairman McCarthy granted the lease to a ramshackle hot dog stand in the park to Edward Stewart, of Rome, who eventually transformed the place into Eddie's Restaurant.

Bill and Theresa's two sons, Buddy and Edward, matured within a vortex of Sylvan Beach commerce. Family dinner table conversation focused on topics like the size of crowds at the "Hop Growers" or "Colored People's" picnics (both events enlivened notable summer weekends), the number of railroad trains that rumbled into the Beach on a particularly busy day, the success of Midway attractions, and the price of walleyed pike. The McCarthy brothers, being children of the lake, naturally gravitated to the fishing business. Read this book's story on Sylvan Beach's "Fabulous Fifties" for details about Edward McCarthy's walleye marketing. Buddy McCarthy's Beach memories end around 1940, however, when he left the village and became an engineer and pilot in the Merchant Marine. He retired in 1980, after a remarkable forty years of service. He and his wife, the former Rita Bosler, raised three daughters–Rita, Ruth, and Evelyn.

I interviewed Buddy during the summer of 2001. McCarthy is an engaging octogenarian, with a crisp memory. I told him that I was writing a volume of stories about the Oneida Lake region and that his nephew, Ed McCarthy, Jr., recommended that I talk with him. He delighted me with several hours of sharp, valuable narrative. As we traversed the lifelines of Sylvan Beach in the '20s and '30s, vivid prohibition stories emerged. Buddy introduced that era by saying, "Jack, let me be frank. Prohibition produced wild times and Sylvan Beach was a wide-open town. You wouldn't believe what went on there." I told him that I would and Buddy McCarthy tapped into his recollections of some not-so-dry times.

> I was lucky to live in Sylvan Beach during my younger years. It was a great place for kids. You could go swimming–always in Fish Creek, where it was cool in summer. There were plenty of barns where kids could jump in the haymows and into haystacks that stood alongside. The farmers didn't care because we'd give them a hand from time to time. We knew where the coldest wells were when we got thirsty. We learned how to fish from the old-timers. My grandfather, Roscoe Cook, was my best friend and he taught me how to make tip-ups from sumac branches and how to wrap the piece of tin foil from a pack of cigarettes around a fishhook and make one of the best walleyed pike lures there ever was. He showed me how to hunt. We shot rabbits, ducks, and deer, even before there was a season on them. Grandpa Cook had a duck blind along the lake near 29th Avenue and one time a flock of geese froze into a little backwater, right near the blind. We had roast goose for several days after that.
>
> Life got even more interesting when I became a teenager. Girls from the city vacationed at the Beach and their house parties were great fun for us local boys. I bought a Model-A Ford and even owned two of them by the time I was twenty. For my first job I worked as a clerk for Ike Head, in his general store. It was interesting. Ike sold almost everything...groceries, shoes, raincoats, fishing tackle, boots, hardware...you name it. I worked there during the Depression and times were tough. Farmers would bring eggs or produce to Ike and he took them in trade for other merchandise. He was a generous, trusting man. Ike had a filing cabinet where he kept the "due bills." He gave credit and trusted farmers all winter, until spring came and they started to make more money. He gave lots of Beach peo-

ple credit and conveniently forgot many bills when people couldn't pay. The bills collected dust in the cabinet. Ike made life easier for people in Sylvan Beach during those hard times.

There was nothing dry about the Beach during prohibition. Take the picnics, for example. The biggest two weekends of the year were the ones when the "Hop Growers Picnic" and the "Colored People's Picnic" were held. The Beach was filled with people! My friends and I used to watch thousands of people as they walked from the Lehigh Valley Station in Verona Beach across the Barge Canal Bridge to the festivities over here. It seemed like an endless line of people. The most fun we had, though, was in the evening. Trains would leave around 8 or 9 o'clock and these hop-pickers and black people would have to get back to the station. Heck, a big portion of them would be drunker than skunks! They'd be staggering, helping each other. They'd be running into each other, laughing, yelling. They'd be singing, dancing their way over the bridge. We used to sit along the bridge and watch the show. Quite the prohibition parade!

These people had absolutely no trouble getting a drink at Sylvan Beach. I'll bet that there were at least twenty places in the Beach where a fellow could take a drink during prohibition. Almost all of the hotels were speakeasies. You could get a cold one at the Windsor and the Eagle, along the lake front. The Forest served the booze and so did Hotel Nobles. The Royal used to show "moving pictures" and had some relaxing refreshment to go along with them. Johnny Rice and Mort Dunn ran a place where the meat market was, at the corner of 5th and Main. Across the street, near the foot of the old bridge, was Paddy Dwyer's. Heck, I think he was serving before he even had a restaurant license. The Owens Hotel, where the Beach Bowl is today, was wet. The Lehigh Valley Hotel, by the Verona Beach train station, was a speakeasy, too. Supposedly the lady that owned it went over Niagara Falls in a barrel. Who knows? She liked me, though, because I brought her muskrat carcasses and she loved to eat muskrat. A Verona Beach gourmet.

It was a wide-open time, but the hotel owners were a little secretive, too. You'd go into these hotels' front rooms and there would be a bunch of people sitting down, eating dinner. All well and good. There was always a little side door, however, off the dining room. That door led to the back room, where they served the beer and booze.

They could be secretive, all right. The Forest Hotel had a trap door, hidden under a mat, behind the bar. They could quickly slide the mat, open the door, and stash the booze in a crawl space under the hotel. The Russells, after they bought Hotel Nobles, used to bury their beer for safekeeping. They'd even bury it all winter...the ground doesn't freeze much at the Beach. One time a couple local guys found where Russells buried a keg. These fellows dug out the keg, found a tap, and took it to a house across the street from Eddie's. They had one helluva party! I remember another time in the late 1920s. Some of my friends and I were playing hide and seek. One of my buddies jumped over this high, wood fence that hid the small back yard behind the Hotel Royal. He saw this hogshead barrel–six feet high, five feet across–and he got into it. Wow! It was the hotel's beer stash! We were only about twelve or thirteen, but we emptied plenty of those bottles. Never a lot at a time, mind you. A couple here and there, so the owners wouldn't get suspicious. All of it was premium Canadian beer.

Then you had your "camp speakeasies." Some people would arrive by train, bringing several big trunks with them, rent a camp and, before you knew it, they'd be serving the public. Word spread and the folks at that camp enjoyed a couple busy weeks. Almost as quickly as they came, they'd leave, profit in hand. A brewery from Syracuse owned a camp and, on occasion, made their products available. Rumor had it that the state police even had their own speakeasy camp, near the lighthouse in Verona Beach. Some hot dog stands sold an occasional bottle of beer, mustard and ketchup included.

Lots of people made their own. My Grandfather Cook kept crocks and barrels on his back porch, where he fermented his elderberry wine and made his home brew. He wasn't alone. There was a big still in town at one time, right across the street from Ray Sawner's Boat Livery at the end of 6th Ave. Some guys from the city ran it. You'd see trucks bringing loads of sugar to the building. One time, I was talking to Ray in front of his house and I said, "Hey, what's that sweet smell?" Ray laughed and said, "Buddy, I wouldn't worry about it. It's all for the public good." Well, next winter, the Beach was snowed in for three weeks. A bunch of local guys volunteered to shovel Main Street. The boys that owned the still were stuck in town and they brought the shovelers some samples of their liquid refreshment. Well, the guys got pretty loaded and, when they

> went home, their wives didn't like it. They called the Feds and the still operators got raided and closed down.
>
> But this was an exception. The Treasury Agents, "Feds" we called them, seldom made a score. We used to love seeing them pulling into town. They had these big touring cars...I think they were Fords...all black, with cloth tops and windows that had pull-curtains over them. Three or four of these cars would come speeding over the bridge and pull up in front of one of our hotels. The Treasury agents jumped out of the car and ran into the hotel, ready to make a bust. It was high drama, just like in the movies. But they never found anything! The Beach had its own police force–men like my grandfather, and a few farmers from up in Vienna. Local guys. Our cops dressed the part, they looked like law enforcers, but their loyalties were here. These guys always seemed to know when a raid was coming, when the Feds were going to try and knock a place off, and they tipped off the hotel owners. You might say that the Sylvan Beach family took care of itself during prohibition.
>
> Prohibition was fun for us kids, but sad things happened, too. There used to be a family that lived in Oneida Valley that made whiskey runs to Canada. These people supplied some of the Beach's hotels. One of the family's sons got involved in a high-speed chase, crashed his car, and got killed. You read of other events like this. Prohibition was a wild time, but it was violent, too, and people got hurt.
>
> Prohibition kept the Beach going after the Depression hit. People didn't have much money, but they still wanted a good time. Sylvan Beach offered nickel beers, even two for a nickel sometimes. Food was cheap, friends were all over the place, and fun was free. What more could you ask for, especially if you were a teenager?

I talked about prohibition with Buddy's former employer, Ike Head, during my first days of researching Sylvan Beach and Oneida Lake's history, thirty years ago. Ike recalled that, when prohibition began and the village was adjusting to this unpopular law, speakeasy owners coined a phrase to warn each other of impending raids. When the Feds were known to be on the way, word spread like wildfire through the Beach that "Murphy's cows are out!"

Considering what Buddy McCarthy recalled about the Feds' success, the cows should probably have stayed in the barn.

– Chapter 21 –

Dollars Through the Ice

Commercial fishing has always provided incomes for Oneida Lake's anglers. In the early nineteenth century, enterprising Yankees marketed salmon that they netted in the lake's tributaries. Eel trapping on the lake's western end and at the shoals by Chittenango Creek's mouth brought lucrative rewards. "Fish pirates" boldly harvested Oneida's bounty until modern law enforcement techniques limited their illicit activities. Walleyed pike dinners used to be a specialty in lakeside restaurants, until sale of this valuable sport fish was banned in the early 1960s. Yellow perch, sunfish, bluegills, and bullheads taken from Oneida can still be sold and, at times, receipts derived from these panfish's harvest more than pay for anglers' expenses.

"Fishing for profit" has long been a controversial issue around Oneida Lake. One of the reasons for the Anglers' Club's organization at Lower South Bay in the 1890s was to combat fish pirates and to promote sport fishing as the sole method of reaping Oneida's offerings. The Oneida Lake Association, started in 1945, led the fight to stop walleye marketing and took pride in legislation being passed for that purpose. Millard Rogers, the Association President who spearheaded the crusade to eliminate commercial walleye angling, noted that "the dollar sign has now been removed from our lake's most important fish" when the law was signed.

On January 26, 1930, the *Syracuse Herald* published articles describing commercial ice fishing in waters off the North Shore, near Cleveland. This was the Great Depression and that fact magnified the importance of any income. The stories revealed the inner workings of Oneida's winter fish business, an endeavor that attracted only the most rugged devotees. In a pair of articles, the paper highlighted ice fishing and one of its noted practitioners, Timothy C. Grow.

From Oneida Lake to Manhattan

Oneida Lake is yielding treasures from its icy waters in the form of pike and perch for the New York markets. Hardy fishermen, numbering possibly 200, are fishing through the ice and sharing that treasure. Fishing this year is good.

Cleveland fishermen shipped 1,000 pounds of pike the week before Christmas. That brought forth protests from sportsmen and the charge that the ice fishermen are "robbing the lake." The latter retaliate with the statement that the 1,000-pound shipment represented the week's catch of almost one hundred men.

This group is fishing on the ice off Cleveland. They bring their catches to the Globe Hotel, where they are weighed.

New York prices, as paid to fishermen, vary from twenty to forty cents per pound for pike and about twenty-three cents per pound for perch. New York retail prices for pike run up as high as eighty and ninety cents per pound.

Great care must be taken in handling the pike because, if they freeze, the eyes turn white and they cannot command the highest prices. They must be shipped carefully, with snow between the layers.

The men who fish through the ice work hard. The nearest operations are about a mile and a half from the shore, which means a daily walk of three miles over ice. That, however, is only the beginning of the toll. The real ice fisherman, if he wants to take his work seriously, has his holes in the ice chopped before daybreak. He is allowed fifteen of them. Each hole must be chopped through ice that now is about ten inches thick.

Above each hole a stick is driven into the ice. A wire extends from the stick. The hook and line is attached to the wire. When the fish strikes the bait the wire sags. The fisherman rushes to that "tip-up" and pulls in his catch.

Each fisherman is allowed to take fifteen pike daily. The pike cannot be less than twelve inches long. The fish range in weight from one pound to six pounds. Three pounds would be a high average. A full catch of approximately forty-five pounds would net the fortunate fisherman about $11.25. There is a joker to that statement, however. They aren't getting full catches of pike. Furthermore, a pound per fish would be nearer the average.

Whether ice fishing or summer fishing yields the highest return is a debatable problem, with advocates for both sides. "When you fish through the ice," the reporter was told, "you have to wait for the fish. When you are fishing from a boat you can follow the fish around."

Following the fish around on the ice is a difficult task. Distances are deceiving. Tip-ups that look comparatively near are more than a mile away. Even little shacks, which some of the fishermen erect on the ice, are much father away than they appear to be. Some of the fishermen attempt to solve the walking problem by driving their automobiles over the ice. Correct form requires that you drive with both doors open, prepared for a hasty exit and the possible loss of one car.

There are air holes and gas holes in the ice to be avoided. One fisherman, who was alone, lost his life last year. "We'll drag for you next spring," is a grim jest among the fishermen.

Careful investigation disclosed that it probably is possible to earn a living by fishing through Oneida Lake's ice. This task can't be done by fishing a few hours, deciding that they aren't biting, and returning to the warmth of the Globe Hotel. Even a full day brings a reward none too large. The "tons of pike" people assume are caught are largely a myth.

The Fisherman in the Cod Liver Oil Ad

We proceeded to the home of Timothy C. Grow, who was in the barn. He had been experimenting with a newfangled gas lantern and apparently had been anticipating an explosion for, when I suddenly appeared in the doorway, my unexpected arrival startled him. But he calmed down so quickly that even when Hermie [note–a photographer who accompanied the reporter] came in with three or four cameras and a couple of tripods he withstood the shock beautifully.

Mr. Grow was fixing the lantern so that he could go down to the harbor and get some minnows. He is one of the fishermen who snatch the pike and perch through holes in the ice during the winter. The pike are purchased by a Cleveland man, who ships them to New York. Some money is made out of the fishing, but it depends on the length of the season and the appetites of the fish.

It seemed to be the pastime that interested Mr. Grow the most. Near the barn was his ice shanty. It is completely equipped for the sport. It has runners, iron ones at that, so that it can be hauled out on the ice. Inside is an oil burner, for the air that sweeps across the lake in sub-zero weather can never possibly be mistaken for a blast from a smelting furnace. In the shanty were fifteen poles, not tip-ups. Tip-ups, said Mr. Grow, are all right if they would tip up every time they tipped down.

"When they are pulled down by the fish," he explained, "They often freeze into the ice. So we use this wire. The fish pulls the wire down and it can be put back in place in a second. This is the best rigging."

Mr. Grow has a small trap door in the floor of the shanty. Through this hole he fishes for perch while waiting for action on the other poles. And he doesn't have to watch this particular line. He has it attached to a "doodad" on the ceiling, which rings a bell when a fish signals that it wants to come up for air.

Mr. Grow, who might easily be mistaken for the fisherman in the cod liver oil ad, fishes about three miles from shore, out near the Shackelton Shoals. His pike average about two pounds in weight and, coming from the cold water, are as firm as a pawnbroker's refusal. "But we don't catch many," Mr. Grow said. "We see plenty of fish but that's as far as it goes sometimes. I've seen a half an acre just boilin' with bass, but not one'd bite. The lake also is crowded with minnows and fish won't bite when they've got a bellyfull."

After Mr. Grow had unraveled one of his fish poles to give us the "philosophy of it," Hermie asked him what kinds of birds roomed in the birdhouses on the premises. Mr. Grow said that they were martins, bluebirds, and white-breasted swallows.

"I thought," said Hermie, who seemed overwhelmed by the angling atmosphere, "that maybe you raised kingfishers."

– Chapter 22 –

"Besting" the Fish Pirates

It took a long time for New York State's game wardens (now called "environmental conservation officers") to gain the upper hand over the savvy Oneida Lake fish pirates. For decades, these outlaws confidently set their gill and trap nets, firm in their conviction that the "protectors," a polite pirate reference to the wardens, lacked the ability or even the desire to apprehend them. Their feelings found justification in the fact that many early game wardens were local residents–neighbors, friends, and even family of the pirates. Arresting a relative or a fishing chum was simply out of the question. Local judges were sympathetic to the fishermen. In addition, the pirates knew Oneida much better than most law enforcement officers and took advantage of the lake's size and secrets.

Technology reversed the situation, however. "Motor launches," prototypes to today's speedboats, were developed in the 1920s and these vessels greatly increased wardens' patrolling range. "Cottaging" (camp construction) proliferated along Oneida's shore and the automobile became affordable during this decade. These developments brought thousands of additional anglers to the lake. The new sportspersons were often hostile to the old-time netters and, armed with better boats and bait casting equipment, they fished more of the lake, often reporting the nets they snagged to appreciative officers. Pirating didn't disappear (it exists even today), but the practice suffered a severe setback.

Harry E. Best was one of the first "high tech" conservation officers. Best was born into a Cleveland glass making family in 1890. His father John was a glass blower and Harry's first job, after high school, was that of a "glass carrier," a person who brought melted glass to the blowers. He loved the outdoors, however, and in 1925 became a state game warden. Best was assigned the Oneida Lake beat and it was a perfect match. He knew the water and, better yet, knew the habits of the fish pirates. Working out of the North Shore, Best arrested scores of violators, one of whom was Upper South Bay's famed Jake Kyser (who eventually switched sides and became a game warden). Harry built a reputation as a tough, determined environmental policeman and his labors brought acclaim in the following newspaper article, published on July 26, 1936.

> A 68,000 acre area that must be patrolled each day–twenty-four hours on duty daily–one hundred miles of Oneida Lake shore line to be kept free of pirate fishermen.
>
> Such is the task which Harry E. Best, state conservation department game protector, has assigned to himself and his twenty-three foot power launch, which is kept in a newly painted boathouse at Scriba Creek, Constantia. The boat has been overhauled recently and its boathouse is newly painted because department officials are realizing the size of Mr. Best's job, and the importance.
>
> While making his rounds last Sunday, he rescued five persons who were at the mercy of Oneida Lake's wind-whipped waves. Although five is an unusual number for a day, rescues are not new job for Best, since nearly every daily trip about the lake turns up someone in distress.
>
> For instance, there was the time not many months ago when two men were stranded on a small island in the lake because South Bay boatmen thought the waves were too rough to attempt a rescue. Best went out in his craft, to the windward side of the distressed pair. Fastening a line to a small rowboat, he set it in the water and allowed it to drift to the island, whereupon the men jumped in and were towed to safety.
>
> His main job, he explains, is to keep nets out of Oneida Lake, since pirate fishermen of days not so long past drew from that body of water literally tons of fish in this illegal manner. He thinks the pirates have been cleared out by now, but the task of patrolling the lake is still not an easy one. He is hoping for an assistant soon.
>
> What gives Mr. Best his greatest theme for oratory, which

rolls out in nautical matter-of-fact language is that, while nearly all lake fishermen resent his daily inspection tour's disturbance of their angling, there is not one who minds in the least when the conservation department boat is nearby as heavy waves roll.

Mr. Best guesses that this is human nature, though, and just keeps on inspecting. When he finds someone fishing without a license, he cites them for justice's court, and if they get "snooty" they are "arrested right there and then and told to come along, whether they like it or not."

Science and progress seems to enter into everything and even Mr. Best has not been immune. An airplane from Albany flies over once a month and, with a two-way radio between the plane and the Best boat, the pilot locates on his map points that look suspiciously like trap nets, and then relays the locations to Mr. Best. After a few such sites have been mapped, the plane flies off and the warden goes to work. He once took seventeen nets from one man on the lake.

Mr. Best, who once was a glass factory worker, has been on the job at Constantia since 1925 and figures that he has brought in some big catches, not the least of which was about $2,000 worth of nets from one fish pirate.

The pirates resent his intrusion, of course, but Mr. Best says some of his best friends are among the convicted fishermen. "They realize that's what I'm getting paid for," is the way he puts it.

Mr. Best, while a killjoy to some lake fishermen, is a welcome visitor to many since, from his years of inspection tours, he has learned plenty of Oneida Lake's secrets, such as where the big fish are, when these fish bite, where hidden shoals await the unwary boatman, and when small boat operators should beware of onrushing storms. He is very free with his expert information.

He deplores the custom, practiced by so many cottagers, of overloading boats. "For instance," he pointed out yesterday as a slow-moving rowboat went by his place, "what chance would those three men have if they ran into a real wind storm out there?" The flat bottom rowboat was sagging precariously from its burden, and had a foot-high wave been there to break on its gunwales, the occupants would have been swimming for their lives.

Mr. Best, the "man who made the pirates walk the plank," is now busily engaged in reconditioning his boathouse living quar-

> ters, recently made over so that hereafter, when an inspection tour is interrupted by a squall, he will not have to return to his Cleveland home. His boat will also soon have a new tie-up dock.

Poachers went to great lengths to avoid or deceive Harry Best. Francis Cooper, of Cleveland, laughed as he told me how some ice anglers fooled the famous warden. In the days prior to insulated clothing, fishermen wore baggy wool pants, long underwear, and big, heavy winter coats. They often stuffed newspapers in their boots and pants. The papers provided added insulation, but were also used for wrapping extra walleyes, that could then be slipped into the pants, well hidden for the trek off the ice.

Harry was probably the only game warden in the history of New York State's Department of Environmental Conservation to have been quoted in Life magazine. Best knew virtually all the fishermen along the North Shore and anglers often stopped by his house to show off exceptional catches. One day in the early 1960s, three anglers arrived at the Best home with a large northern pike. Harry admired the big fish and accompanied the fishermen to his dock, where they scaled and eviscerated the northern. The fish's stomach looked unusually distended, so Best recommended that they open it. Dissection revealed a "Zippo" lighter! They dried the lighter and, to everyone's surprise, it fired on the first try!

Harry wrote the Zippo Corporation and told them the story. An official immediately contacted him. The company's advertising department thought that the incident would make excellent copy. "Could we send a representative to talk with you, Mr. Best," they asked. "Sure, anytime," responded Harry. A Zippo official came to Cleveland and the resulting story ended up in an advertisement in Life. In appreciation, Zippo gave Harry a special lighter, engraved with his name and every year thereafter the company sent him another engraved lighter.

The *Life* ad described the event as follows:

> Mr. Harry Best, recently retired fish and game protector for the New York State Conservation Department, told this remarkable but true story to the Zippo man.
>
> "A party, just west of Cleveland on Oneida Lake, was fishing for Great Northern Pike in Three Mile Bay. They caught a Pike that weighed about eighteen pounds. When they dressed the Pike, in the stomach was one of your lighters. The Pike must have picked it off the bottom or could have grabbed it

before it got to the bottom. The lighter was in fine shape, which showed that it had not been lost long. The best part of it was that the Zippo lit the first time."

Colleen Goodale, Harry Best's daughter, lives in Cleveland and shared the Zippo tale with me. She also told about her father's benevolent side. Every year the veteran warden acquired a good number of deer that had been killed either illegally or by motor vehicles. He gave the deer to poor families in the Cleveland area. Some families wouldn't have had "meat on the table" if it weren't for Harry. Best's environmental food stamp program enabled many people to enjoy proper nutrition in days when unemployment's grim reaper took its toll.

Paul Brown, of Leonardsville, is a retired New York State Conservation Officer who, although assigned primarily to southern Madison County, occasionally worked with Harry Best. Brown and Best dragged Oneida Lake for nets in summer. In spring, they checked anglers along Fish Creek prior to walleyed pike season's opening (this can be a prime poaching time). Their job required patience. Sometimes they'd wait all night, hoping for violators to show, only to be rewarded by a good case of field fatigue. Paul vouched for Harry's expertise and equanimity, saying that Best "knew every stone and shoal in Oneida Lake" and had a reputation for coolness on the job. When astonished, perturbed, or needled, all Harry would ever say was, "Golly sakes."

Brown had warm memories about his colleague and he chuckled as he told one noteworthy story. Harry Best enjoyed a relaxed, laid-back retirement, seldom venturing too far from the lake. One day he and his wife, Alta, decided to take a leisurely drive. They cruised west from Cleveland, along Route 49, and turned onto Route 81 at Central Square. There was one problem, however. Harry turned into the wrong ramp and drove north on Route 81's southbound lane. Cars and trucks swerved and honked at the Bests. Drivers gestured frantically as Harry motored northward. According to Brown, Mrs. Best got nervous and asked, "Why are all these people waving, Harry?"

The veteran game warden thought for a second and answered, "Honey...they must be folks I met on the lake."

– Chapter 23 –

Boats Built In Brewerton

Like cabinet making, blacksmithing, and coopering, boat building was once an important American craft. Boat builders thrived in the nineteenth and early twentieth centuries and their workshops were centerpieces of many waterfront communities.

Several families stand out in Oneida Lake's boat building history. Loren Damon and his sons, Leon, Ceylon, and Raymond, who lived near their namesake point east of Bridgeport, crafted "Damon boats." These were rugged fishing vessels whose owners must have been reassured by a legendary local saying, "No one every drowned because a Damon boat capsized." Nearing L. Emmons and his son N. Corey also fashioned superb Oneida Lake angling craft in their shop, north of Brewerton. In addition, the family enjoyed a national reputation for their "Snipe" and "Lightening" class sailboats, racing sloops that finished first in many a regatta.

Thomas Milton was another famous Brewerton boat builder. Assisted by several workmen and, later, by his son J. Elet Milton (the Brewerton historian who wrote two of this book's stories), Milton built canal barges, sailboats, private steam launches, fishing vessels, and even speedboats. One local historian said of Milton's prodigious work that, "if put side-by-side, all the boats Tom Milton built would stretch from Brewerton to Frenchman's Island." Syracuse newspaper reporter and Brewerton native Joe Beamish interviewed Milton in 1931 and wrote this biographical sketch.

Rambling 'Round Brewerton

When vagabond dreams come true! For years I have been reading about the famous "Stone Crusher" [his photographer's auto] and, last Monday, I not only saw it and sat in it, but I had a ride in it.

Hermie, heavy pilot of the S.C., adjusted his goggles, warmed up the motor, sealed the barograph, and motioned for me to climb into the cockpit. He gave it the gun and the Stone Crusher, gaining momentum, took off for Three Rivers.

As we hummed along by the old salt vats, the big photographer noticed a number of bait signs announcing bass bugs and crabs for sale.

"It's a good thing we haven't got Steve with us," he asserted, "or we would have to stop and buy some bait."

I guess most of you known Steve–the fisherman who nearly caught a fish in Otisco Lake. (He told me confidentially that he would like to buy Otisco Lake himself, and drain it, just to prove there're no fish in it.)

Nearing Liverpool, the Stone Crusher developed a slight sniffle. It was apparent on the radiator cap. No doubt S.C. caught it from me, as I have been under the pressure of a summer cold for the past week.

However, the new road north from Liverpool was balm to the Stone Crusher, and we crushed along beautifully. Three Rivers came into view and we made as pretty a three point landing as you could wish for, right in front of Barnum's. I inquired for the residence of a certain Mr. Perry of as many people as I could find. He was to be the subject of our ramble this glorious Monday morning and we tried our best to find him, but without avail.

"Have you and Joe ever rambled 'round Thomas Milton, the boat builder at Brewerton?," I asked Hermie.

The master of photography replied in the negative, so we pointed the Stone Crusher due east and drove along the Oneida River on a fine country road, until the town without a bridge came into view.

After a satisfying meal at the old Washburn House, we drove a few blocks west to the home of Mr. and Mrs. Milton and their son, Elet.

Elet Milton greeted us heartily. He knew me when I used to wear Buster Brown's suits, as the majority of my boyhood was spent in Brewerton.

While waiting to see Mr. Milton, senior, we were shown around their charming garden. A fishpond caught Hermie's eye and he wanted to catch some of the gold fish but, with difficulty, I restrained him.

"Would you like to go into the boat shop?," asked Elet.

We would and we did. Some very fine boats were in the process of construction and others were ready for the water. As we were listening to a description of the manner of building the boats, Thomas Milton joined us.

At seventy-five, Thomas M. Milton, who is recognized as the pioneer builder of speedboats in this country, is still to be found every day, working in his shop. For the past thirty-two years the firm of T.M. Milton & Son has been in business in Brewerton, and its boat products are well known throughout this section of the country.

Mr. Milton is descended from a long line of boat-building ancestors who originally came to this country from France, in the seventeenth century. His grandfather, William Milton, settled in Brewerton in 1849, building the house that is even now occupied by Thomas Milton and his family. It is the oldest house in the village, and one of the nicest appearing.

After his marriage, the young Thomas Milton began building rowboats in an old barn on his property. As the market for boats increased, Mr. Milton took his son into partnership and erected larger and better-equipped shops.

Later, the Miltons experimented with power craft with such success that they were kept busy by the new development–the increasing demand for speedboats. And they are still engaged in the production of pleasure craft of all kinds.

In a private office we found evidence of Mr. Milton's hobby. Standing on a shelf was an exact replica of a locomotive, about four feet long and weighing about fifty pounds. Mr. Milton, who is an expert machinist, made each part in detail in his shop. The model took a year of spare time for the making, and it runs.

On another shelf is a model of the old side-wheeler, the Manhattan, which used to run on Oneida Lake. A five-foot model of a Great Lakes' sailboat, in which more than 700 feet of fishing line were used to rig it up, reposes in a large glass case. And there is still another model of a tugboat, which would run under its own power, a small steam turbine built entirely by Mr. Milton.

Hermie was like a boy in a toyshop before Christmas. He was so interested in the miniature locomotive that he nearly forgot to take a picture of Mr. Milton. I didn't know he liked models so well.

"Gosh," he cried, "I wish Harry Bull was out here with us. Harry would just eat this thing up."

"Why," I asked, "Does Harry need iron in his system?"

Luckily for me, Hermie has a wonderful disposition. While he was sitting on the floor, playing with the locomotive and the boats, I was wandering around the shop. My attention was called to a sign on the wall. This is what I read:

"I have been in this business since 1887. I have been pleasing and displeasing the people ever since. I have been cussed and discussed, boycotted, talked about, lied about, lied to, hung up, held up, robbed, etc. The only reason I am staying in this business now is to see what the hell is going to happen next."

By this time Mr. Milton was as anxious to interview us, as we had been to question him.

"Is that the Stone Crusher out there?" he asked, pointing to the curb.

Hermie admitted it. So Mr. Milton trotted out to look it all over. In the meantime his son, Elet Milton, who had been instrumental in effecting the preservation of the old fort [at Brewerton], showed us some Indian relics that he had found in the fort and its vicinity. He has a very rare and valuable Indian necklace, among other things, which is worthy of a place in the Smithsonian Institute. The younger Mr. Milton is almost as interesting as his father to listen to, which is paying him quite a compliment.

Finally the senior Milton came back, his face wreathed in smiles. He didn't quite say, "Well, now I can die happy. I've seen the famous Stone Crusher," but it had given him great pleasure to gaze upon the slick lines of the renowned enemy of stones.

We had had such an interesting afternoon that neither Hermie nor I cared to leave, but we just had to get the Stone Crusher back to the city before its sniffle should become a cough.

Note: Elet Milton donated his father's models to the Fort Brewerton Historical Society and they can be viewed at that organization's Oliver Stevens Blockhouse Museum.

Ann Hopkins

Sylvan Beach's Main Street in the 1920s–lots of cars, lots of John Barleycorn-seeking tourists

John Clements

The Forest Hotel, built by Lyman Spencer in 1879, became a speakeasy during prohibition.

Jean Kowalski

Hotel Nobles, at the corner of Akehurst Avenue and Main Street, was another popular speakeasy. William Russell continued the wet tradition when he purchased the inn in 1920. Russell, however, transformed the old Nobles into "Russell's Hotel and Danceland" in 1939. The Dorsey Brothers, Harry James, Duke Ellington, and other "big bands" entertained tens of thousands at this Sylvan Beach landmark.

Isaiah and Minnie Head

Oneida Lake can freeze to a depth of over two feet. When the ice breaks up in spring, a stiff west wind can pile it to impressive heights on shore. This photo was taken at Sylvan Beach around 1925.

Rob Ziegler

Buddy McCarthy worked for Isaiah Head at his general store, a Sylvan Beach landmark from the 1920s to 1980.

Oneida Lake Association

Ice fishing has always been a popular Oneida Lake sport. Syracuse newspaper cartoonist Steve Schilder captured the Big Bay angling scene in January of 1934.

Colleen and Norman Goodale

Game Warden Harry Best proudly displayed the famous Life magazine cover that featured a "Zippo" lighter and the northern pike that swallowed it.

Syracuse Post-Standard

John F. Cook's, "Joe Beamish," prose enlivened Syracuse newspapers for over three decades. He served as a director of the Oneida Lake Association.

Fort Brewerton Historical Society

Brewerton boat crafter Thomas Milton takes a break from hull repair in his boatyard, around 1925.

Fort Brewerton Historical Society

Thomas Milton (on the dock, in the foreground) poses by a prized creation–the steamboat *Frances*, named for his wife. The steamer *Nancy Peer* rests behind the *Frances*, circa 1900.

Fort Brewerton Historical Society

Milton boats were elegant and stylish. The motor launch *Adois*, piloted by Herbert J. Leighton in this 1920s' photo, was a Milton gem. The photo shows the *Adois* entering Oneida Lake near Brewerton.

Fort Brewerton Historical Society

Milton enjoyed experimenting with faster boats. This sleek, trim vessel was photographed during a test run on the Oneida River, around 1905.

– Chapter 24 –

A Beach Family Tradition

Eddie's Restaurant, a Sylvan Beach landmark, has been operated by the same family for nearly seventy years. It's the restaurant where a "big band" leader of the 1940s entered the kitchen, cooked dinner, and then sang for the owners. Listed among that restaurant's customers are Frank Sinatra, Harry James, Nat "King" Cole, Duke Ellington, Desi Arnaz, Liza Minelli, and George Foreman. A complete census of the restaurant's patrons during the past seven decades would overflow the Manhattan phone book. The restaurant is the largest in Sylvan Beach and its menu sports items like "our famous fish dinner," the "original hot ham sandwich," and lunch and dinner specials named for its founders, Edward and Florence Campanaro Stewart. Founded in 1934, Eddie's Restaurant occupies a unique place in Sylvan Beach history. Herbert Leneke, Canastota High School Class of 1939, articulated this importance. "For us," Leneke said, "Sylvan Beach meant Eddie's and Eddie's meant Sylvan Beach." His words echo the beliefs of legions.

Edward "Eddie" Stewart's story personifies the American dream and his history mirrors America's immigrant heritage. Eddie was born in 1914 in Rome, New York, the youngest of Edward and Marcellina Martini Stewart's nine children. Both his parents emigrated in the late 1890s from Piete Monte D'Alive, a small Italian village. His father, whose given name was Gaetano DelGuidice, was the first of five brothers who resettled in America. Gaetano couldn't speak a word of English when he arrived in New York

City. When an immigration interpreter asked him about his vocation he replied that he was a railroad worker. The interpreter nodded and summoned a man to his table. “Hey Tom, here’s another railroader. Can you use him?,” inquired the interpreter. “Sure, I’ll take him,” answered the man. Tom was a railroad “line boss” and needed experienced workers. He offered Gaetano DelGuidice what every immigrant so desperately sought–a job.

Gaetano’s benefactor was no ordinary employer. Tom and his wife were good people who owned a small hotel where they housed and helped their workers. Their hotel sheltered a salad bowl of ethnicity. Poles, Germans, Irish, Russians, as well as Italians, made it their first American home. Tom’s wife was a teacher and, at night, she schooled her boarders in reading, writing, math, and civics–subjects that they had to understand when they took citizenship exams. Her husband, whose full name was Tom Stewart, helped the men complete citizenship papers. Tom believed that anglicizing difficult European names would give his men a better chance to succeed. When Gaetano DelGuidice brought his papers to Tom, the latter had trouble spelling both the first and last names.

“Gaetano, I mean no offense, but I think you should change your names. You’re in America, now.” Tom advised. “Changing names will make life easier for you. Easier to get jobs. Easier to get paid. If you don’t mind, I’ll give you my last name. How about ‘Edward’ for a first name? From now on, you’ll be known as ‘Edward Stewart.’” Gaetano agreed. When his four brothers arrived in the United States, he explained to them that changing their name would facilitate life in America, especially earning a living. The brothers listened and believed. All of them became Stewarts. Incidents like the DelGuidice to Stewart name change were commonplace in American history and, generally speaking, abetted immigrants’ assimilation.

The new Edward Stewart possessed a solid old-country work ethic. He moved from New York City to Rome and worked on the New York Central Railroad through the World War I era. He and Marcellina raised a family of six girls and three boys. They liked Rome and felt comfortable within the Italian-American neighborhood that centered around East Dominick Street. When the railroad wanted to transfer Edward to Virginia, he opted for employment at a Rome wire factory and worked there until his death, at age eighty-two.

Eddie Stewart inherited his parents’ industriousness. When he was eleven years old he washed dishes and helped an old Italian chef at Sam and Scotty's Restaurant in downtown Rome. Although he had to work throughout his high school years, Eddie was graduated from Rome Free Academy in 1932. Limited by the Great Depression's sluggish economy, he joined the Civilian Conservation Corps in 1933. The "CCCs" shipped Eddie cross-country, via railroad, to Idaho where he and his co-workers built a camp that housed Corps' employees. The Corps offered Eddie a job in nearby Boonville when his western enlistment expired, but he declined. Instead, he went to work for his brother-in-law Frank Uvanni, who ran a restaurant near Rome's New York Central Railroad Passenger Station.

Fate and Frank Uvanni brought Eddie Stewart and Sylvan Beach together. As Eddie tells it, his genesis unfolded this way:

> It was the spring of 1934. My brother-in-law Frank read an ad in the paper offering a boat for sale at Bill Cottman's Boat Yard, at the Beach. Bill's marina was across the Canal, where Snug Harbor is today. I was familiar with the Beach because my parents used to take me there for the picnics. The "hop growers' picnic," the "colored people's picnic"–those were great times. We used to ride the *Colonial*, a tour boat that took people from Rome to the Beach. I was just a kid, seven or eight years old. That boat trip, the Beach picnics–they were fun. I looked forward to them.
>
> Frank asked me if I wanted to take a ride to the Beach. I remember that it was a cold spring day. There were patches of snow on the ground and ice chunks from Fish Creek floated on the canal. The Ontario and Western railroad tracks still ran down Main Street and, when we got to the Beach, a train of coal cars was parked on the tracks. They used to ship coal on the canal and the railroad connected with barges at the Beach's harbor. When we drove by the village park I noticed a hot dog stand–you might better call it a shack–with a sign on it. That sign said, "For rent or for lease–inquire William McCarthy."
>
> We went to Cottman's and looked the boat over and then we stopped and saw McCarthy. He had returned from Florida that morning, about ten minutes before we arrived! He controlled the lease on the hot dog stand, but he hadn't been running it because he was busy with a new place, the Elk Restaurant. That was located where the Crazy Clam is now. A guy named Walter Richie was the first person to operate the hot dog stand, but the tenants after him neglected it. The place was pretty run down.

> McCarthy got the key and we drove up to the stand. We climbed over railroad cars to get to the building. We didn't need any keys because the back door was wide open! There was water all over the place. It was a mess, but I liked it. I thought that I could make a go of it. I made arrangements with McCarthy and with Bill Cottman, who was also chairman of the Park Board, to open the place.

And, with that modest economic move, Eddie's Restaurant was born. The first Eddie's was a far cry from its present self. Eddie Stewart remembered it, in every spartan detail.

> I just had hot dogs, hamburgs, and soda when I started. That's all. A hot dog cost a dime, a soda a nickel, and a hamburg fifteen cents. The front of the building opened up and we had a counter there, with ten stools. My first remodeling job was our porch. It was on the left, the south end, of the restaurant and it held four tables. The eel flies and other bugs used to come off the lake every summer and they made eating outside next to impossible. I screened in the porch and made it into a dining room. Customers liked it. Lots of them came just because we were sheltered from the bugs. I did this in 1936, after I got married to "Fifi" [Florence Stewart's nickname].
>
> Fifi and I stayed upstairs. You got there by climbing a ship's ladder! There was a bathroom and storeroom in the upper floor when I took over. We used sheets to separate areas of the storeroom into bedrooms because our help stayed with us and you had to have some kind of privacy. All the heat from the grill went up, and it was summer besides. Upstairs was sometimes so hot that it was almost unbearable.
>
> Our first few years were rough. All the action was in the Midway area. There wasn't much to attract people this way. Then, the big bands and dances at Russell's started catching on. [Russell's Hotel and Danceland were located on the northeast corner of Akehurst Avenue and Main Street, near Eddie's. It became a major Sylvan Beach attraction.] People started coming uptown but, guess what? They walked on the other side of the street! That side had a paved sidewalk. Our side had a cinder walk, with curbs made from old railroad ties. They'd stop at places like Polly's Inn [where the Beachy Clean Laundromat is today] and we'd sit on our stools, watching them eat hot dogs–across the street!

> Then, around 1940, we added Italian food to our menu. Business picked up. People liked the Italian food. I made my own ice cream in Rome and brought it to the Beach. People liked this, too. But, just as our place was starting to take off, World War II broke out. We kept the stand open, but business was terrible. The government rationed gas and people couldn't drive to the Beach. On one gorgeous 4th of July, a picture-perfect day, we took in a grand total of $6. We had to do our part for the war effort and couldn't spend as much time here. Fifi worked in Revere Copper, in Rome, making artillery shells. I cooked in Revere's cafeteria.

The post-war era witnessed renewed prosperity and Sylvan Beach thrived. Starved for consumer goods throughout the war, bolstered with savings, employed in vigorous manufacturing jobs, Americans spent as never before. New cars, rare during the war years, were purchased almost as fast as they left Detroit's assembly lines. Fresh autos gave families mobility and Central New Yorkers flocked to Sylvan Beach by the thousands. Eddie Stewart recalled that he "never saw as many cars at the Beach" as he did in the late 1940s and 1950s.

Eddie's grew within America's robust economy. He remodeled in 1946, changing the business to a point where it was more of a restaurant than a hot dog stand. He added overhead doors to the building's front, enlarged the counter to accommodate thirty-two people, added a soda fountain, and screened in the entire place. He renovated and expanded the kitchen. New walk-in coolers and a walk-in freezer facilitated food storage. The most significant growth occurred around 1960, when Eddie enlarged his dining room to its present size (the restaurant holds around 250 customers). Large picture windows replaced the screens and brought Eddie's patrons sweeping views of Sylvan Beach's village park and Main Street. Central air conditioning added spa-like relief for customers during the Beach's steamy summer days.

A major factor that contributed to Eddie's popularity was his menu's appeal. He and Fifi developed broad-based, Italian-American offerings, served in satisfying portions that attracted a family-oriented clientele. Like the restaurant itself, the menu evolved slowly, efficiently, and often with a bit of lady luck. Eddie recalled a few savory details.

When we expanded after the war, our business grew. The minute we fixed up our place, the people came. A big break was the hot ham sandwich. I ran out of hot dogs one day. Imagine–running out of hot dogs at Sylvan Beach! I had some capicola, Italian hot ham, in the cooler. I heated it on the grill, got it sizzling hot, put it on a bun and offered it as an alternative. The people loved it! They ordered more–and more. I reheated the capicola and it got hotter–the more you do this the hotter it gets. The people didn't care. They wanted hot ham sandwiches. That sandwich's popularity took off beyond my wildest dreams!

We always had an "Eddie's Special"–an Italian sandwich–so we added a "Fifi's Special"–a dinner with meatballs, sausage, hot or sweet peppers, covered in sauce. Adding Italian dinners was an important change. Spaghetti, pasta, Italian soups–parents would order these while their kids ate the hot dogs, hamburgs, and hot hams. It gave us a wider appeal.

Our sauce is made from an old family recipe. I used to make fifty-five gallon kettles of it...two, sometimes three times a week. I taught my son Eddie how to make the sauce. We both taught his son Rick the secret. No one else cooks our sauce.

Fish wasn't on our first menus. The fish man from Syracuse used to deliver to Gary's Restaurant and stop here for a cup of coffee and a sandwich. He'd always say, "Eddie, you're on the lake. You've got a natural location. Why don't you serve fish?" I said that Fifi didn't want anything to do with fryers. She was afraid of them. He said, "Don't worry, there's nothing to it." I drove to Syracuse a couple times to look at his operation. He fried fish there.

One day he came by and said, "Look, Eddie, I'll show you how to bread the fish and how to fry it. I even brought you a small fryer. If things don't work out, just return it." He gave us five pounds of fish. We cut it into sandwich pieces and put it on the board as a special. I'll bet that he hadn't even left the Beach before we ran out of it!

I phoned him and told what happened. He asked how many pounds of fish we wanted. I ordered twenty-five pounds. My God, we put it on Friday's menu and went through it in forty-five minutes! So, here I am, out of fish–again! I called him and he said that he had to make a special trip to Gary's and would bring me one hundred pounds more.

I thought we'd have problems selling the one hundred

> pounds, but we didn't. People loved our fish dinners and sandwiches. Now, we sometimes sell nearly a ton of fish per week in the summer.
>
> And–just think–I was afraid to buy five pounds.

Eddie and Fifi Stewart's work ethic was another major factor contributing to the restaurant's success. They were an inseparable team whose business dominated their lives, seven days a week, April through October. They took time off only for funerals and weddings and, for the latter, they attended the formal ceremonies, never the receptions. Fifi's day started at 7 A.M. Morning was baking time, when she created the restaurant's mouth-watering pies. It was also time for selecting and preparing lunch and dinner specials. Fifi handled food orders and deliveries usually arrived before noon. She worked until about 2 P.M., when she went home for a brief rest, returning for the dinner hour and staying until nine. Eddie's day began at noon and continued, non-stop, until 3 A.M. He handled all beverage orders, functioned as a general manager, and greeted patrons with what one observer termed "an unequaled, million-dollar smile."

John DePerno, owner of Captain John's Restaurant in the Beach, operated concessions in the Midway during the post-World War II era and also owned the Forest Hotel. DePerno spent many an early morn at Eddie's and fondly recalled the restaurant's past.

> A lot of Midway concessionaires would head for Eddie's after we closed our booths. The Stewarts were among the best friends we had. You wouldn't believe what Fifi cooked. It was like we were a part of her family. Every night she'd prepare something different. One evening it might be pasta faggioli, another night she'd make greens and beans, or mushroom stew, or sausage and peppers. None of these dinners were on the menu. She'd make them especially for us–and charge us twenty-five cents! We'd help them make coffee and clean up the place. After their customers left they'd sit down with us and talk about the Beach, about business, about how to make things better. We'd sometimes talk until four in the morning.
>
> Eddie and Fifi worked as a team all day and into the wee hours of the morning. Every day. Every night. They lived above the restaurant then and, from time to time, one of them would dash upstairs to check on their children and the baby sitter. They would hug them, change diapers, make sure bottles were

> prepared, and then dash downstairs to their grindstone. Fifi and Eddie were well-respected business people, who earned that title through sixty years of hard work. They captured the "American Dream" and were excellent role models for our younger generations

Eddie's has been blessed with a core of loyal, efficient employees, whose labors have enhanced the restaurant's quality, consistency, and achievement. The Stewarts published a souvenir brochure entitled "A Step Back In Time" in 1994 that commemorated Eddie's 60th anniversary. The publication contained a "Hall of Fame Honor Roll" that listed employees with noteworthy longevity. The honor roll included thirty-eight people who had worked five or more years and twenty-one who had a decade or more of service. Four employees–Jean Bertollini, Terry Dixon, Geraldine Helt, and Patricia Merrell–boasted between twenty and thirty years and two–Stella LaParne and Roberta Wolff–had been with Eddie's more than thirty years!

Eddie's served millions of customers during its tenure and, while the restaurant appeals primarily to middle America, it has hosted the famous as well. Listen, as Eddie Stewart tells about some renowned patrons.

> Jack Palmer was a trumpet player with the big bands of the '30s and '40s. I knew Jack all my life. In fact, he lived across the street from our house in Rome when he started playing the trumpet. We were old friends. Jack was playing with Harry James' Band at Russell's and, after they closed, he brought the band members to the restaurant. With them was a young vocalist named Frank Sinatra. Yes, Sinatra...at Sylvan Beach.
>
> Frank was a skinny kid then, just starting out. He was an unknown, traveling with Harry James, trying to make a name for himself. I'll never forget him, though. While the rest of the band came in and ate, Sinatra sat on the old wooden curb, our railroad tie curb, just looking at traffic along Main Street. Times had to be tough for him. I could have invited him to eat with the rest of us, but the idea never occurred to me.
>
> Every once in a while Frank wandered in, bought a nickel candy bar, and went back to the curb. Finally he walked up to me, pointed to the curb, and asked, "Why do you guys use railroad ties for curbs in this town?" He had a big smile on his face. We shared a good laugh. Then I decided to make him feel bet-

ter. I asked him for his autograph, but I couldn't find a piece of paper, so I took a Dentyne Gum poster off the wall. The poster had a big picture of Roy Rogers riding his horse, Trigger. Frank signed his name in big letters–right across Trigger's rear! The two of us had another good laugh.

We met all the big band musicians. Duke Ellington, Tommy Dorsey, Paul Whiteman, Cab Calloway, Lou Prima. All the big names. Dagmar, Desi Arnaz, and Nat "King" Cole. They'd walk around the Beach during the day and stop here, get a coke or ice cream, relax in our screened dining area. After playing at Russell's they'd come back for coffee, dinner, sometimes just to talk into the morning hours.

Lou Prima was funny. He came into our kitchen and put his arms around Fifi. He sang "Angelina, My Angelina" to her. Fifi shook her head and corrected him. She said, "My name is Florence, not Angelina." He just laughed. Then he saw a big round bread and asked for it. We gave it to him. He dipped it into our sauce, took a bite, and said, "Wonderful." He asked if he could cook his own spaghetti! We were happy to let him do it. He sang the entire time that he cooked.

Russell's was still open in the early 1950s when my son Eddie Jr. was a little kid. He liked to sneak over there and get the performers' autographs. One night he came running back into the restaurant and yelled to me, "Hey Dad, I brought the singers back from Russell's!" In came the "Ink Spots," a pretty famous group. Eddie ran behind the counter, grabbed a handful of cigars, and gave one to each singer. We gladly fed them–they were nice guys. They appreciated our generosity and, in return, they stood in the middle of our dining room and sang a few numbers. Then they walked around the room and sang as they walked. A funny thing happened after they left. Several people came up to me afterwards and asked if I was going to be hiring entertainers on a regular basis! I had to laugh.

Liza Minelli made a movie called "The Sterile Cuckoo," back in 1968 and they shot scenes in Union Chapel and Oudin's Court [now called Sunset Cottages]. She came by several times while she was here, but she wasn't overly friendly. The movie company hired Eddie Jr. as Liza's chauffeur and one of his duties was teaching her how to drive a Volkswagen. She had never driven a standard shift car. She made Eddie nervous and he advised her to pay more attention to the road. Guess what? He got fired for saying that!

> The largest celebrity that walked through our doors was ex-heavyweight champ George Foreman. He was being inducted into the Boxing Hall of Fame in Canastota and came down with his whole crew for dinner. Lord, was he big! My son's big. My grandson Rick lifts weights and he's even bigger. George was larger than the two of them combined!
>
> We took him into the kitchen to see how we make sauce. He looked at our sauce, kept looking, looking. He saw all the big chunks of beef and pork in it and said, "Eddie, what I could do with a loaf of Italian bread!" I told him to take a loaf off the rack and help himself. He said, "No, I can't do that because when I go back into the dining room, I want *another* piece of pie." That man was one tremendous eater.

Eddie's has always been a family business. The Stewarts' children and grandchildren matured there and some remain involved with the restaurant today. Eddie and Fifi raised two children, Barbara and Eddie, Jr. After college, Barbara married Robert Corona. She and her husband recently retired from successful teaching careers in the Oneida Public Schools. They have two children, Robert and Brian. Both boys worked at the restaurant throughout their high school and college years and Barb still substitutes as a hostess-cashier. Eddie, Jr., married Leslie Woolcott and they also have two children, Alison and Edward III, better known as "Rick." Alison, a music teacher at Camden Central School, serves Eddie's part-time as a hostess and waitress. Rick, Leslie, and Eddie Jr. manage Eddie's today. In addition, Rick operates "Harpoon Eddie's," a beachfront, Key West-style restaurant and the Beachy Clean Laundromat. The family also owns Sunset Cottages, a lakeside rental facility next to Harpoon's.

A visit to Eddie's today is a voyage through the restaurant's and Sylvan Beach's history. Patrons entering the main door are directed into two lines–one for "parties of one to four," the other for "parties of five or more." A "specials' board" greets them immediately when they enter. Three large, mounted photos, however, quickly draw customers' attention away from their appetites. One print depicts Fifi and Eddie, his hand placed lovingly on her shoulder, posing in the counter area of the old stand. Another photo frames a kitchen scene, with Eddie, Fifi and staff posed within their cluttered stage of culinary delight. A third print shows the restaurant's exterior in the post-war era. Vintage autos parked bumper to bumper in front of the building testify to Eddie's popularity.

Posted between the prints and the specials' board is a resolution adopted by the New York State Legislature in 1994 that commemorates Eddie's 60th anniversary. The restaurant's photo-proclamation display tells patrons that heritage and history are important here. To keep people from getting too distracted, however, the Stewarts have placed a see-through cooler just past the old photos. The chiller's mouth-watering desserts, especially its dynamic pies, create a visual caloric explosion, loudly broadcasting their rich tastes and reminding patrons that, although history matters, this place is primarily about good, all-American food.

An ever-smiling hostess greets customers by the cashier's counter, just beyond the dessert cooler, and escorts them to their tables. Eddie's dining room is actually two rooms, a smaller one off the kitchen that occupies the approximate area of the restaurant's original screened-in porch, and the big dining room that was added during Eddie's early 1960s expansion.

The small dining area is conservatively decorated, but the large room radiates a collage of Sylvan Beach's vibrant, fun-loving carnival colors. Orange chairs by the family tables (groups of twenty can enjoy meals together at any of these four rows) and orange naugahyde seats in booths facing Park Avenue reflect the rays of fifty yellow globe lights on the ceiling. Deep blue naugahyde coats the seats and back rests in booths that overlook the village park while green seats, contrasted with their purple-plaided fabric backs, color the booths facing Main Street. Blue carpeting, emboldened with striking red flowers, bursts from the floor and the expansive picture windows that surround the room import every color from Sylvan Beach's seasons. Red, pink, green, and blue neon strip lights, attached under the building's overhang, happily glow through the windows. Marbled mauve wallpaper adds a conservative contrast to the walls surrounding the room and actually unites the myriad colors.

You might think that a terrible color clash occurs here but, to the contrary, Eddie's rainbowed dining room hues blend together in a kind of celebration of Beach life–the Midway's neoned rides and games, the waterfront's muscle-boated, jet-skied power, the lake's anglers, bathers, beach walkers, the people who revel in the village's basic nature–the colors of these places, these persons, thrive in a Beach metaphoric abstraction at Eddie's.

And the rooms in which the colors merge can be justly called the "Metropolitan Museum of Art of Sylvan Beach History." The "Museum" evolved in this manner. Eddie examined his Beach postcard collection in the late 1960s and thought, "These pictures might make nice paintings." He hired local artist Lorraine Clark to make the card to canvas transfer and her paintings now adorn the dining rooms' walls. Clark's work brings vivacious color to vintage images of the Beach's former St. Charles Hotel, a luxurious facility built by Louis Chesebrough of Vaseline fame, and to the Forest Hotel, the village's first commercial resort facility.

In Clark's paintings, tourists stroll by a tintype studio on the boardwalk, swimmers frolic by the Rowe Brothers' bathhouse and toboggan slide, and travelers wait for trains by the Ontario and Western Station (which formerly occupied Eddie's building's site). One Clark oil depicts a wooden vessel–perhaps a Damon or Milton boat–bobbing atop the waves by Buoy 109, its occupants intently focused on netting a big fish. In another painting nurses relax in front of Dr. Cavana's Sanitarium, a large building located at the intersection of 13th and Park Avenues. The hospital's owner, Dr. Martin Cavana, led Sylvan Beach during its first golden era.

Railroad Avenue, the thoroughfare that became Main Street when autos replaced trains, tracks its way through Clark's work. The glorious gingerbread gothic St. Mary's Roman Catholic Church, once located kitty-corner from the restaurant, returns to its sanctuaried life in still another canvas. Lorraine Clark's tapestry of Sylvan Beach history celebrates the village's rich past.

The dining rooms' rear wall holds several noteworthy items. Most prominent is a large painting of the famous clown Emmit Kelly. An artist who stayed at Verona Beach's Dwarf Line Motel painted it for Vic Farina, the inn's former owner, but Farina didn't have a place for it. He offered it to Eddie and the latter accepted. Formal photographs of Eddie and Fifi and an enlarged, extremely clear print of the Stewarts' original hot dog stand, also hang on the rear wall.

You can still experience a touch of the old Eddie's at the restaurant's lunch counter. The counter meanders around two horseshoe-shaped serving areas and its patrons sit atop old-fashioned, kid-loving swivel stools. A wood-framed, fully enclosed telephone booth nestles in one corner and a gumball machine near the door patiently awaits a coin. Artist Iva Money's pretty painting of the Verona Beach lighthouse hangs behind the machine. Two metal poles from the first Eddie's building occupy amusingly bothersome places within the horseshoe spaces. Children's drawings and a neon clock decorate the red and white tiled wall that divides the lunch counter world from the restaurant's kitchen.

Waiters and waitresses scurry about, hustling in the horseshoes, bursting through the swinging kitchen doors, attending patrons at the take-out window. Despite the activity, the counter is a very casual place. Customers relax at this twenty-first century soda fountain spa–they sip cups of coffee, savor each sweet bite of Eddie's famous homemade pie, make the most out of every heat-relieving lick of an ice-cream cone.

Time has almost stood still at Eddie's counter. You can sit on a stool, swivel a couple 360°s, sip a cool coke, and imagine the door opening. Tommy and Jimmy Dorsey and company enter. Russell's has closed and the guys are tired. They flop on the stools next to you and order hot hams, fries, and sodas for the band. One musician hums a tune, another's fingers beat big band rhythms on the counter. Swivel a 180°, look outside at the curb, and you see a man sitting there. Is it a skinny young singer? Could that be a candy bar that he's eating? You pause and wonder. Is that a concrete curb or a railroad tie? Quite the town, indeed.

Eddie's Restaurant's history is an anthology of many tales, more than can be told within this story's confines. There's one last memory, though, that needs to be repeated. It flows like this:

Times were tough for Eddie and Fifi during their first few years at the Beach. The Depression. The war. Starting a restaurant in an era of national crises. Business was inconsistent, often slow.

Eddie fondly recalled that, every spring during those difficult years, Fifi asked him, "Are we going back to the Beach this year?" He'd think about the question, mull over their options, and answer, "Well, let's go up and just see the place. We'll look things over and decide." His response always prompted Fifi to say, "Eddie, if we go there, I know what you're going to tell me."

They'd drive to Sylvan Beach. They'd usually have to wade through snow banks and shovel out the stand's doors. Once they got inside, looked around, wiped the dust off counters and shelves, Eddie would say, "Fifi, let's try one more year."

She'd laugh and shake her head. The words almost smiled with her as she said, "I knew it, Eddie."

– Chapter 25 –

Shipwrecks

We had not been more than two or three hours upon the Oneida Lake when the loons set up a general cry from every part and sometimes screamed as tho' they were in great distress or striving to outdo each other. This was new to me. I inquired of my Indian brother what was the occasion or what could be the meaning of such an outcry among the loons. He answered a high wind before night and perhaps a storm tomorrow. We had sailed for two hours longer and the wind rose and blew almost like a hurricane. At our right the lake seemed to be all in foam, with now and then great swells and then breakers.

–*Samuel Kirkland*
Journals, April 1765

Imagine walking along Sylvan Beach on a calm, but cloudy evening, the lake tranquil and beautiful. In the serenity, a distant noise catches your attention. Like the sound of a speeding freight train, headed straight for you, but you see nothing. A dark line appears on the lake's horizon, stretching from the North to South Shores. Jet black, it steadily grasps the entire lake as it moves. The sound intensifies and the water begins to surge, up and down, pushed by a powerful, unseen force. The din becomes almost deafening and, as the darkness on the water approaches, you can see whitecaps building. Suddenly the wind reaches you and gusts reach thirty-five miles per hour as an Oneida Lake gale manifests its full force. Waves rise to six feet and crash on the beach's outer sandbars. You stand amidst a spectacle of overwhelming power.

Oneida Lake's fabled storms have claimed many vessels, and even more lives. An early example occurred around December 6, 1854, when the *Syracuse Standard* reported, "A couple of loaded canal boats were lost on Oneida Lake near Constantia on Sunday last. They had been towed as far as that place, but the storm was so severe that the steam tug could take them no farther, and they were obliged to stop. The storm increased, and the boats broke loose and drifted into the lake, where one of them sunk and the other, which was loaded with lumber, broke into pieces."

Both large boats and small have succumbed to the lake's tempests. The lake is a part of the Barge Canal system and, during the canal's commercial heyday from the 1920s through the 1950s, large fleets of tugs and barges used the water. More vessels meant more chances for tragedy. Margaret Cullen, of Utica, sent me an article "Barges Are Washed Ashore By Terrific Oneida Lake Storm," that illustrated one such disaster.

> *Sylvan Beach, June 30, 1925*–One barge loaded with 15,000 bushels of wheat was split open and its contents lost, and another was grounded during a severe storm which swept the Lake Tuesday. Considerable property along the shore was damaged.
>
> Jake Kyser, of South Bay, in company with John J. Yusaitis, succeeded in rescuing a captain, cook, and deckhand only after Kyser's rowboat had been capsized once by the heavy waves.
>
> The Transmarine Corporation of New York proved to be the biggest loser when Captain Trel of New York, commanding a fleet of five boats, was unable to reach the channel because of the high seas and ordered the last two barges cut loose. One of these contained 15,000 bushels of wheat and was broken open as the waves grounded it on Verona Beach. The other, laden with 13,000 bushels of rye, was washed high and dry but, so far as is known, its cargo did not suffer from water.
>
> Captain Trel had signaled to Cleveland, eight miles away, but during his approach the *Grant* received another call, this one from the Belle, commanded by Captain Whalen of New York. The tug succeeded in bringing two of the *Belle's* fleet of five boats to shore, but it sprung a leak and water three feet deep filled its hold, preventing it from answering the second call. The *Belle* brought its other barges safely into the channel.
>
> Jake A. Kyser, of South Bay, and John G. Yusaitis, seeing the waving figures aboard the two loosened barges of the Trans-

> marine fleet, set out in a rowboat to rescue them. The high seas capsized their frail craft, but they swam to shore and secured another. Reaching the barge, they rescued Captain Hull of Rensselaer, cook William Lulik of Brooklyn, and a deckhand.

Kyser, a South Bay hotel owner, fish pirate, and boatman nonpareil, became an Oneida Lake legend who saved scores of people caught in the lake's storms.

Many tugs and their fleets of barges experienced difficulties on Oneida. On November 8, 1930 the Syracuse Post-Standard reported the story of the *Elsie K*, a tug that fell victim to the lake's fury.

> The *Elsie K* tugboat, which sank in Oneida Lake yesterday after her crew of four had been taken off, can rot on the bottom, so far as her master and owner, Captain Patrick J. O'Neill of Lockport, is concerned. At least that is his sentiment today, although the boat represents his livelihood and fortune.
>
> The sixty-two-year-old grizzled veteran declared that he would make no attempt to salvage the *Elsie K*.
>
> "I guess old *Elsie* has made her last voyage," Captain O'Neill said after he and his crew had taken their duffle from the *Seneca Sun*, the ship that rescued the crew of the tugboat. "She was a good boat in her day, but I guess she's done for."
>
> There was the suspicion of a tear in the sailor's eyes and the working of his weather-beaten face showed his emotion. He had made many a good, rollicking voyage as captain of the *Elsie K* and it was hard to give her up.
>
> Although sea and wind had tried many times to wrest the *Elsie K* from him, Captain O'Neill, until yesterday, had always managed to pilot her to a safe haven.
>
> Death, too, had threatened before, but it had not come so close as it did yesterday when O'Neill; John Bigelow, his engineer; Harold Clair, fireman; and James Glenn, deckhand, clung to the wave-washed decks of the old tugboat until Captain Frank Stewart of the *Seneca Sun* reached them in the nick of time.
>
> The buffeting of the waves as the tugboat proceeded down the lake opened the seams of the *Elsie K*, the crew said, in telling how they fought to ward off disaster. The inrushing waters proved too much for the pumps, however. When it was seen that the vessel could not be saved, Captain O'Neill blew the siren four times, the distress signal of lake mariners.
>
> Bigelow, the engineer, after he was safely aboard the *Seneca*

> *Sun*, remembered that his license and his papers were still in his bunk on the tugboat. By that time the decks of the tug were awash. Bigelow could not be restrained from an effort to retrieve his license, however. He went below on the sinking ship, while his mates watched and prayed that he would come out before the tugboat took its final dive to the bottom.
>
> A second after Bigelow had left his ship with the papers, the Elsie K nosed down and settled in her grave.

Barges towed by tugs were particularly vulnerable to Oneida's storms. The barges were connected to the tugs and to each other by cables and wave pressure could stress metal to the limit. The *Post-Standard* described a broken cable incident on October 19, 1936.

> *Sylvan Beach*–A northwest gale was gradually blowing itself out Sunday night after driving three barges loaded with pig iron aground early Sunday at the eastern end of Oneida Lake.
>
> Two of the three craft grounded about midway between Verona Beach and Nabor's Grove, the places where two soda ash barges were stranded last Monday morning.
>
> As cables started to part under the thirty-eight-mile-per-hour wind, three men who were on the three barges made their way to safety on the tug *Transco 5*, which had the fleet of five pig iron barges on tow. The tug managed to keep two barges in tow.
>
> The fleet, *Flex Fleet B*, left Brewerton shortly before 6 P.M. Saturday and was about to be brought into the shelter of the breakwater when the gale broke, about 3 A.M. Sunday.
>
> One of the barges went aground about 500 feet off the southern edge of the entrance to the canal. The other two, still lashed together by a single cable, drifted several thousand feet south.
>
> Drawing approximately ten feet of water, each of the barges was about a foot above the surface of the lake. High rollers were breaking over the barges, with one of the pair almost hidden beneath the waters. Only a part of the shelter house showed.
>
> Each of the seven men on the fleet had put on life preservers. The trio, driven off the barges as they broke away, was forced to leave their clothes behind.

The "Nabor's Grove" cited in the article was a small commercial picnic area, located in the south end of what is now the Verona Beach State Park. Margaret Dobson Druse, whose Canastota family built a cottage just north of Oneida Creek in 1921, remembered visiting Nabor's to enjoy the grove's refreshment stand. "We never wore shoes when we walked there," Margaret recalled, "because the grounds were covered with sand. No one had to mow a lawn. Sometimes we'd row our old flat-bottomed wooden boat to Nabor's. I'll never forget the grove's trees–tall, stately pines–majestic evergreens reaching upward to the brilliant blue skies. Children used to play on the barges that were stranded on the sand bars off the beach. The big boats became their fortresses, castles, and battleships. The young folks' imaginations transformed the barges into stages for delightful childhood fantasies."

Another sudden Lake storm brought tragedy to the crew of the tug *Thomas H.* The vessel was towing six barges filled with iron ore on May 30, 1945. The *Post-Standard* reported the details:

> One man was believed drowned and three of a chain of six barges were lost when high winds whipped Oneida Lake early yesterday.
>
> Captain Herluf Dallard of Brooklyn, in charge of the ore-laden barges, and eleven of his twelve-man crew were landed safely at the Sylvan Beach pier at 2:15 P.M. by the Standard Oil tanker *Poughkeepsie*, which rescued them.
>
> Seventy-three year old Charles Blanchard, of Kingston, who was manning the last barge in the convoy, was unaccounted for. Two of the barges were seen to go down when a twenty-seven mile an hour wind struck the convoy about 1:30 A.M. and Blanchard's boat was believed to have been sunk in the vicinity of Cleveland.
>
> The story, as Captain Dallard told it to State Police, was that the tug hauling the barges left the pier at Sylvan Beach at 11:40 P.M. Tuesday to cross the lake.
>
> When the wind began tossing the barges, the captain ordered all the crew off the vessels, with the exception of Blanchard.
>
> Shortly after the crew boarded the tug, that vessel was discovered to be leaking. Pumps were brought into play, but the tug began to sink rapidly.
>
> Abandoning the tug, Captain Dallard and his men managed to board the first barge. This was also shipping water and, at 2:30 A.M., an hour after the storm began, it sank.
>
> The men had managed to climb back to the second barge, the *Margaret Hutton*. A distress signal made of a white sheet and a black blanket was hoisted and the men went to work at

> the gasoline and hand pumps.
>
> Many a prayer was offered while the men worked frantically and heroically to keep their barge above the water.
>
> At noon, after State Police had been notified of the convoy's distress, the Standard Oil tanker put out from Sylvan Beach, pulled alongside the barge and took off the men.
>
> Late in the afternoon the barge from which the crew was rescued was sighted floating near Scot Noose Park [by 16th Avenue in the Beach], listing badly.
>
> Two of the other barges were located later, one near Oneida Creek and the other near South Bay.
>
> Cold and hungry, the eleven survivors expressed the highest admiration for the men who manned the *Poughkeepsie*.

Most Oneida Lake shipwrecks remain on the lake's bottom, forgotten by all except those connected with the vessels. The story of the *Thomas H* and its barges resurfaced over forty years after the tragedy, through the exploits of scuba divers James J. Allen and Timothy Caza. The divers searched for the tug for over eight years and, using sonar, found the wreck south of Cleveland in 1986. Reporter Patricia Cappon documented Allen's and Caza's triumph in an article for the *Post Standard*, published on July 2, 1987.

> Nearing the limits of their strength and the last of their oxygen, two divers rose from the murky depths of Oneida Lake Wednesday with the pride of their underwater odyssey–the ship's wheel of the *Thomas H*.
>
> The eight-spoked wheel, its fine wood grain hidden beneath a sooty glaze, once guided the eighty-nine-year-old tugboat through New York Harbor and the waters of the Barge Canal.
>
> By 11:15 A.M., more than an hour after they made their descent, Timothy Caza and his diving partner, James J. Allen, broke the water's surface and raised their fists in triumph.
>
> "She's all wood, and that brass pedestal will shine up just like a trophy," cried Caza as they lifted the wheel onto the back of Caza's boat. "But that was more of a job than we thought."
>
> The *Thomas H* met its end in a gale wind on the lake forty-two years ago and lies tilted slightly to the starboard in the fifty-foot deep solitude of the lake. The rear of its nineteen-foot wide hull is buried to the tip of its rudder in mud.
>
> For both men, the raising of the ship's wheel marked a moment of glory in their eight-year journey and in the friend-

ship that had deepened through it all.

Since discovering the sunken vessel a year ago, Caza and Allen and a team of divers have made their descent many times to painstakingly reconstruct the history of the doomed voyage in their archaeological expedition.

Each artifact from the wreck is being located, measured, and photographed before it is removed and restored, in hopes of complying with New York State requirements for such expeditions.

"Since the wheel is up now, there's going to be an emptiness each time we go down to the pilothouse, because that beautiful sight will be gone," Caza said.

Inside the silent world of the *Thomas H*, time has lost its meaning. Milk bottles rest unbroken in a cabin icebox. Chunks of cheese appear to be floating inside. China plates and bowls lie on the floor. Wooden letters once affixed to the pilothouse have fallen to the deck. Half of a pair of binoculars was found outside the captain's quarters. A carved sailboat was perched on a shelf in the pilothouse.

Crew member John J. Vetter's wallet contained a baby's pink hair ribbon and his daughter's birth announcement. Diver Dwayne Pardee found the wallet.

Among divers, the *Thomas H* is what is known as a "virgin wreck." Its significance is more archaeological than economic.

"It's one of the best wrecks in New York State because it's intact," Caza said.

For Allen, it's a bounty of historical treasures.

Caza, a thirty-year old United Parcel Service employee from West Monroe and Allen, a forty-three year old Brewerton resident who works in quality control at New Process Gear, began searching for the *Thomas H* eight years ago. They pieced together its history with library visits and combed the lake bottom with their chart recorder, a $600 instrument that uses sonar to detect submerged objects.

Seven years ago, Caza and Allen found the *Jackie Eagen*, one of three barges that sank with the *Thomas H*. Three years later they found its sister barge. All the while, they were researching the *Thomas H* in the library and writing to anyone who could provide information. An author of a pictorial history of tugboats helped locate a photo and a detailed description.

In late May last year, Caza and Allen pinpointed the tug with sonar. They descended together.

"My eyes were as big as teacups," Allen said. "For me it's

> been fourteen years of searching for something like this."
>
> Allen said the dive was an education for him and for those he hopes will one day see the artifacts in a museum. They are paying for their expedition themselves and estimated they have spent about $50,000 in search of the fleet.
>
> The divers asked that the precise location of the wreck be withheld to prevent scavenging. "Other divers will come and strip it and it never would be presented to the public," Caza said.
>
> Bound for Oswego, the *Thomas H* was pulling six ore-laden barges when high winds whipped up the lake at 11 P.M. on May 29, 1945. Pounding waves opened her seams, and she began taking in water. The pumps were unable to handle the flow, and she sank after midnight on May 30, along with three of the barges. Olin Haakonsen of New York City owned the tug.
>
> Captain Herluf Dallard of Brooklyn and eleven of his twelve-man-crew were rescued by the Standard Oil tanker *Poughkeepsie*. Charles Blanchard of Kingston, who was manning the last barge in the convoy, drowned.
>
> Abandoning the tug, Dallard and his men managed to board the first barge before it sank. When that began sinking, they climbed to the second barge, the *Margaret Hutton*. They hoisted a distress signal of a white sheet and a black blanket. The *Poughkeepsie* noticed the signal and the crew were rescued.

There are two beautiful postscripts to this story. James Allen and Timothy Caza donated the *Thomas H*'s artifacts to the H. Lee White Marine Museum in Oswego. The museum staff developed an informative exhibit that educates the public about the tug's history.

The divers, helped by Syracuse Channel 3 newsman Tom Miller, located crew member John J. Vetter, and told him that they found the *Thomas H* and his long-lost wallet. Vetter was living in Florida and came back to Oswego where, in an emotion-filled ceremony on September 10, 1987, Allen and Caza presented him with the wallet and other mementos, including his daughter's pink hair ribbon.

Speaking to the *Oswego Palladium-Times*, Allen summarized his view of diving's rewards, "It shows that you don't necessarily have to have a chest of gold and jewels to make a shipwreck valuable."

I talked with Jim about the *Thomas H* chapter of his life. The veteran diver characterized the event as a "dream come true. No other diver had explored the vessel. I had a feeling after the discovery that I had found a long lost friend. In a nutshell, the *Thomas H* was a living history lesson that brought life to a bygone era."

– Chapter 26 –

An Unforgettable Duck Hunt

Throughout history Oneida Lake has been a refuge for Upstate New York's middle and working classes. Groups such as farm laborers, industrial workers, school and church organizations, Grangers, ethnic singing societies, and African Americans picnicked at Sylvan Beach, Frenchman's Island, Brewerton, and Lower South Bay in the late nineteenth and early twentieth centuries. The Beach burst its touristy seams when upwards of 75,000 people jammed the village for the annual hop-growers' gathering every July. On the lake's West End, steamboats like the *Sagamore* and the *Manhattan*, based out of Lower South Bay and Brewerton, offered reasonably priced excursions to all lakeside locales and were jammed with patrons on every summer weekend. Numerous hotels around the lake advertised rowboats for the sportspersons, sailing craft for the romantics, and cold liquid refreshment for the tired laborers from the foundries and mills of Utica, Rome, and Syracuse. Waterfront building lots and camps were relatively inexpensive until the Reaganomic boom of the 1980s. At times, property was downright cheap. In 1923, the *Syracuse Herald* offered lots close to Oneida's South Shore near Lakeport and Bridgeport for $58.50, if a person would subscribe to that paper for six months! Upstate's middle and working classes could afford Oneida's offerings and the lake became their playground.

John and Ancilla Togni lived in Solvay during the Great Depression. They took in boarders, ran a tavern, and John worked for the WPA to support their eleven children (eight girls, three boys). Around 1939, Ancilla decided that the Tognis needed a retreat from Solvay's industrial environs so she and John scraped up $400 to buy property on Beach Road along Oneida Lake's Lower South Bay. One of their daughters, Angie Togni Capella, purchased an adjoining lot the year prior. The whole family pitched in to construct Ancilla's and John's camp. They nicknamed the place the "Labor Camp" because of the seemingly endless array of work projects needed to perfect it.

Eventually, Togni family members owned six camps at their Beach Road enclave. They savored Oneida's delights together every year. Music highlighted the Tognis' summers. Mary Togni Frizzi played the piano and accordion and Bruno Davia, who married Alma Togni, bowed a violin. Other family members added their instruments to the family ensemble and lively Tyrolean melodies bounced through the South Bay breezes. Old country cuisine like chicken polenta, a family favorite, complemented the tunes.

Judith Togni Armani was John and Ancilla's oldest daughter. She and her husband Barney lived in Solvay, but spent weekends at the family's retreat. Judith and Barney's son, Arnold, grew up amidst South Bay summers and enjoyed Oneida Lake's outdoor sporting world. After serving in the Navy during World War II, Arnold trained as an electrician and worked for General Electric in Syracuse for thirty-five years. He married the former Betty Scaia in 1949 and the couple raised three daughters–Barbara, Beverly, and Patricia. He and Betty invested in a camp amidst the Togni properties and they still summer there. Arnold's love of the outdoors deepened in his retirement and he has served as a Director of the Oneida Lake Association for nearly three decades. The lake's preservation and protection rank among his highest priorities.

Arnold's Uncle Ed Togni was his hunting and fishing mentor. Ed became more of a best friend than a relative to the teenage Armani. Together they experienced the gamut of Oneida's sporting life, but one duck hunt in particular stood out from all of their other shared days. Recalling the event, Arnold noted, "I remember this hunt as if it occurred yesterday. This was an incredible day."

> My Uncle Ed Togni was an electrician, first at Halcomb Steel and then at Frazier and Jones, both in Solvay. Uncle Ed was a good spirited, industrious man who became my best friend and my idol. He taught me about hunting, fishing, and the joys of the great outdoors. My dad was a hard worker,

always busy with his many jobs. Ed was like my surrogate father.

We fished all over the Syracuse area–Cross Lake, Warners' Clay Pits, Nine Mile Creek, but after our family bought their property on Lower South Bay, we spent most of our time on Oneida Lake. Ed liked to fish for walleyes, especially near Frenchman's and Dunham's Islands. I'd steer our old five horsepower "knuckle buster" motor, attached to our wooden Thompson boat, while Ed directed me to the hot spots. It was a two-mile drive to the islands and we didn't get there very fast. We fished with June Bug Spinners, tipped with worms. We drifted and cast. I always caught the most fish, which seemed to make Ed mad, but his anger was only an act. We had loads of fun every time we went out on the water.

Ed liked all types of hunting, but his luck wasn't the best. He hunted whitetail deer for thirty-seven years without getting a buck. Then, he and some friends traveled to Steuben County, where deer are plentiful. The first morning was beautiful–sunny and warm, maybe too warm. After seeing nothing all morning, Ed got bored and sat down. He leaned against a maple tree and fell asleep. As he told it, he was "awakened by some rustling leaves." He looked around and there, thirty yards away, was a nice buck. He shot the deer and ended his whitetail jinx.

We drove to our family's camps to duck hunt. We took Uncle Ed's Model A Ford from Solvay to Mattydale and got on South Bay Road, which gave us a quick shot to the lake. This road was dead straight, not a curve in sight. They built it on the bed of the old Syracuse to South Bay Trolley. People nicknamed it "Politicians' Highway" because it led to the Yacht Club. A few of Syracuse's pols belonged to the club and they made sure that the road was well maintained.

We passed a few crop farms in the muck land that bordered South Bay Road. There weren't many farms. There weren't many cars, either. Once we got on the road we might meet six other vehicles during the whole trip. You could test your car's speed on South Bay Road and feel safe doing it.

We turned onto Beach Road when we got to the lake. That road was rough! I'm almost exaggerating by calling it a "road." It was made from dirt and gravel. It often flooded because it bordered the lake on one side and a swamp on the other. Potholes, washouts–you name it–Beach Road had them. The road ended where Aero Marina is today. The Conway Home Improvement Company was located there in the 1940s.

Staying at camp was a "roughing it" experience. We had no electricity, no running water. We used an outhouse. We got water from a hand pump. The upstairs was like a big dormitory room–lots of beds, lots of people. Uncle Ed and I slept there. We were usually the only ones at camp in duck season. The place was cool and we slept well. Lots of barges traveled up and down the lake in the fall and I remember listening to their sounds as I drifted off to sleep. Their engines made a kind of throbbing, pulsating hum as they motored down the channel to Sylvan Beach. There was something about that sound that I liked–it was comforting, in a way. It was part of being at camp.

Uncle Ed was a "quick trigger" hunter. He taught me all that he knew about wing shooting. That's what we called shooting at flying birds. I learned to shoot just like Ed. There was a problem, however, because Ed was a terrible wing shot. He went by the motto, "If you can see the ducks, shoot 'em, 'cause they're in range." This philosophy only helped ammunition companies. Ed and I burned up two boxes of shells [twenty-five per box] on a typical morning's duck hunt. On a good day we'd kill two ducks. I never read the game laws and it was years before I realized that the limit was not one duck apiece!

Our decoy spread was a sight to behold. We bought a few "dekes," and these looked nice bobbing in the waves. Uncle Ed, however, thought that he could carve his decoys to make our spread more attractive. He spent hours working on those wooden birds. When he finished carving he painted them black, for a silhouette effect. Ed's masterpieces were the scrawniest decoys I ever saw. They looked like a flock of floating, malnourished crows! No wonder the ducks avoided us.

Now, let me tell you about the one trip that I'll never forget. We drove to camp well before daybreak on a Saturday morning. It was very, very cold. The lake's surface formed an icy skim. We shivered as we loaded our sack of decoys and our other gear in the Thompson. Lastly, we placed our shotguns in the driest, part of the boat. I had an old Remington 870 pump, while Uncle Ed used a twelve gauge Belgian Browning automatic.

When the boat was ready I started the knuckle buster motor. I eased into the bay, passed Short Point, and then turned around Peck's Point. This was the old name for Long Point. I followed the shoreline west for a couple hundred yards down to Old Man's Point. We set our decoys in the water off Old Man's, beached and hid the boat, and then got into our blind on the end of that point.

The ducks started flying at sunrise. Thousands upon thousands filled the air! Bluebills, redheads, canvasbacks, all sorts of flight ducks. Rafts and rafts of ducks covered the lake's channel. We called these huge flocks "rafts" when they were on the water. From a distance they looked like a solid mass of birds. It's normal for ducks to fly in the early morning and late evening. That's their natural time for movement. On Oneida Lake, however, lots of barges traveled down the channel, even late in the season. They disturbed the duck rafts and kept the birds airborne for most of the day. Flocks of a hundred birds commonly flew in what we thought was range of our decoys. This made for exciting hunting.

Exciting, it was. Productive, it wasn't. Our shotguns roared as we vainly threw lead in the ducks' direction. We used up the customary box of shells apiece and killed our two duck quota. When sundown arrived we were tired, but happy. We enjoyed the lake but, more important, we enjoyed our time together.

Sunday morning came and we repeated our hunting ritual. The day duplicated Saturday in all aspects, even the results–two more ducks. We packed our gear in late afternoon, closed the camp, and started home.

We had a strange feeling when we got to North Syracuse...a feeling that something was wrong. Despite the cold weather, groups of people were standing on the sidewalks, talking, shaking their heads. They looked so serious. A lot of people were standing alone, staring blankly into space. All the way from North Syracuse to Solvay there were hundreds of people, outside in December. Everyone was somber, sad, distant. No one smiled. No one laughed. It was like a scene from "The Twilight Zone."

Uncle Ed and I couldn't believe what we saw. We didn't know what to make of it. Finally, we reached Solvay. Ed dropped me at my parents' house. I thanked him for the trip, unloaded my gear, and walked upstairs. My father gazed out a kitchen window, lost in his thoughts. My mother's head was in her hands. She was crying. I asked them what happened and they told me.

That Sunday was December 7, 1941.

– Chapter 27 –

Inside Xandria

Two marvelous estates along the South Shore have graced Oneida Lake's history. John Chapman's English-styled "Orchard Cottage" is all that remains from his gentleman's holdings on Messenger's Bay. This house, on Route 31 across from the Oneida Lake Congregational Church, is meticulously preserved and has been cited in architectural surveys of noteworthy Madison County homes. Charles Brown's "Xandria" Estate on Shackelton Point, east of Bridgeport, has been home to Cornell University's Biological Field Station since 1955. The Field Station is a research-teaching facility that monitors and investigates Oneida Lake's environment.

Charles Brown's father, Alexander, was a prominent Syracuse businessman who made his fortune through typewriter and firearms innovations. Brown was a blacksmith by training, but technical genius inspired him to create several typewriter inventions. Rumor held that Brown received income from almost every typewriter manufactured in the United States. The inventor built a cottage on Shackelton Point and came there to relax with the locals, whose company he enjoyed. When Brown passed away, he left seven million dollars to his wife and his sons, Charles and Julian. When Mrs. Brown died she willed her money to her sons, but litigation reduced each brother's portion to about $50,000.

Julian received the Shackelton Point property and wanted to turn it into an amusement area, similar to Sylvan Beach's Midway. Nineteenth century Shackelton Point boasted a steamboat landing, a dance hall, rental cottages, a picnic area, and a hotel–in short, the seeds of a full-fledged resort. Charles disagreed and persuaded his brother to sell him the family's Oneida Lake property. He named the place "Xandria," in memory of his father.

A brief history of Shackelton Point, written by Town of Sullivan historian Clara Houck, describes how Brown expanded and developed his estate. He purchased cottages and land along the adjoining shore. One larger property was the Groesbeck farm. He razed some buildings, and moved and renovated others. His father's Greek revival home was turned to face the east and remodeled into what is now known as the "Main Cottage." Charles married Iola Warior in 1936, and they spent many summers in this house. "The Lodge," one of the original camps, was remodeled and used as their servants' quarters. The old "Longhouse," formerly a dance-hall, was moved next to the Lodge and became a six-car garage. The "Clubhouse," where Cornell's students live in summer, was also one of the original camps. Brown built a large kennel in the late 1930s for Iola's Great Danes. Iola's first dog was brought from Germany by a "nursemaid," who was paid to stay with it until it learned to take commands in English. These huge canines' barking discouraged uninvited guests. Brown valued privacy and enclosed his original estate with a fence and a row of poplar trees.

In subsequent years Brown enlarged his holdings to over 400 acres by buying the Fred Deyo, Frank Deyo, and John Pindle farms that bordered his land on the west, and the Delmarter and Thurlow Roberts shore property to the southeast. He demolished Fred Deyo's home and remodeled Frank Deyo's house. The Laible family moved into the latter dwelling. Paul Laible, one of Brown's employees, was hired in as a professional landscaper for the estate in 1936.

Brown had more plans for Xandria when he passed away on April 22, 1953. He bequeathed the estate to Cornell University. Brown's wife Iola died in Fayetteville on April 15, 1968.

I interviewed Paul Laible at his home at Richland, New York, several years ago. I wanted to find out more about Charles Brown, Xandria, and the inner workings of this unusual Oneida Lake enclave. Paul was a gracious host and a morning of clear, delightful memories passed all too quickly.

Laible was born in Lyons, New York, in 1913. After finishing high school he entered the horticulture program at Cornell University and was graduated in 1936. He worked briefly at a nursery in Painesville, Ohio, but was subsequently hired by Brown to maintain Xandria's extensive grounds. Except for a three-year service during World War II, Paul spent the rest of his career working for Brown and then Cornell, after the University acquired the estate. He and his wife, the former Caroline Lucas of Bridgeport, raised two sons–James and Charles.

Paul Laible's memories portrayed a meticulously organized Charles Brown whose omnipresent perfectionism manifested itself in Xandria. "Mr. Brown planned his property in great detail," recalled Paul. "He was incredibly picky. His engineering background showed in his detailed planning." What follows are some Laible recollections of "Mr. Brown" and his estate. Employees always addressed him that way. Xandria was a unique creation and Brown a unique person in Oneida Lake's history.

> I worked for Mr. Brown for much of my life. My wife, Caroline, and I lived on the estate. We had the "run of it," so to speak. We could use the facilities, and these were the very best. I enjoyed my job. I lived on an estate. An estate! You might say that it had all the advantages, and none of the worries, of having money. I was rich in many ways. My family lived in a beautiful place. The estate was a great home for raising children and my boys loved being there. You can't put a dollar value on that.
>
> I was Mr. Brown's Superintendent of Grounds. I landscaped the great lawns. Mr. Brown, of course, drew up and approved the plans for everything. The east lawn, that faces Dutchman's Island and Delmarter Bay, sloped one foot downward for every hundred feet it went toward the water. The north lawn, that faces the lake itself, sloped two feet for every hundred. Mr. Brown bought 10,000 yards of topsoil and had it trucked in so that the lawns would slope perfectly. I supervised the grading and he checked the work.
>
> I also watered the lawns. They were kept in flawless condition. No one wearing spiked heels was allowed to walk on an estate lawn. The big maple trees were all planted in distinct patterns. One year, forestry worms got into the maple trees. Mr. Brown ordered me to put planks across the lawns for the sprayers to walk on, just so they wouldn't damage the grass. Our lawns were never disturbed.
>
> I also took care of the orchards. I had to prune the trees and harvest the fruit. Mr. Brown had a kind of "don't bother me, just do your job" attitude toward his workers. If you did good work Mr. Brown trusted you. I earned his confidence.
>
> A number of people worked at Xandria. Most were older

men who wanted part-time employment to add to their retirement checks. Mr. Brown hired a carpenter, a plumber, an electrician, a mason, and a tinsmith. He and his wife also kept a maid and a cook. The cook had worked for Mr. Brown's father, Alexander.

Mrs. Brown loved Great Danes so much that she persuaded her husband to hire a dog trainer, who had sleeping quarters in the "kennel house." The kennel's construction was delayed for three years because Mr. Brown kept modifying its architectural plans. When it was finally completed it cost $60,000, and this was back in the 1930s. The Browns even had a cemetery where their Great Danes were buried.

Mr. Brown was a planner like you can't imagine. He hired Dwight Baum, a famous Boston architect, to design Xandria. Baum modeled the estate a lot like Williamsburg, Virginia. Big lawns. Trees laid out in perfect patterns. Everything worked together within a master plan. Mr. Brown changed Baum's ideas to meet his specifications. He paid an expensive architect's fee and then modified all the designs.

The big garage on the estate used to be a dancehall. Mr. Brown wanted it to be rewired, so he hired electricians to install the fixtures and wiring–using baling twine! He carefully examined the garage, made his changes, and then we did the actual wiring. He was that kind of man.

Mr. Brown was brilliant. He designed the first roadside grass mower ever built in this country. He never marketed it, even though it was a fine machine. He was rich. He didn't need more money. Mechanics was his hobby. He also designed and built the small tractors that we used on the estate and, just before he died, he was planning a sawmill. He planned and planned. Every tree, fence post, pipe, board, everything was planned and surveyed. In winter, I'd make mechanical drawings for some of his plans. He'd look at these and usually say that he liked them. Then, of course, he changed them. We did everything his way.

Mr. Brown hated cars driving through Xandria. The road that goes through the front gate once lead to several camps on what they called "Eagle Bay," an area southeast along the lake. People use Hamilton Brown Road to get there now. Mr. Brown paid for Hamilton Brown Road's construction just so these camp owners wouldn't drive through the estate. That road goes through a swampy area and Mr. Brown let the road crew dig fill on his land just to get the road completed. When they made the road they dammed up the swamp's creek. This formed a wetland, actually a large pond. Local people sarcastically called it "Lake Charles." Once Hamilton Brown Road was finished Mr. Brown installed a gate at the entrance to Xandria.

Mr. Brown didn't care much for hunters and fishermen. Duck hunters snuck into the estate and built blinds. He personally chased them off. Sometimes he only had his bathrobe on when he did the chasing! After this he paid a man to sit on Dutchman's Island and shoot at ducks during season–not to kill them, but to spook them and discourage hunters.

One time, Mr. Brown and some of his guests were sitting by the big flagpole, just visiting, relaxing. There was a fisherman in a small rowboat by Dutchman's. The fisherman stood up in the boat and, with his back turned, relieved himself. Mr. Brown was extremely offended. He was bound and determined to stop what he considered to be antisocial behavior. So, he designed and installed an electronic noisemaker that floated in the lake and could be activated from shore. This was supposed to scare the fish away. No fish–no fishermen. He'd go to any lengths to protect his privacy.

Mr. Brown died from a heart attack in Syracuse. Before that, he had another attack while he was in Baltimore. He didn't want to be alone there so he paid me, Guy Moore, and Clarence Dilthy to stay with him in one-week shifts.

I took pride in what I did for Mr. Brown. The estate was a wonderful place. Everything fit. Neat, clean, the way it should be. Buildings, trees, lawns, flower beds–there was a kind of balance between them, like every part of the estate was a piece of a beautiful puzzle and, together, they fit into a master plan. It was relaxing to walk around Xandria. It was pleasing, too. You felt comfortable within the order of things.

I always hoped that Xandria, in the future, would be maintained properly. It was a memorial to Mr. Brown's high standards. To honor his memory, the estate should be kept that way forever.

Note: You can visit Charles Brown's Xandria Estate today. The grounds are located at the eastern end of Shackelton Point Road, Bridgeport. A phone call ahead (315-633-9243) would be appropriate and appreciated.

– Chapter 28 –

Life With Pop

The late Milt Kellogg, formerly of Long Point, fished Oneida Lake for over half a century. He began angling during the 1940s. His father John, whom he affectionately called “Pop,” was his partner. In spring the Kelloggs set “long lines,” heavy lines that stretched for 1,500 feet, on which were attached 300 hooks, all baited for bottom-feeding fish such as catfish and bullheads. In other seasons they used more traditional techniques to catch Oneida’s walleyes, bass, and yellow “jack” perch. Milt was a painter at Bristol-Myers and John was an engineer for the New York Central Railroad. They fished together until John’s death in 1978 and logged many joyous hours in pursuit of Oneida’s bounty.

Milt’s memories of “Life with Pop” encompassed a variety of topics. He loved to share his lake stories and called me regularly just to chat about Oneida, until his death in 2000. Milt enjoyed the lake’s sporting life and this feeling helped color his words.

The First Snowmobiles

When you think of snowmobiles today, you picture these customized, sleek Arctic-Cats and Ski-Doos that can speed across the ice at over one hundred miles per hour. These fancy machines, powered by the best that modern technology offers, carry a hefty price tag. Old time snowmobiling was a totally different matter.

A new era dawned on Oneida Lake when the first snowmobile arrived from a Canadian manufacturing company. Winter sports on the lake have never been the same.

My father John and I bought a Polaris "KC 95 SnoTracker" from A.C. Lamb of Liverpool in the early 1950s. We paid $1,400 for it. The snowmobile had a 9.5-horsepower motor and a belt-driven torch clutch. This machine was a far cry from today's models. The engine was mounted on the back! The throttle was a "stick" type that you'd push in and out. One seat was in front of the driver and there were no brakes. It was a very heavy machine. When it got stuck you needed a block and tackle and a tripod to free yourself.

This snowmobile's track was lined with metal cleats. This gave the machine good pulling power. The track ran into a chute, located under the seat. The track's rotation produced strong suction. If the chute filled with slush and low temperatures made it freeze, you were in trouble. There was no hope for moving that machine. You simply left it, walked home, and came back with a propane torch to thaw it the next day. You never worried about anyone stealing the machine. It would take a team of horses to move our Polaris!

That snowmobile gave us a nice ride. Depending on the slope of the land and the amount and condition of the snow, the Polaris could travel in speeds ranging from ten to eighteen miles per hour. A governor kept it under control. Since the engine was in the rear, its noise didn't bother us too much. Our Polaris could easily carry my father, our black lab "Laddie" who loved to ice fish with us, and me.

Snowmobiles greatly changed ice fishing on Oneida Lake. They could pull sleds that contained tackle, tip-ups, and bait. They hauled ice shanties for fishermen, making that difficult task easy. Back then, New York State law allowed anglers to use fifteen tip-ups. Twenty walleyes per day was the legal limit and very little law enforcement occurred. My dad and I probably averaged between thirty and forty pike per day. Just about every family in the Lower South Bay area had their share of tip-ups "cut in" the ice. These simple fishing devices suspended a minnow above bottom. When a pike took the bait a "flag" [a small piece of red cloth], attached to a wire, popped up. We put our tip-ups in at first ice during December and took them out just before the spring thaw. We used golden shiner minnows for bait and bought these at Millard and Chuck Rogers' Brewerton Bait Shop.

Ice fishing was a big social event in those days. People were friendly. They respected and trusted each other. Almost anyone would give you a hand if you had some trouble on the ice. On some weekends there would be hundreds of ice anglers in the South Bay area, all catching walleyes, perch, and northern pike.

Snowmobiles were, at first, good for the ice fishermen but, as they increased in number, bad things happened. Some snowmobilers took advantage of their speed and mobility. Sledders raided the tip-ups at night when the fishermen were home. Walleyes bite well after dark and often got hooked on the tip-ups' lines. Snowmobilers stole all the fish. Sometimes they left the lines on the ice, which ruined them when they froze. Sometimes they just ran over the tip-up tops, bending them to the point where they couldn't be used again. Fishermen got discouraged. Many gave up the sport. Others removed their tip-ups at the end of each day. This was a lot of work. Complaints to the police and the game wardens never resulted in better law enforcement. Oneida is a big, wild lake and "the law" has trouble patrolling it.

A Night On the Ice

Once my father and I spent a night on Oneida's ice, trying to catch the fish pirates who had been running tip-ups after dark. "Running tip ups" meant stealing fish and these pirates had it down to a science. After selecting a particular bunch of tip-ups that were producing, they snuck into the tip-up area between 11P.M. and 3A.M. Fishermen seldom tended their tip-ups at night and stealing fish was pretty easy pickings.

One night in late February during a driving snowstorm, Dad and I tried to catch the pirates. We snuck into our ice-fishing shanty, which was then near the shore of Long Point, opposite from a landmark we called the "old stone house." Our shanty measured six by eight feet and was built of wood and canvas. There were four fishing holes in the floor. We lit it with a kerosene lantern and heated it with a kerosene stove. We built the shanty on sleigh runners that dad got from the New York Central Railroad. When you tipped the shanty into position the runners were off the ice, nice and dry.

Oneida's winds are notorious. They rise suddenly and powerfully. About 1A.M. a violent wind hit us. It tipped our shanty over while we were inside! The shanty acted like a sail and, catching the wind, took Dad and me for a ride of several hundred yards to Conway's [Short] Point. Finally our shelter shattered. What a mess! Kerosene soaked everything. Gear was scattered all over. Wood and canvas littered the area. Luckily, we were unharmed.

We didn't catch the pirates who had been raiding our tip-ups, but we caught something else–a nice dose of humility. Oneida Lake can do that to you. There's something about the lake that makes you feel pretty humble at times.

The Best Damn Way Imaginable To Catch Bullheads

On an early spring night in the 1940s, Pop and I were fishing in South Bay. We anchored off the tip of Long Point, by a spot called "Peck's Point." This was bullhead time, but they didn't bite that evening. We tried everything–worms, cheese, and even chicken livers, but the bullheads wouldn't cooperate.

We were frustrated so we decided to move. We took a shortcut. The water was high and flooded much of the point. We beached our wooden boat and started to drag it through the shallows across the point, aiming for Old Man's Bay. The water was about three inches deep. When we first started, the dragging was easy. Then the boat got heavier...and heavier...and heavier. Finally, Pop said, "What's going on, Milt? The water isn't any shallower. What's wrong with the boat?" I confessed to being puzzled and suggested that we flip the boat and check the hull.

We overturned the boat. There were dozens of bullheads fixed to its bottom! The wood must have softened from being in the water so long. The bullheads' hard dorsal fins were stuck in the wood! Pop said, "Can you believe it, Milt? I've never seen anything like this!" I said, "Pop, we'd better act fast." Quickly, we plucked the fish off our boat and filled two five-gallon pails.

Now, if there's an easier way to catch a mess of bullheads, I have yet to hear it. I hope that when someone comes up with a better way, they share their "wisdom" with me.

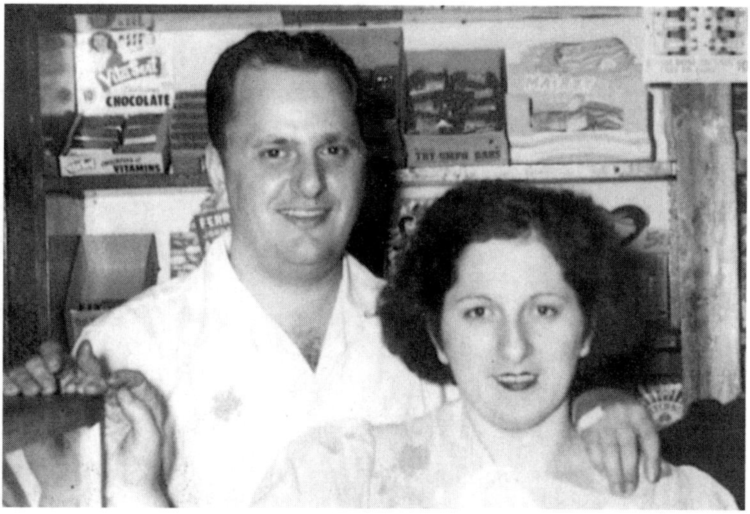

Eddie Stewart

Eddie and Fifi Stewart pose behind the restaurant's counter, around 1945.

Eddie Stewart

The original Eddie's Restaurant–a far cry from today's enterprise.

Bill and Janeen Fariel

Strong winds on Oneida Lake can generate great waves, as evidenced in this 1912 photo.

Fort Brewerton Historical Society

Oneida Lake was a part of the Barge Canal's course when that waterway opened in 1917. Boat traffic on the lake increased exponentially. The potential for shipwrecks rose in kind. These barges and tugs were moored in Brewerton harbor in 1936.

Ann Hopkins

Many will recall the Morania and Peckinpaugh tugs and barges, carrying their cargoes of oil and cement through Oneida. Here, a tug propels an oil barge into the lake at Sylvan Beach in the 1950s.

Jean Kowalski

The Barge Canal accommodated a variety of pleasure craft. This large yacht cruised into Sylvan Beach harbor on a calm day in the 1950s. Oneida's storms could even give boats this size a troublesome voyage.

Arnold Armani

John and Ancilla Togni's family gathers around them during a feast day celebration at their Oneida Lake camps on October 4, 1938. Arnold Armani is on the far right in the back row. Edward Togni is kneeling in the front row, holding a child, third from the right.

Edward Togni and Arnold Armani enjoyed Lower South Bay's sporting life during the 1930s and 1940s. This photo was taken on Beach Road.

Cornell University

Charles Brown's plan for Xandria, completed in 1933, shows the intricate sense of order that influenced his estate's design.

Cornell University

Xandria from the air. Paul Laible maintained Brown’s property with care and precision. Note the immaculate lawns. Laible took great pride in his work.

Brown’s “main house” on Shackelton Point radiates a classical flair.

Doric-capitaled columns are part of a classical nook that frames a Cornell research vessel in Xandria's harbor.

Milt Kellogg

John Kellogg stands behind the snowmobile that he and his son Milt used for Oneida Lake ice fishing trips. It was one of the first machines on the lake. This photo was taken in January 1954.

Milt Kellogg

The Kelloggs' knowledge of Oneida Lake produced ample fishing success. John proudly displays a forty-two-inch, twenty-three-pound northern pike that he caught in Old Man's Bay in 1969.

– Chapter 29 –

Brewerton's Bait Shop

Chuck and Millard Rogers were, for half a century, synonymous with angling on Oneida Lake's Western End. The brothers established the "Brewerton Bait Shop" on the corner of Library Street and Route 11 in 1946. They moved their business to the intersection of Bartell Road and Route 81 in 1975 and renamed it "Brewerton Sports." Tens of thousands of Oneida Lake enthusiasts have relied on the Rogers family for outdoor sporting supplies and, perhaps more important, fishing and hunting advice. In peak seasons the shop still handles hundreds of calls per week, inquiring about topics ranging from how the fish are biting to what lures work best, what spots are "hot," what Brewerton's weather forecast is and, of course, what hours they're open. Millard and Chuck and Chuck's son Steve, who owns the business today, always believed in honesty with their customers. They'd tell you if the fishing excelled and, if it reeked, they'd be equally candid. Oneida Lake anglers know that they can rely on Brewerton Sports' data.

The shop celebrated its 50th anniversary in 1996 and, to commemorate the event, *Syracuse Post Standard-Herald Journal* outdoors columnist Fred David wrote an article highlighting the store's history. David regularly fished with Millard and Chuck and visited Brewerton Sports often. The brothers provided Fred with information for his popular, well-rounded column. David is an Oneida Lake advocate and belonged to the Board of Directors of the Oneida Lake Association for fourteen years, during which time he edited the organization's newsletter, *The Oneida Lake Bulletin.*

Millard and Chuck Rogers were tremendous sources for my research of Oneida Lake's history. I met them twenty-five years ago and have visited their shop on many occasions to verify information, enjoy their lively stories, or just talk a little "lake fishin'." Millard contributed some fascinating fish pirate lore to my last book, *Tales of Oneida Lake.* Both brothers influenced my second work, *Oneida Lake–Place Names and History.* I interviewed Chuck for this volume and recorded a few of his valuable, colorful memories.

What follows is two-fold. Fred David's story, taken from the *Herald-Journal* of September 15, 1996, leads. Following that are several Chuck Rogers' stories, creeled from his life of Oneida Lake fishing. I encountered some of Chuck's material in an article entitled "Oneida Lake Fishing–The Way It Was," published in the Spring 1995 edition of *The Oneida Lake Bulletin.* Charlie Engel, a member of the Oneida Lake Association's Board of Directors, wrote the piece and I used his work as a springboard for my interview's questions.

Brewerton Bait Shop Grows With Changes

Chuck Rogers doesn't know what he'd be doing today if events sixty-one years ago hadn't turned his world into a pot of gold.

The seventy-five year old's recollection of a mid-September duck-hunting trip in 1935 is as vivid as the bright sun. It wasn't much of an outing, because the ducks weren't flying, he said. He was a fourteen-year-old high school sophomore (he was graduated with the Class of 1938, North Syracuse High) and, on that day, was especially observant of the happenings in front of his makeshift cattails–reeds blind in a shallow bay on the outskirts of Brewerton.

"Suddenly the water began to boil," he recalled. "It lasted almost twenty minutes. I could see thousands of buckeye minnows thrashing in the water and I got so excited that I ran home to find a minnow seine."

After locating a net, Chuck jogged back to the bay to catch bait for future fishing trips. A motorist stopped to ask if he had any minnows.

"I will in a minute," he replied. The man followed him to the lake.

"I sold him a pail (about ten quarts) of buckeye minnows for

$1. He bought several pails and asked if I could supply him with minnows a few times a week," Rogers remembered. The customer was Joe Wallen, a bait shop owner from Binghamton, who often cruised Oneida Lake's shore, looking for minnows to stock his popular Southern Tier sports shop.

Young Rogers hurried home to tell his parents, Jack and Ruth, about the sale. They were grocers, proprietors of the successful Red & White Grocery Store, at the corner of Railroad Street and Route 11, in the hub of Brewerton. Railroad Street was renamed Library Street when the village library opened. Jack and Ruth helped their son set up a few tanks in a twenty by forty foot storage room behind the market. Chuck then contracted to supply minnows to the popular Vad's Bait Shop, on Syracuse's North Side.

"I was the richest kid in high school," the smiling Rogers said. "Not many high school kids had $10 in their pockets back then. This was the Depression and I was making a lot of money selling bait behind our family's store." He sold between twenty and thirty pails per week before graduating and enlisting in the Army Air Corps.

During Chuck's tour of duty, his father died and his mother kept the market going. Young Rogers returned home in 1945 and, while the grocery business was good, the bait business thrived and kept getting bigger. In 1946, Chuck's older brother, Millard, left a physical education teaching position at Syracuse University and, together, they opened the "Brewerton Bait Shop."

"I was making more money selling minnows than Millard was teaching," Rogers said, "so he quit and we went into business. He was a very intelligent man, but got discouraged when a fire at Archbold Stadium destroyed his just-completed doctoral thesis. All that work went up in smoke, so he left the teaching profession."

The brothers became well known around Oneida Lake and Central New York. They cleared the grocery shelves and restocked with lures, rods, reels, guns, hunting equipment, and a smattering of other sporting goods. Nothing for archers, however. "Hunting with a bow and arrow wasn't heard of then," Chuck recalled.

"We served a major portion of the bait and sporting goods market in this area," he said. Fishermen had to pass the store to get to the lake. They stopped to buy their bait. Many came from the city by train. The station was only a few blocks away.

Rogers remembers anglers standing in line during the winter to buy minnows for ice fishing. "Big Bay was the hot spot for walleyes and panfish through the ice and, to get there from Syracuse, fishermen had to go by the Bait Shop. There were so many people on the ice that it was like a city. Most of them bought their bait here."

There was always a reminder of the grocery store days around the shop. Ruth Rogers was still a part of the business. She helped with everything, from selling tackle to counting worms. "If the door was open, Mom was working," Chuck stated.

On many occasions, Ruth would take eggs in trade for bait and sell the eggs to townfolks. The store even took in dry cleaning for years. It became the information center of Brewerton. "The shop was the general meeting place in the village," Chuck said. "People always stopped in just to say 'hello' or to talk about town politics with Millard." The elder Rogers was active in Cicero politics and served on the Town Board and as Town Supervisor.

Then, one day, Brewerton changed. Its "downtown" section became a virtual ghost town. Interstate 81 opened and diverted traffic around this once bustling village. "Our business dropped by 50% immediately," Chuck said.

The brothers owned a farm on Bartell Road near the Route 81 exit and entrance ramps. They decided to get out of town and relocate next to the superhighway.

"Everybody thought we were crazy," Rogers said. "They'd ask, 'Why are you moving out to the country?'" A half-mile from the village was apparently "in the country" to some.

"They thought we were crazy to leave town," Chuck related. "Certainly we felt sorry to leave the old building but we knew that if we didn't get in the flow of traffic, we would soon be out of business."

The Rogers clan planned a fifty-year celebration. They invited sporting goods representatives to display their wares under a huge tent and in the spacious 5,000-square-foot store they built twenty-two years ago.

"It's a new ball game now," said Chuck's son and co-owner Steve Rogers. "Trolling was the technique used to catch walleyes when Dad and Uncle Millard opened the shop. Today, it's artificial bait, designer lures, and high-tech equipment."

The big lures used to be "Little Wonder" spinners and Heddon "River Runts." Now, Rapalas and Storm Thunder-

Sticks catch the walleyes.

I asked Chuck what the greatest change he's seen in fishing in five decades of involvement in the bait and tackle business and he echoed his son. It's the emphasis on artificials, on catch-and-release, and also the switch from skinny, locally hand-picked worms to plump, commercially grown worms, raised fat in soybean fields. Different times, different methods.

CHUCK ROGERS REMEMBERS...
POPULAR LURES IN THE PAST

My mother, Ruth, loved the "Oneida Lake Pike Spoon." She trolled with it all the time. The spoon was actually a long (about three inches), willow leaf spinner, attached to a stiff wire shaft. The first ones were silver, but they painted 'em other colors later on. A double hook set-up joined the bottom of the spinner and you'd attach a worm to it. You'd troll or drift the spoon real slowly. This lure just killed the walleyes.

The "Little Wonder" was our biggest seller for years. It was a funny looking lure. It consisted of a large streamer fly on a hook, attached to a spinner. This was linked to a leader that had a sinker on it, about eighteen inches above the spinner-fly combo. At the sinker end of the leader was a loop that you could tie to your line. Fishermen hooked a crawler to the fly and trolled the Wonder. Catches were "wonder-full."

The "Buffalo Spinner," a two-toned silver/gold spinner, caught a lot of pike. Pflugger made this. The Gusto Company, out of Binghamton, made "Dixie Spinners" in many colors and these were very popular and effective, too. Fishermen added worms to hooks on both these spinners. They'd catch walleyes, bass, perch, silver bass–you name it, they'd catch it.

The first casting lure I ever used was a Heddon "Spook." It was what you now call a "stick bait" and it came in several colors. There's a funny story here. My father Jack was a confirmed troller and, when casting reels came out, he wouldn't use 'em. Didn't make sense to try casting if his own methods worked so well. I tried to convince him, but I didn't have much luck. Then, one time, the walleyes were in the Oneida River. Lots of 'em. At night you'd shine a light and you'd see nothin' but eyes. Nothin'. I persuaded Dad to join me at Smith's Pier, west of the Route 11 Bridge. I brought some Heddon Spooks and cast for pike. I used a Bronson steel rod and a Green Hornet reel. I even pushed a wheelbarrow to the pier to bring the fish home. I was that confident.

Well, on my first cast I got a hit. It felt like a big pike. My lure was a six-inch Heddon Spook. I caught two walleyes on that lure–one on the front hook, the other on the back! Dad and I landed our limit quickly [fifteen per person] and filled the wheelbarrow. Best of all, I made a believer out of him.

The Old Bait Shop

We netted our own buckeye minnows. Never bought 'em. There were lots of 'em back then. We'd net 'em in the shallows of the bays–Big Bay, Muskrat Bay. There'd be tons of 'em in the river from time to time. We sold bluenose chubs and golden shiners, too. You'd use the chubs for walleyes and the shiners for northerns. Used to be a lot more northerns than there are now.

We got our crabs from ponds. We'd drag a crap scoop along the bottom and net 'em. This was a big round net with a stiff handle. There used to be ponds along the abandoned railroad tracks. They were dug when the railroads were first put in, probably as emergency water sources. There were a few ponds along the old South Bay trolley tracks. We'd net these and get all the crabs we wanted.

At first we picked our own night crawlers. Back breaking work. Eventually we had to buy 'em. We got 'em from other pickers and from worm farms. Those farm-raised worms were fatter. Wiggled more.

I remember our first bait prices. Wow. One dollar for a scoop of buckeyes. There were many, many minnows in a scoop. If people complained we'd give 'em more. Always wanted happy customers. We sold crabs and "bass bugs" for twenty-five cents a dozen. [Note–"bass bugs" was Oneida Lake vernacular for dragonfly nymphs.] Worms were a penny apiece. About 1960 we went to two cents. Didn't want to do it, but had to.

It seemed like we hardly ever closed the shop. On weekends we'd be open from 5 A.M. till dark. Six A.M. until dark during the week. At first we lived upstairs. People rang the doorbell if they needed bait when we were closed. We always served 'em.

My mom Ruth counted worms. We used to kid her and say that she had a million worms in her life. Our wives and kids helped us run the business, too. Marv Ladd worked for us for years.

Brewerton back then was a real small town. You knew

everybody's first name. Now it's just another suburb. The old shop was in the center of Brewerton. It was a "hang out" for townspeople. In winter they'd sit and stand around our wood stove. The coffee was always brewing. Guys like Marv Ladd, Harry Wing, Bob Belknapp, Jack Bolton, Ken Miller, and Emerson "Red" Abbey–they'd be there. Old time fishermen. Lived on the lake. They'd come in, warm up, have a cup of coffee, and tell their stories. Big walleyes, big bass, bigger northerns. Pails of perch and sunfish. Bullhead catches that filled boats. Talk and laughter, talk and laughter, over and over. You could fill a big book with the stories that went around our Shop. My God, it was nice.

His First Boat

Elet Milton built boats in a workshop behind his house on Library Street. It was a big shop. Elet's father, Thomas Milton, started the business. Milton Boats used to be famous around the lake. They were made from cedar and had ribs that gave them strength. The boats had three seats and two sets of oarlocks, so two fishermen could row and get out a little faster. The rowers had to work together to have their timing down. Good rowers like Millard and me could make a Milton boat move.

I lucked out when I went to see Elet. I got the last boat that he had. It was sixteen feet long and about four feet wide. Milton tapered the bow to a point and squared off the transom so you could attach a motor. The boat cost me $90. This included two sets of oars and custom-built rod holders for holding trolling rods on the back of the boat. I bought the boat around 1940. Imagine, $90 for a high quality fishing boat today!

These Milton boats could take whatever the lake threw at 'em. If you'd maintain 'em, they'd last a long time. I used to draw the boat out in late fall. I'd get it under cover and turn it over. Had to dry it. Then I'd scrape it down, get all the loose stuff off. I'd caulk the seams and let them dry. Later, I'd repaint the boat and then varnish it. Both sides of the boat.

That boat was a great fishing machine. Wish I had a dollar for every fish that we hauled over its sides.

Trolling for Walleyes With Copper Line

This was a two man operation. One person sat in the back of our boat and tended the rods. The other rowed. The rods were sixteen-foot cane poles. The guides were fastened to 'em with tape, wrapped around the poles. The copper line was wrapped around the base of the pole. There was no reel. You'd stick a pole in a hole in each side of the back of the boat. These holes were our rod holders, so to speak.

You attached your lure to the end of the copper line. You let out as much line as needed to get the lure just off bottom. You could hold the line in your hand and feel the lure hit bottom. Then, you'd bring in some line and raise the lure. The deeper the water, the more copper line you'd let out.

You needed teamwork when a fish hit. The rod tender in the back of the boat set the hook and brought the fish in. He'd get the pike to the boat and swing it along the side, to the rower. The rower grabbed the copper line and pulled the pike into the boat, took it off the hook, rebaited the lure, and set the lure back into the water. My parents were experts at this. They taught Millard and me how to troll.

There was a lot of rowing in the days before we had a motor, but we had a way that made it easier. The canal was busy back then. Barges were constantly going through Brewerton. We'd row out into the river and ask the barge crew for a ride down the lake. Usually they'd agree. They'd throw us a rope, we'd tie it onto our boat's bow and away we'd go. We'd often go as far as the Pancake Shoals, off Constantia, and troll back.

The pike limit was twenty-five per boat and we caught it often. We sold our pike in town. The Washburn Hotel bought 'em, twenty-five to fifty cents each. They wanted cooking size pike, up to two pounds, not the big ones.

His Parents and Fish Piracy

My father Jack was a good fish pirate. He knew the lake like the back of his hand. A big reason for his success was my mother. They had a great marriage. They were a team. She made his nets. Used heavy cotton twine. If a net wasn't balanced to her liking, she'd sell it to another pirate.

These were trap nets. Four to six feet across. Fish would swim into 'em and couldn't get out. My dad would check 'em once or twice a week, always at night.

Dad had his favorite spots. Old man Downer lived on Muskrat Bay and he had a big oak tree on his property. Dad used to set a net in the bay and tie it to that tree. The spot was good for at least one hundred pounds of walleyes a week.

My father set nets in all of the bays. Toad Harbor and Big Bay were great places for bullheads. He'd keep everything except bass. There wasn't any market for 'em.

Ciscos used to be common in Oneida Lake. These were lake whitefish. They were only good to eat when the water was cold. My father set his nets around Wantry Island, just before freeze-up. Caught hundreds of pounds of ciscos. People would pay good money for 'em. Used to smoke 'em. The fish would run about fifteen to eighteen inches. Weighed about two pounds apiece.

I went out with my father all the time. I remember a night when we caught three huge catfish. God, all total they must have weighed over one hundred pounds. The lake got rough as we were coming home. It was rolling pretty heavy. Big, big waves. Those catfish must have gotten seasick or something because, all of a sudden, they vomited handfuls of this stuff they hadn't digested. Must have been fifteen pounds of it. Imagine–a seasick fish.

My father quit pirating before the war. My parents' market was taking more time and he was making good money there. Dad trained as a butcher. Pirating became tougher, too. More people were fishing the lake. With casting reels they covered more water. They hooked nets. More people and more boats equaled lost nets. Pirating just wasn't worth it.

Ice Fishing

The law said you could have fifteen tip-ups, but it didn't matter. Heck, you wouldn't see another person on the lake on most days. Might be a few in Ladd's Bay on occasion, but that was all. Millard and I used to set one hundred tip-ups apiece.

We baited the tip-ups with buckeyes or bluenose chubs. We wouldn't tend them during the day. We'd come out in early morning, take the "hangers" off the line, and rebait. Walleyes usually bite best at night. On a good morning we'd get anywhere from twenty-five to fifty pike. We sold 'em, of course. You could do that legally back then.

Loren Camic and I built one of the first snowmobiles on this lake. Well, it was kind of a snowmobile. It was more like a motorized sled–ten feet long, with tracks like tank tracks on it. Wasn't fast, but it was useful. Once we rescued a bunch of people on the ice off Constantia. They'd gotten tired and the weather was cold, windy–real tough. They were shivering and could hardly walk. They easily could have frozen to death. We took 'em into Spruce Grove Marina. Boy, were they happy to get there!

The Scandinavian Twirlers

When I was a kid in the 1930s I used to take a few city people fishing. I was their guide and they'd pay me. There were these two doctors from Syracuse who'd come every summer. They were in their sixties. One was Swedish, the other Finnish. They'd give me $5 to take 'em fishing. Big money back then.

They fished in a very unusual way. I called it "twirling." I rowed our big, flat-bottomed boat up and down the Oneida River. They put boards across the back and front ends of the boat. One doctor sat in each end. These guys didn't have rods and reels. They looped linen fishing line in perfect circles on the boards. They tied a homemade spoon to the end of the line. They made these lures from actual spoons! They'd twirl the spoon above their heads, kind of like a cowboy twirling his lariat. When they got the spoon up to speed they'd let it fly. Boy could they cast! Accurately, too. They could throw that spoon fifty feet and put it right on target.

I'd row 'em up and down the river. They'd cast to each dock. They'd catch northern pike after northern pike, many over ten pounds. They loved it! They'd hook a pike and pull it in, hand over hand. They'd get it into the boat, hold it up, and admire the fish. Then, I'd take it off and throw it back. They were "catch and release" guys. Conservationists, before it became popular. Never kept a northern.

We'd fish down to the "cut," where the canal branches off from the river. They always brought a gallon jug of wine with them. By the time we reached the cut they were in high spirits. Nothing bothered them. They were happy as larks. Their casting suffered, but they didn't care. They always had a chauffeur to take them home.

One time they wanted to keep some fish, so we rowed out to Three Mile Bay. Bass and perch were biting. They brought this old fish bag, which we tied to the boat and hung over the side. And, of course, they brought their wine. Well, the fish bit like crazy and we filled that bag. Lots of fish. When it was time to go, one of the doctors picked the bag up and the bottom fell out. All the fish swam away. Boy, did they laugh! Laugh and laugh! When we got back to the dock, one of them paid me and said, with a smile, "Here Chuckie, here's $5. We want to go out again next week."

They showed up a week later–with a strong, new fish bag.

A Favorite Spot

Dad had a place in Three Mile Bay that he always fished. Probably went there since 1920. He showed me the place and I've gone there ever since. Can't begin to count the fish I've caught there. It's my favorite spot on Oneida Lake.

The water's ten feet deep. You line up with the lighthouse on Frenchman's Island. Then you triangulate with–hey, wait a minute, why am I telling you about my spot?! Ha!

Well anyway, trust me, it's there. Last Sunday I took two friends to the Bay. I told them that, after we anchored, we'd have a smallmouth bass on within a minute. I was wrong. We lowered our minnows and almost immediately we had three bass on! Three, not one! Guess I have to be wrong sometimes.

This spot has never failed me, never disappointed. Millard and I even took Governor Nelson Rockefeller there. Caught the limit, of course. The Governor was mighty happy.

Postscript

Fred David still spends many a fine hour fishing with Chuck Rogers on Oneida. Whenever they go bass fishing, if Chuck drives the boat, they motor to Three Mile Bay and anchor in "the spot." Fred jokes that if you blindfold Chuck and put him behind the wheel of a motorboat on Oneida Lake, that boat will end up at Three Mile Bay.

One time, after a fishless hour at Three Mile, Fred told Chuck, "You know, there are other spots for smallmouths on Oneida Lake."

"I know, Fred," Chuck answered, "but the bass have been here before and I know they're going to be here. I just know it."

Just then Chuck's rod dipped. The veteran Oneida Laker set the hook and a big smallmouth bass cartwheeled atop the surface of Three Mile Bay.

– Chapter 30 –

A Fabulous Fifties Fanfare

The World War II era meant sacrifice for Oneida Lake's communities. Like the rest of the country, the lake region gave its young people, paychecks, scrap metals, clothing, tires, and foodstuffs in unwavering support for the country's war effort. The war years were quiet times around Oneida Lake. Gasoline rationing greatly reduced mobility and tourism waned. The post-war years, however, witnessed a dramatic turnaround. Americans were flushed with the cash of their war-era savings. They also had good jobs. The electronics and appliance industries thrived. Cold War military spending flowed from government coffers, the auto giants competed to sell stylish, colorful new cars, and the economy boomed. Upstate New Yorkers prospered and, drawn by the lake's attractions and proximity, they cruised to its shores by the thousands. Sylvan Beach, Oneida's premier resort, literally burst its seams as tourists, businesses, and the lake's bounty combined to produced a decade of fun-filled memories.

The Utica *Observer-Dispatch* echoed the Beach's fabulous fifties theme in an article published on June 6, 1951. The reporter captured the spirit that enveloped the village.

> It's a wide place in the road. It's a place where they sell more neon signs than washing machines, more cotton candy than chocolate bars. It's a place where there are more cars than parking places, more people than beds. It's a place where 800

> natives move over for 35,000 pleasure-bent city folk for nine of the busiest, noisiest, most wondrous weeks of the season.
>
> It's the Beach–Sylvan Beach to those who haven't enjoyed the fine, white sand, savored fresh-caught Oneida Lake pike, or deposited their last penny in one of the 150 clicking coin machines in Pennyland.
>
> Sylvan Beach is the playground of the workingman, the man who wants his vacation with a generous dose of gaiety, laughter, and good clean fun. He hasn't time for rocking chairs.
>
> It's the Coney Island without the salt, but with a beach that its old-timers say has Coney "beat a mile."

The Beach's fabulous fifties are best described by those who experienced the era. To compile this story, I interviewed four people whose lives were a part of the village fiber–Lilian Sawner, Ernest Money, John DePerno, and Edward McCarthy. Their recollections provide a fine picture of Sylvan Beach in the years when Americans liked Ike, contained communism, settled suburbia, and be-bopped their way through a unique decade.

Lillian Sawner

Lillian Esengard Sawner was a sharp, ebullient octogenarian when I talked with her in the summer of 2000. "Lil," the daughter of George and Catherine Albicker Esengard, was raised in the Beach and married Raymond A. Sawner, another Beach child. She also wed the fishing business because "Ray" and his father, "Raymond J.," operated Sawners' Boats and Bait, the Beach's largest livery. The marina was located at the end of 6th Avenue on what locals call "National Lake," an ancient oxbowed backset of Fish Creek. Lil worked with her husband and father-in-law, and also waitressed and cooked in many of the village's restaurants. She and Ray had two sons, George and Charles.

Listen, as Lil Sawner walks you through her village in the 1950s.

> I worked in restaurants in Sylvan Beach since I was eight years old. I used to help my grandmother, Anna Davis, who ran the Auburn Restaurant. That building was at the corner of 4th Avenue and Main. I worked in the Elk Restaurant, in Eddie's, the Forest Hotel, Ron-Nell's, the Owens Hotel, in Midway food stands, and in the bowling alley. After my husband had a stroke that left him totally disabled, my father-in-law and I ran the

boat and bait businesses. We did this until 1960, when Raymond J. passed away. Later on, I taught bowling in Rome. I had to support the family. I worked my whole life. There was no other way.

I'll never forget one 4th of July when I worked at Mamie's. This was a small Midway stand, located by the back of the Hotel Royal. My stepmother Mamie Esengard ran it. We served one ton of potatoes that day–2,000 pounds of French fries! The lines of customers were endless, from ten o'clock in the morning until late at night. A man named Sable peeled Mamie's potatoes and he finished off forty bags in a day. Each bag weighed fifty pounds! Can you imagine peeling a ton of potatoes?! Our deep fat fryers never stopped.

The Beach, in the 1950s, was a collection of many small, family businesses. We called these places "mom and pop" operations. Let me talk about them by taking you on a walking tour of the village around 1950. We'll start on Main Street, by the Pancake House, at the corner of 6th Avenue. It's a landmark that you can't miss, with its big white pillars. Moe LaBella didn't open that restaurant until the late '50s. The building housed the Victory Market in 1950, a chain store now called Great American. Prior to that, it used to be a post office. A man named Charles Bell built the place back in the early 1900s. Bell was one of the first village postmasters.

Let's walk from the Pancake House south, down Main Street toward the Barge Canal. We'll stay on that side of the street. The next building was Head's Store, a general grocery store at 5th Ave. owned by Ike and Minnie Head. Then came Koster's Meat Market, followed by "Rouge" Martin's barbershop. The Beachcomber variety store occupies the meat market building today. A small gas station followed and, next to that, was my Aunt Anna Davis's Auburn Restaurant. The Parkview Restaurant bordered the Auburn and Bill Coon ran a garage on the other side of the Parkview. Mickey Rizzo's Bar and Grill came next. This place was once called the Clark Hotel, and afterward it became known as The Casino. There was a roller skating rink behind it that the kids enjoyed. After Mickey's we had another gas station and, on the bank of the canal, was Paddy Dwyer's Tavern, where they played Irish songs on the jukebox. All the businesses from the barbershop to the canal were demolished when the state replaced our old bridge with the current one, around 1960.

Now, let's go from the Pancake House up Main Street, north on Route 13. There was a small camp at the corner of 6th and Main and after that came Victor Serby's Sylvan Beach Department Store. Vic's parents, Louis and Sarah Serby started this old-time variety store in the early 1900s. Another barbershop bordered Serby's, followed by Saint Mary's of the Lake, our Catholic Church. It was a beautiful building, kind of rustic. Ray and I got married there. Next was a nice gingerbread cottage in what is now Eddie's parking lot, followed by a small icehouse on the bank property. The Cook and Beneke Ice Company, run by Charlie Cook and Howard Beneke, cut ice on the lake every winter and maintained this small shop for the fishermen, who used to patronize it in early morning. The business was a relic from an era when ice harvesting was a major source of off-season employment. An older fire hall occupied the site of today's modern structure. Next we had Vanertfelda's Block, a large building with apartments–you've got the Beachy Clean Laundromat and Eddie Stewart's house there now. Hank Hoffman's Hotel followed. It was called the Owens Hotel before that and, originally, it was known as the Ontario Hotel. It was named for the Ontario and Western Railroad, the "O&W," whose trains used to rumble down the tracks that stretched along Main. Gene Aubeuf bought Hoffman's in 1957 and made it into the Beach Bowling Center.

You'd walk past two houses after Hoffman's and then you'd come to Akehurst Avenue. Across the street sat Russell's Hotel and Danceland–it was still going strong in the early '50s. I loved Russell's. I went there all the time when I was young. It was open every night, even on Sunday. Couples had to pay ten cents per dance, or three dances for a quarter. The "Big Bands" brought the crowds, but some of the lesser-known groups were great, too. Russell's used to hold dance contests. Couples paid their fees and everyone went out onto the dance floor. Then the music began! Judges circulated through the crowd, tapping the shoulders of unlucky dancers who had to leave the floor. Finally, the winning couple remained. I'll never forget the night that Bill Donlon and I won a trophy for doing the best jitterbug. We were so proud and happy. I felt extra special on that evening. Hundreds of dancers, and we were the best. There was another dance hall called Pardee, Sennett, and Quinn's, in back of the Forest Hotel, down by the bridge. It was a large, pavilion-type building, not as fancy as Russell's. They held dance contests, too. So did the Forest. Bill and I once won a waltz contest there.

The other side of Main Street didn't have as many businesses. Ron-Nell's Restaurant was located at 16th Avenue, right by the big parking lot. The McKenzies ran it–wonderful people, great employers. They had the best pike dinners in the Beach and their bar, shaped like a ship, was very popular. You had to walk down to Eddie's to find another restaurant on that side of the street. Our police station was also in the park, but it was situated more towards the Midway than the present barracks. The Honeydew Restaurant was in the park, across from 4th Avenue. And then, of course, you had the Midway.

There were two distinct Midway areas and they bordered each other. One ran alongside the canal and the other centered around Cottman's Carousel. The Elk Restaurant was located where the Crazy Clam is today. Sam and Evelyn Grieco took over the Elk during the '50s and renamed it the Fishnet Restaurant. This building was unique because it was open–you could walk through it. After passing through the Elk, going toward the lake, you entered the canal-side Midway. The first things you encountered were concessionaires' stands like Ed and Norma McCarthy's Cork Guns games. After passing these you entered the Midway proper, with its rides, cotton candy, hurdy-gurdy music, and carnival atmosphere. Emory and Ruth Sauve owned the area and ran most of the rides until 1953, when they leased them to Francis and Iva Money. Niles' Midway lunch was situated in the middle of this entertainment area. El and Zilpha Niles ran this famous stand for years and served hot dogs, hamburgs, hot sausages, and fries to long lines of people.

If you turned right, or north, after exiting the Elk Restaurant, you came to the Royal Hotel. Part of the building was used as a bingo parlor, but the main section was still called The Royal. It was known for its huge, long bar. Joe Sullivan, who ran the place in the early 1950s, used to have a pulpit that he bought from a church, at the end of the bar. He'd sit in the pulpit and watch over his bar, visiting with the customers all the while.

Cottman's Carousel was a focal point of the other Midway area. Bill Cottman started this in 1896. All of his horses were hand carved masterpieces. The Carousel building is still there and the Carello family owns it. Their horses are replacements for the originals. It still has its unequaled, old-time amusement park charm, though. Across Park Avenue from the Carousel were businesses owned by the Donlon family–Laffland, Fascination, Playland, and the old Arcade Building, in which they had a bingo hall. They had high-class bingo at Donlon's. It cost ten cents to play, but they had much better prizes than their competition. Now, if you walked toward the canal from Donlons, Bubble's Lunch and the Lake Shore Hotel were on the same side of the street. The Thomas family operated Bubbles and used to advertise their famous hamburg–hot dog sauce. The diner was named for "Bubbles" Love, whose sister married Archie Thomas. DiCastro's nightclub was located just up, or north, from the Donlons' businesses. The DiCastros had some big name entertainment there, groups like the Jimmy Cavallo Band. The club was what we called a "jacket and tie" place. Guys had to wear these to be admitted. Pfohl's Beach House occupies the building now.

If you walked up Park Avenue from DiCastro's, you'd first come to The Shack, owned by John and Betty Aubeuf. They also rented beachfront cottages. You'd find more rentals along Park Ave. if you walked uptown. Oudin's Court was one of them. A movie company shot scenes for the "Sterile Cuckoo" at Oudin's, and at Union Chapel.

There were several businesses on the Main Street side of the Carousel. The Forest Hotel, Treasureland, the Fun House, and a big arcade in which you had gift shops that sold souvenirs were among these. The DePerno brothers bought the Forest from Bill McCarthy in the '50s and they also ran a Carmelcorn Stand nearby. Their sister, Betty, and her husband Lou Dontino operated The Dog House, a hot dog stand next to the Forest. There was also a photo shop and a popular ice cream parlor along the road that leads from Main Street to the canal. Bill McCarthy owned the Fun House. I'll never forget the first time I walked over the bridge in that place. Bill had a fan underneath the bridge and it blew my dress all over, creating a sort of "Marilyn Monroe effect." The girls used to laugh and scream and the boys loved it, of course.

The Beach in the 1950s was an incredibly busy place. But it was a small town, too. You knew everybody that lived here. There was a tight sense of community. You knew a lot of the summer folk, too, because they came here year after year. People made money during the '50s, but they had fun, too. Lots of fun. Family fun. When I think back to this time...a great time...all I can say is that it was wonderful to be a part of a place like Sylvan Beach.

ERNEST MONEY

Ernest "Ernie" Money is a son of Francis and Iva Money, an enterprising couple who bought Emory Sauve's carnival rides in 1953 and leased the Sylvan Beach Midway until 1965. Ernie was more than a son, however. He and his brother, Dean, were partners with their parents. The Money family worked side-by-side, summer after summer, to make the Midway a superbly crafted, smoothly functioning unit.

After his family sold their rides, Ernie worked as a journeyman carpenter for ten years and then moved to Jupiter, Florida, where he became a scuba diver, specializing in fishing for grouper, snapper, and lobster. He and his wife, the former Phyllis Grieco, have two sons–Koby and Gy. The Moneys winter in Jupiter and summer at the Beach, where I interviewed them in 2001. Our discussion centered on Ernie's memories of the Midway during the 1950s.

> My father started as a storekeeper. He and my mother ran a grocery store, kitty-corner from the Verona Beach post office. My mother was postmaster. They lived on Jug Point Road but, in 1944, they sold the store and their home and bought a house on 2nd Avenue in the Beach. My father was away a lot during the war because he worked for Grumman Aircraft, in Connecticut. He designed an aluminum seat that made planes lighter and faster.
>
> Dad got into the Midway in 1945. He operated rides that summer for Art Martzloff, in the carnival's "kiddy area." The following winter, my parents went to Florida and dad bought a miniature train ride. He tried to repair it but, after a lot of effort, he decided that the ride was beyond fixing. So he built his own version of that train. Built it from scratch. He didn't buy any materials. Even the train's tracks. He got those from an abandoned coal mine in Pennsylvania.
>
> My father was a natural mechanic and had expertise that you'd expect from a college-educated engineer, not a farm boy from rural Oneida County. He was a self-taught technician. After he built the train, he made other rides in '46, '47, and '48. All kiddy rides. Little boats, little airplanes, little fire trucks. Over the years dad built three boat rides and two trains. My

parents gave the trains names like the "Kookamonga and Dogpatch Special." Cars were called "L'il Abner," "Daisy Mae," "Moonbeam McSwine," names like that. There were seven boats in the boat ride and each had one of the seven dwarfs' names on it. The fire trucks were a part of the "Sylvan Beach F.D." and they all had bells, steering wheels, and ladders. Everything in the kiddy ride area was built from scratch. Even the lights. My father got these from an old chicken farm. Mom worked right beside dad. My parents had a pole barn workshop across the street from their home on 2nd Avenue and they created these rides in that building.

You wouldn't believe how children loved those rides. Kids lined up to get on them all through the summer. Parents felt at ease when their children enjoyed my dad's rides. My father's reputation as a ride maker spread. Norman Rockwell, the artist, heard about it and bought a custom-built Money train ride.

At first, my parents rented space from Emory Sauve but, in 1953, Emory offered them the opportunity to buy all the rides in the Midway area. They accepted and "Money's Midway" officially began. It was a big operation. My brother Dean, and I, worked right with mom and dad. Dean's wife, Carolyn, was a part of the business, too. She helped mom take tickets. She also painted and repainted the rides, and she pitched in wherever needed. There's a nice sidelight here. Carolyn's maiden name was Grieco–she's my wife's sister. Two brothers married two sisters. And each couple had two sons. Ours are Gy and Koby, theirs Mark and Wayne.

We employed over twenty people every summer, mainly high school and college students. There was a lot of responsibility in our operation. Every ride had to be inspected regularly. Cables broke. Joints and fixtures had to be lubricated. Spark plugs failed. Touch-up painting was a continual chore. Clutches on the cars had to be rebuilt. Wiring had to be checked. That was Dean's specialty. Mom and dad were masters with sewing machines and they did all of our reupholstering. And we had to keep things clean. Spotlessly clean. The rides, the grounds, everything. My parents insisted on it. Interestingly, the rides that required the least amount of maintenance were the ones that my father built.

We had some exciting rides in that Midway. Exciting, of course, for the 1950s. There was the "Scooter," where people slammed their bumper cars into each other and the

"Caterpillar," where customers whirled about in a chain of cars that looked like a big, green caterpillar. The caterpillar was like a miniature roller coaster. You dipped fast and came right back up–you felt heavy at the bottom and light on top. It got the best of a lot of stomachs. We had the "Hammer," where people got into a plane and swung back and forth, like they were on a pendulum. We'd stop it at the top, just for thrills. People would scream as they fell back to the bottom. Then there were the "Octopus," with eight cars on heavy beams that extended outward from the center and the "Silver Streak," where people also rode in cars. Both rides twirled in circles at high speeds. Our most expensive ride was the "Hot Rods," a racecar simulation. Each car had a five horsepower motor and mag tires, like the old Indy-Daytona speedsters. We also had a merry-go-round and a small Ferris wheel. And, of course, my father's kiddy-ride area.

My mother took charge of selling tickets and keeping the Midway's account books. We sold nickel tickets and you could buy twenty-five for a buck. The number of tickets needed for each ride varied. For example, the Hot Rods cost seven tickets, the Scooter five tickets, and the kiddy rides three. We started the practice of having "bargain days" on Wednesdays. Our rides' ticket costs went down from five tickets to three or whatever. They still use this practice today. We set a couple other precedents, too. Our Midway was the first in Upstate New York to receive full state inspection. Dean and I explained each ride's details to the inspectors. We highlighted all the critical, sensitive parts...places that had to be checked thoroughly. I'll never forget how one inspector was bothered by how much the Ferris wheel's cars rocked. Dean offered to weld it in place, if the inspector would take the first ride. The man thought for a second and then declined. He realized that the car would be upside down when it reached the top of the wheel! We also had several concessions' booths in the Midway...things like "dunk the ducks," "break the plates," and "tip the milk bottles." We were one of the first concessionaires to give Sylvan Beach t-shirts as prizes.

We spent our winters in Florida and came back to the Beach in March. There was always prep work. We kept the wooden kiddy rides and the cars from the other rides in a storage building that fronted the canal. It had a big, smiling clown face and the words, "Take Time For Fun–Sylvan Beach Midway" painted on the canal side. We stored the rides' heavy metal pieces in the Scooter building. We usually started to put things together around April 15, weather permitting, and we opened on Memorial Day weekend. We stayed open through Labor Day. And we were busy! Hundreds, thousands of people! Big lines at every ride. Weekends and bargain days saw non-stop action and the 4th of July was a wild time!

Dad, Dean, and I sold the rides in 1965. My parents were in their mid-sixties and they felt that it was time to retire.

I enjoy great memories of that Midway. When I'm asked what I recall about the Beach, a half century ago, I think of things like the friendships that developed between our employees and us. We spent a lot of time with them...water-skiing the lake in the early morning, having a couple nickel "Sylvan Beach head" beers before work. One summer I even got the guys pumping iron. They came to my house every day to lift weights. Mom bought the boys tricolored muscle shirts. We had the fittest, toughest-looking workers that any carnival ever dreamed of employing. We shared big, family-style barbecue parties with them. It paid off, because they were a loyal, hard-working crew.

Talk about laughs. I remember wearing a clown suit, getting on stilts, and parading through the Midway on kiddies' bargain day. Fun times, but it was awfully tough for a nine foot six inch clown to dismount! Pretty hard landings. The best memories I have of the '50s Midway, though, involve working with my family. The six of us...mom, dad, Dean and Carolyn, Phyllis and I, worked together as an inseparable, efficient team. We were six united, self-directed people who invested twelve years of their lives in a business whose main purpose was making people happy.

I wouldn't trade those years for anything.

John DePerno

John DePerno has spent most of his life within Sylvan Beach commerce. DePerno, a Utica native, took his first dip into the Beach economy after World War II when he, with his brothers Carmen and Joseph, opened several concessions in the Midway. The DePernos expanded their interests during the '50s by purchasing a carmelcorn booth, a hot dog stand known as "The Dog House," an amusement hall called "The Fun House," and The Forest Hotel, a restaurant–tavern (John and his brother, Larry, owned this endeavor). John purchased the Rex Inn, at the corner of

15th Avenue and Main Street, in 1973 and transformed it into a steak house called "Captain John's Steer and Beer." Later, he changed his menu's theme, redecorated in a nautical motif, and renamed the business "Captain John's Prime Rib, Pasta, and Seafood House." Today "The Captain," as he is affectionately known, guides diners through a unique, popular Sylvan Beach culinary voyage, assisted by his wife, the former Mitzie Leonard, and their four daughters–Elaine, Mary Anne, Dorothea, and Joni.

John and I discussed the life of a concessionaire in the Midway of the '50s, and other salient elements of the Beach milieu of a half-century past.

> You simply cannot imagine the business that the Beach did in the 1950s. You cannot imagine it. Cars were always jammed into Main Street on weekends and holidays, hundreds of cars. Every style, every color. Main Street was a mile long "American Graffiti" cruise. The people packed the Midway like the State Fair. The bingo halls brought in hundreds of players every week. Restaurants had lines of customers just waiting to get in. There were dozens of picnic tables in the park and every one was taken. Families–big families–this was the "baby boom" time, remember? They came to the Beach. They had fun here because we had something for every member of the family to enjoy.
>
> I was a partner with my brothers Joe and Carmen in the Midway. The first things we got involved with were the concessions' stands. You had to work hard to make these succeed, long hours and lots of talking, barking your game's appeal.
>
> I ran several games through the '50s. I had one called "Dunk the Dolly," where the slide is today, by Laffland. I hired this good-looking girl and got her all costumed up...flashy hat, shiny dress, fancy shoes, the works. She sat on a stool, in a protective cage. Customers paid fifty cents and got three balls. They threw the balls at a metal plate and, if they hit it, the chair's support gave way and the girl got dunked in a tub of water. Bright lights flashed, sirens blared when they hit the plate! People got a big kick out of this. They also liked my "kewpee doll" prizes. Those dolls are antiques today.
>
> The "Flasher" was another popular game. I had this one in a booth by the old Lake Shore Hotel. Older people liked the game. They could sit down and play it. Cost ten cents. Ten cents! Everyone had a button that, when you pressed it, stopped

the flashing lights. The lights moved continuously–red lights, blue lights, orange, yellow, white lights. People were almost mesmerized by them. The object of the game was to stop the flashing when the red light was on and then you won a nice prize. You'd win something for stopping it on blue, but the prize wasn't as good.

Then there was the "Cat Game." I had forty metal cats, all lined with fur, on a moving rack. Three rows of moving cats. You'd get three balls for fifteen cents, six for a quarter. Knock over three cats and win the prize.

There were more games. The old "milk bottle knockdown" game. This was across from the Fun House, by Treasureland. Three balls for a dime. Knock the bottles down and you'd win a kewpie doll, teddy bear, ashtray, and lots of other prizes. You had to have a lot of prizes. You had to give the customers lots of chances to win. We also had an archery game...three arrows for a quarter...three chances to make a bulls eye. Our cork shooting gallery was popular, too.

Other concessionaires worked the Midway. The Moneys had some booths and the McCarthys had stands by the Elk Restaurant. Emory and Ruth Sauve had a shooting gallery where the targets popped and ducked as they moved across the line. It was popular, and challenging. Jack Paidy, from Rome, ran his "Horse Racing" game in back of the Royal Hotel. We used to call him "Paidy Gatey," for letting his horses "out of the gate." He had an interesting game. Patrons sat along a counter and each had a wheel in front of them. By turning a small wheel, they controlled one horse in a race. The quicker they turned the wheel, the faster the horse would run but, if they rotated their wheel too fast, their horse would balk, stumble, or fall over. Jack's horses were numbered. When he started the game, the #2 and #9 horse would win lot, but then he'd adjust the machine and other horses came in first. He kept the patrons guessing. People liked the challenge of playing this game, and they also liked Jack's prizes. He awarded boxes of chocolates. Nice, nice prizes.

You can't talk about the '50s Midway without mentioning "Big Hearted Leonard," another concessionaire from Rome. His name was Leonard Doria–what a guy! My brother Larry used to needle him by saying, "Big hearted Leonard–with a heart as big as a pea!" Everybody knew Leonard. You could say that he was a "Midway institution." He had a "Flasher" game, somewhat like ours, in a stand right across from Paidy's, behind the Royal. The big difference between the games was that Leonard, not the customers, controlled the buttons. People just put their money down and watched the machine flash.

Eddie Stewart told me a couple good stories about Leonard. Concessions' prize companies used to exhibit their merchandise at the Royal before the season began. One year a company had these unique birdcage prizes and Leonard bought a bunch of them. First week into the season–Memorial Day Weekend–a customer won three cages in three consecutive games! The customer walked off with the cages and told Leonard, "Can't wait to come back and play this game again." Leonard panicked. He called the company and asked them to take the cages and give him cheaper prizes!

Here's another story. Leonard used to sleep in a small room in back of his concession stand. One night, a couple of the state troopers decided to play a joke on him. They wadded up a bunch of newspapers and set them on fire by the Leonard's window. Then they yelled, "Fire! Fire!" at the top of their lungs! Leonard burst out the front of the stand, panic-stricken, wearing only his long underwear. He looked at the troopers and asked, "Where's the fire? Quick–call the fire department!" The story gave Beach folks a good chuckle.

Bingo parlors were big draw that brought huge, regular crowds to the Beach in the 1950s. The village had five bingo halls. The Donlons operated one in the old Arcade Building, near Fascination. George Esengard owned a bingo parlor in a building that adjoined the Royal. The third parlor was located across from Ron-Nell's Restaurant, by 17th Avenue. The fourth was housed in the big cinder-block building at the corner of Akehurst and Main. Then there was A.J. Johnson's Bingo, across the street from today's Cinderella's Cafe. These halls were packed almost every night. From 5P.M. on, the ladies flocked to the Beach to play bingo. Their husbands went fishing, took the kids to the Midway, or visited the hotels. After bingo, whole families went out to dinner or grabbed a snack at the hot dog stands. When New York State outlawed commercial bingo, it hurt the Beach badly.

But the '50s are years of great memories. I'll never forget Jimmy Powell and his ice cream stand. He was the first to dip cones in melted chocolate and, man, was he popular! I remember when Larry and I bought the Forest. I crawled down to see what was in the cellar and, good God, I found hundreds of dusty whiskey bottles! Old bottles–most dated back to the 1920s. So much for prohibition! We managed the Forest like the DiCastros ran their club, jackets and ties required for the men. That didn't last long, but it was nice, a little formality in the Beach. Speaking of hotels, I remember how Pete Maurtano, who ran the Lake Shore, showed movies every night from Sunday through Thursday. "A cocktail and a film"–the combination worked. Pete hired Tony Zito to entertain on Friday and Saturday evenings. Tony was kind of a throwback to the "big band" era. He played the harp, sang the old tunes, walked around the hotel while serenading the customers. They loved him. He'd probably be successful today.

We had some colorful people in the Beach during the '50s. Let me tell you about Charlie Findout. Now there was a character. Probably landed here off a canal boat. Nobody knew. We all loved him. He lived down on 2nd or 3rd. He was a nice guy, but he liked the bottle. Worked in the bars every morning, cleaned the floors, the stools, polished the woodwork. Bar owners used to feed him and give him free beers. In any case, one time Charlie got arrested for public intoxication. He appeared before the judge and the conversation went something like this:

Judge:	Please state your name.
Charlie:	My name's Charlie.
Judge:	Your last name, too, if you will.
Charlie:	Findout.
Judge:	Excuse me, your last name.
Charlie:	Findout.
Judge:	I'm asking you. It is not up to me to find out your name. Now, what is your last name?
Charlie:	Findout.

The judge blew a gasket! He gave Charlie the stiffest possible sentence and added a "contempt of court" on top of it. Well, some Beach folks got together and hired a lawyer for Charlie and, by jeepers, the judge had to take back his sentence!

Sylvan Beach in the '50s. Life at its best. Oh, yeah...yeah...

Edward McCarthy

You might call Edward McCarthy the "Grover Cleveland of

Sylvan Beach politics" because he, like the former president, served two non-consecutive terms as the village's mayor. Eddie comes from a family with a rich Beach history. His great-grandfather, William T. McCarthy, migrated to the village from Buffalo around 1900 and played a significant role in building the Midway. His grandfather, William "Bill" McCarthy, owned the Elk Restaurant, the Forest Hotel, several Midway businesses, and was chairman of the village's park board. His parents, Ed and Norma McCarthy, were Midway concessionaires, commercial anglers, and worked in the Beach's restaurants. Eddie, who has lived in Sylvan Beach for his entire life, is a retired hospital administrator. He and his wife, the former Carol Heintz, have six children–Kathleen, David, Richard, Robin, Edward, and Kevin.

Eddie was a teen during the 1950s and our interview began on the topic of growing up in the Beach during that decade.

> I was a "Sylvan Beach kid," a part of what you might call the extended Beach family. People from this village looked out for their children and gave them special treatment. Restaurants fed you, refreshments were cheaper, if not free, because you were a member of this big family. One time Carol was on her lunch break from Johnson's Bingo Hall. She walked down to Eddie's and sat at the counter. Eddie Stewart noticed her and said to his waitress, "Serve her first. She's got to get back to work." This kind of incident was repeated hundreds of times during the 1950s.
>
> In summer we worked. All Beach kids worked. Tourism created scores of jobs for teenagers–Midway jobs, restaurant work, Bingo, village clean up–it was impossible to be unemployed. Of course we played, too. Couples went on dates to the Forest, Lake Shore, DiCastro's. Beach kids munched at The Shack and Eddie's. The Midway was filled with inexpensive diversions. Bring your nickels and have a great time! We went swimming at the railroad bridge that crossed the canal at Fish Creek's mouth. The water was always clear and cool. We tied a rope to the bridge and used it to swing far out into the water. We played sandlot baseball and football in fields that used to be a part of the Adam Miller farm, along Vienna Road near Harbor View Drive. And we fished. The fishing was "huge." Every Beach kid knew how to catch pike. Fishing was important in our lifestyle and even more vital to the local economy. Cars jammed the lake and canal fronts on opening weekend of wall-

eye season. Fishermen's vehicles were parked all the way from the canal to beyond Eddie's. You couldn't rent a boat because every one had been reserved well ahead of time. Thousands of anglers crowded the village. The entire east shore exploded with a kind of "walleye fever" that you don't see today.

My parents raised my sister Patti and me in a small house on 10th Avenue. They ran concessions in the Midway during the summer. Their stands bordered the canal, just west of the Elk. They had a "penny pitch" game–land the penny on the prize and win it. They drew circles by cigarette packs. If your penny stopped in the circle, you won the pack. They also had a "cork gun shooting gallery" and a Daisy air rifle game. In their games, no matter what happened, you'd win something. It only cost pennies and nickels to play the McCarthy games. Imagine what their income totaled at the end of the day.

Ice fishing was my parents' real passion. They loved the hours spent together on the ice and they sold the walleyes they caught to support our family. My parents' reputation for always having fresh pike was known as far away as Syracuse and Utica. Many, many people went out of their way to buy "McCarthy pike," especially as Friday approached. Patti and I hated to see that day come because we knew that mom and dad's fish supply would be gone and we'd have to eat "Oneida Lake caviar" for dinner. Mom saved walleye and perch eggs when dad gutted the fish. She dipped them in pancake batter and fried them in lard. They didn't taste too bad, if you were hungry.

The building that houses the Beach Bowl today was Hoffman's Hotel during the 1950s. Hank Hoffman, from Utica, ran the place. He and my parents were friends and he helped them market their walleyes. Hank spread the word that mom and dad had fresh pike. Hoffman's was a busy place and Hank talked to lots of people during an average week. They'd phone in or leave their fish orders at the Hotel. My parents stopped after fishing to check these requests. They never sold to restaurants, only to individuals. They charged 50 cents per pound for pike. The fish were scaled, gutted, totally cleaned. Mom did the cleaning and she was very fussy. Her walleyes were perfectly prepared.

My parents fished every day. *Every day*. Sometimes they'd go out two, three times a day. If the wind blew twenty miles per hour, they'd fish. If the temperature was ten below zero, they'd fish. They'd even go out in blizzards. Whiteout conditions disoriented them and several times they started for the Beach, only to end up in North Bay. My father believed the old saying, "One inch of ice will hold a horse. Therefore, it's safe for fishermen." First good freeze, out they'd go. Sometimes the ice would separate from shore and they'd have to detour a long way to get in. My parents endured great discomfort, but you have to remember that fishing provided our family's sustenance in winter. Fishing was the paycheck.

You wouldn't believe the number of walleyes they caught. They knew the time-tested spots, knew when to move, and knew how. You could say that my parents had a feel for the lake, a sixth sense for where to be. A person was allowed to fish fifteen tip-ups in the '50s, which gave my parents thirty legal sets. If the fishing slowed in a particular spot, dad would move five tip-ups to another area and maybe another five to a different place. When he found the walleyes, they'd move the entire thirty tip-ups to the new location. He always wore a heavy Woolrich coat, with huge side pockets that could hold a good number of fish. Sometimes when he came home after fishing, he looked like he put on fifty pounds!

Dad taught me how to fish for pike on the pier. That had to be one of the neatest methods of fishing there ever was. We used the old bamboo poles, strung with linen line wrapped around two knobs on the poles' butt ends. We "walked buckeye minnows" that were hooked through both lips, along the pier's lake edge and, when a walleye struck, we set the hook and lifted the pole. Pike flew through the air! Sometimes scores of fishermen lined the pier and the sheer number of flying pike made you think of tuna fishermen on the ocean. A man named "Doc" Nichols made pier poles in a small shop on Main Street. Doc was also a barber and a chiropractor. An interesting businessman. You could have your hair cut, your back adjusted, and get equipped for pier fishing all in one shop.

New York State banned the sale of walleyed pike around 1960 and that ended my parents' winter trade. My father got a job working on dredges in the Barge Canal. He retired from that position. My mother cooked for several restaurants in the Beach. They made a comfortable living, but it wasn't the same. They missed commercial fishing.

The Beach boasted excellent bait shops during the 1950s. Carl Yahnke operated a boat livery–bait shop on Vienna Road. Bill Krahl had a busy shop in back of the Pancake House. Mose Poppleton ran one of the most colorful bait shops I've ever seen on 12th Ave. The place was right out of a movie–tackle hung everywhere, snapping turtle shells were nailed to the walls, and aromas of fish, bait, and lake water blended into a smell that said, "This is a real fishermen's place." Matthau and Lemmon would have loved Mose's. Then there was Sawner's, at the end of 7th Avenue. This was my second home.

I started working in Ray and Lil Sawner's boat livery when I was eleven years old. I learned so much from those good people. They taught me that if you work hard you'll move up the ladder. It's a lesson that most Beach kids learned. You've got to apply yourself if you're going to make it. The old American work ethic. Sylvan Beach still teaches that lesson. Every day.

The Sawners depended on me to be there–very early in the morning. They taught me to honor my commitments, to be a man of my word. For a kid who loved the outdoors, Sawner's Boat livery was a truly cool place. I took the early morning shift whenever I could. I liked those hours. Just prior to sunrise, the customers started arriving. Non-stop action on weekends and few rest periods during the week. The street would be packed with cars. It was fun to mingle with the fishermen, talk a little walleye, listen to their stories. You could fill books with the tales that passed over Sawners' counter. Depending on the season, we sold all varieties of bait. Worms, buckeye minnows, bass bugs [dragonfly larvae], crabs [crayfish], and butter crabs [soft-shelled crayfish, in a molting stage]. Bass fishermen swore by the bugs and butters. Walleye anglers took the worms and buckeyes. We also sold the usual assortment of Oneida Lake tackle. You could buy June Bug and Dixie Spinners, and all kinds of hooks, sinkers, and line at Sawner's. The Beach boasted hot fishing in the 1950s and Sawner's could equip a person with whatever they needed to capitalize on it.

I did every boat livery task you could imagine. Bailed and cleaned boats. Stored equipment. Untangled anchor ropes. Rented boats. Sold bait. Counted bait. Cleaned fish. I even helped the Sawners pick night crawlers. I'd receive a dollar for every coffee can of worms I picked. It doesn't sound like much but, for a young Beach kid, it was riches.

The riches of Sawners' Boat Livery went beyond money, however. My parents taught me how to ice fish. My father schooled me in the basics of cane-pole pier angling. The Sawners broadened my knowledge of fishing as a lifestyle, as well as a pastime. I learned how, where, when to get bait, how to keep it fresh, and how to use it in the most effective way. I learned that, when you understand how and when fish feed, and how to present your bait or lure, your fishing rod becomes an extension of yourself. Ray Sawner's father taught me that. They used to call him "Raymond J." He was an unbelievable sportsman, the kind of guy that always caught his limit, always decoyed the ducks, and always tagged his buck. He helped Lil run the livery after Ray had his stroke. We spent hours together...talking, working, fishing, hunting, being outdoors around Oneida Lake. Here I was–eleven, twelve years old–and one of my best friends was in his seventies! It was great. Really great. Raymond J. taught me how to live off the land. He was a gifted fish and game cook. We ate turtle soup, fried muskrat, raccoon stew, as well as the usual venison steaks and fried fish. You just don't meet this kind of person anymore.

Another friend of mine and an unsung heroine of Sylvan Beach's history was Fifi Stewart, Eddie's wife. She was one of the kindest, most generous people I've ever known. Few knew what she did for this community because she preferred anonymity. The women that worked at Eddie's kept Fifi informed about everything that happened. If she heard that someone had lost money through tragedy, she'd make sure that they got some back. Whenever a family lost their belongings in a fire, Fifi sent them clothing, furniture, cash. She'd hire people who needed jobs, even people who had quit on her in the past. She and Eddie opened their restaurant for the annual spaghetti dinner that benefited Saint Mary's and Saint John's Churches and she donated everything. Communities need people like Fifi. The warmth and love that she gave to this village simply cannot be understated.

What was the Beach in the 1950s? It was weekends, beautiful weather days, girls galore, bumper to bumper cars, scores of "mom and pop" businesses, and fishing beyond compare. It was Midway games, screaming rides, women shouting "bingo!," water skiers and pleasure boaters, fishermen who didn't need fish finders, dancing couples, happy children, picnicking families, relaxing cottagers, and an ice-cream cone at midnight after a long day's work. It was friends and neighbors who taught you life's lessons, who cared about you, people in whom you trusted and who influenced you to become someone worth knowing.

It was, quite simply, a fantastic place to be.

– Chapter 31 –

The Flutter Spoon King

Anglers know there are lures that catch fish and lures that catch fishermen. Fish-enticing creations with names like June Bug Spinners, Mirro-Lures, Hot-N-Tots, Flex-Eels, and Erie-Dearies have all inspired walleyes, perch, and smallmouth bass to strike with reckless abandon. I have caught scores of game fish on bucktail jigs, on various Rapalas, on Heddon sonars and, of course, have often turned to the old reliable–natural bait–to fill my stringer. During my years with Oneida Lake, however, there has been one constant offering, one amazing lure that, when all else fails, never ceases to awe me with its productivity–the Anthony "Tony" Verno "flutter spoon."

Tony Verno was born on Mill Street in Canastota in 1921, the son of Natale and Philomena Verno. He enlisted in the armed forces after high school and served in Europe during World War II. After his discharge, Tony was hired as a pneumatic drop hammer operator at Oneida Limited. He held that position for nine years before being promoted to master mechanic, a task that entailed troubleshooting the factory's machines. He worked at that job for thirty years, until retirement. Tony married the former Majorie Rouck and was blessed with forty-nine years of marriage. The couple lived in Tony's parents' home on Mill Street and raised five children.

Inspired by a dare, Tony started crafting his famous flutter spoons in 1961. He only fished with live bait until a friend challenged him, saying, "You're quite a fisherman, but I'll bet that you can't make any tackle." Endowed with an Oneida silversmith's expertise, Tony began by sketching rough drawings of fishing spoons. His plans multiplied, but remained on paper until one finally satisfied him. He traced the pattern on light gauge copper, then cut it out and buffed it. Facetiously, he dubbed his creation the "crazy lure." Little did Tony Verno realize that the effectiveness of this lure, and its spinoffs, would cast all laughter aside.

After successfully testing the crazy lure on Adirondack lake trout and whitefish, Tony expanded operations. He made his own metal punches and leather-pounding blocks, on which he rippled a "corn cob" (resembling fish scales) texture into his spoons. He kept the crazy lure's plain finish on other spoons. Both spoons produced and Tony's lures began to acquire a local following.

Over the years Tony designed more than sixty flutter spoons. He custom crafted spoons, even inscribing anglers' names on the lures. His six basic metallic finishes were brass, copper, gold, chrome, nickel, and silver and he experimented with variations and combinations of them all. The longer spoons worked well on Oneida Lake's walleyed pike, while the smaller ones took walleyes and yellow perch. He fashioned flutter spoons designed to catch northern pike, lake trout, and salmon and exported them as far away as Texas, North Carolina, and even the United Kingdom.

Most Verno flutter spoons are fished using an old-fashioned method that is becoming rare as years pass. The technique involves lead-core line, a color-coded, braided or plastic-covered line with lead in its center. This line is used for trolling (fishing while the boat is slowly motor-powered). Every thirty feet of lead core line is colored differently. This makes it easy for anglers to know how much line they're trolling. For example, you might hear a lead-liner talk of catching walleyes while trolling five colors of line on the north side of Buoy 113. Around twenty-five feet of monofilament line is attached to the end of the lead line. Fishermen tie snap swivels to the monofilament and the flutter spoons are secured in these. A heavy, salt-water type reel holds the line and is usually attached to a fairly rugged fishing rod.

Unlike standard fishing lines, lead-core sinks. This enables anglers to present their lures to fish that live in moderately deep water (up to seventy-five feet). The slower a fisherman trolls, the deeper the line dives. At the trolling speed I use, for example, each color of lead line takes my offerings approximately six feet down. Thus, in thirty feet of water I'll use around four colors of line, in forty feet about five and one-half colors, etc. I'd use less line if I trolled slower. It is important to keep the lure within ten feet of the bottom–the depth in Oneida Lake where walleyes and perch thrive.

Flutter spoon lead lining is more than fishing. It's exercise. To impart proper action to the lure, the lead line must be swung back and forth. On the back swing, the resulting slack lets the spoon flutter from side to side inspiring, ideally, a fish's strike. Most lead liners perform this technique by placing the rod slightly ahead of them in the boat, pulling in about five feet of line, grasping the line around two or three fingers, and then swinging their arms like pendulums. Sitting along either side of the boat makes this motion easier because the angler's arm can be swung freely over the vessel's gunwale. A hooked fish is sensed on the upward arm swing, if the line becomes noticeably heavier. When this occurs the angler stops the pendulum motion and plays the slack line out until the rod can be grasped and reeling begun. Fishermen always keep pressure on the line as they release the slack so that the hooks remains implanted in the fish's mouth.

Sitting in the stern of their boats, arms swinging away, lead-liners work Oneida's depths from opening day of walleye season until winter's first freeze. They harvest considerable quantities of fish. Tony Verno became a dedicated lead-liner after inventing the crazy lure. This was the only angling method that he used for over three decades. After the Verno children matured, Marjorie accompanied Tony to the lake and became an accomplished lead-liner in her own right. She perfected a slightly different swinging technique that, until Tony caught on, enabled her to consistently out-fish the flutter spoon king. Tony and Marjorie trailered their boat to Lewis Point on countless summer evenings, launched it at Oneida Limited's club grounds, and spent delightful hours together. Musing about those angling days, spent with "the finest wife that a man could ever have," Tony spoke about his life and his favorite sport.

"All fishing days are memorable," stated Canastota's master lure craftsman, pipe in hand, resting on his venerable workbench. "As long as you're on this lake, especially with those you love, you can't help but be happy. There's nothing better. Nothing."

Postscript: Tony Verno passed away in 1997, two years after his beloved Marjorie. His memory endures on Oneida Lake, however–in the thousands of flutter spoons that occupy honored places in anglers' tackle boxes, and in the fishing joys that these marvelous, hand-crafted lures create, year after year.

– Chapter 32 –

North Wall

I often retreat to a few special spots on and around Oneida Lake that afford a sense of being and belonging. There, I am comfortable and relaxed, savoring feelings that inspire me to write and spend quality time with Oneida, researching and discovering the lake's people and their fine past. Let me share brief images of two places with you.

On the lake itself Messenger's Bay, where my grandfather and I first rented a boat and met Oneida, has always been special. Messenger's is a broad, open bay that occupies the lake's expanse just west of Lewis Point. The bay's rock, rubble and sand bottoms, punctuated by weed beds that extend outward from the shore, are rich nurseries for all forms of aquatic life. There, in years past, I boated my first walleye, shared fascinating Oneida exploration trips with friends, and caught a wonderfully addictive dose of "lake fever," a blessed affliction that prompts the sufferer to spend as many hours on this lake as is humanly possible. Despite its location, close to the heavily used eastern lake basin, the bay is relatively uncrowded and privacy is blessedly common. Every year I return to Messenger's and the bay never fails to reward, with fish, frolic, and an intangible feeling that this place is a part of me.

On land, I often gravitate to a small, man-made peninsula that shelters the marina where I dock my boat. I call this spit "North Wall," a directionally appropriate term since the wall defines the marina's northern boundary. Now, while North Wall rests within an absolutely beautiful setting it is, in itself, no aesthetic delight. The wall is a breakwater that buffers the lake's fury away from major human investments. Its purpose is protection and it serves that purpose well. None of the lake's storms, floods, or ice pile-ups has ever breached the breakwater. North Wall was constructed from a base of broken concrete slabs, a kind of mega-rip-rap if you will, that have been covered with tons of gravel and soil. A few slabs still peer at visitors from openings in the wall's sides. A recent dumping of concrete blocks fortified the wall's eastern tip that, because it's exposed to the brunt of east wind's erosive power, must be rebuilt every few years. People burn driftwood and dock debris on North Wall. Piles of this scrap accumulate throughout the open water seasons, awaiting the occasional bonfire. All kinds of discards wash onto the wall. Civilization's plasticked, styrofoamed flotsam and jetsam reminds visitors of our era's wastes, while nature's lake-crafted driftwood sculptures soothe the senses with their smooth, though often gnarled, character. Errant grasses sprout from crevices amidst the wall's blocks and a few scraggly bushes maintain a tenuous existence. A buoy marks the marina's navigable channel at the wall's east end and an oversized ceramic frog, perched atop one of the concrete slabs, greets lakefarers. If Oneida spawned a Lorelei legend like that of Germany's Rhine, North Wall would not be the temptress's magical home.

What makes North Wall special is the life that teems around it, life that literally bursts at the observer's feet. The wall brings the interested observer into close contact with the lake's vitality. The shallows on the wall's lake side warm quickly in spring and attract schools of emerald shiners, bullheads, and panfish. Walleyes and other predators follow and, on May's pike season opener, nice fish are landed on the wall. Northern pike cruise both sides of the peninsula and, once, I was treated to the sight of a tiger muskellunge sequestered between slabs, awaiting dinner's arrival. As the lake warms through summer, weed and algae growth proliferate. The aquatic vegetation is regularly "mowed" within the marina but it thrives on the opposite side of the wall. Scuds and other insects hatch within the verdant mass, zebra mussels cling to weeds and rocks alike, mallards gorge on the abundance, huge carp swirl and rile the aquatic jungle, and largemouth bass grow even larger amidst this overstocked lake pantry. The plants and algae emit a rich, fertile odor that bothers some people, but reassures those attuned to Oneida's aquatic heartbeat.

North Wall's neighboring biomass undergoes a transformation

each autumn. Fall's cooling temperatures cause weed growth to break up and decay. Vegetation that once clogged the shallows settles on the lake bottom and washes ashore. Baitfish, attracted by the weeds' abundant invertebrate population and urged to feed by tumbling temperatures that herald winter's freeze, migrate to the shallows. Walleyes and yellow perch, similarly driven by weather conditions, follow and angling often reaches spectacular levels. Thousands of gulls and terns mass along the shore, biding their time until predator fish force bait to the surface. Migratory waterfowl find the verdant area near the wall to be an inviting cafeteria.

Nature's autumnal activity often peaks as darkness falls, making this a superb angling time. On one brilliantly colored October evening I relaxed on the wall, awaiting sunset's life. Several hundred gulls, with similar thoughts, floated atop the steady west wind-driven waves. Two blue herons, oblivious to my presence, stealthily worked the wall's outer perimeter. The waves resounded off the wall in a deep bass percussion rhythm, perfect for the scene. Autumn's sun burned to the west. It penetrated the streaked cirrus clouds and illuminated the Eastern Shore with golden, color-enhancing hues. The vanishing sun created a surreal blending of reds, oranges, and lavendered blue-grays above the horizon. I stood on the wall's eastern tip and cast my lure into Oneida's rollers. Colors faded into darkness's blend while wind and waves played the evening's overture, but the walleyes refused my offerings. After a while, I set my rod on a block, faced the breeze, felt the disappearing day and listened to the lake's symphony. I could not imagine a better place.

More often than not, however, cooperative fish visit the North Wall. A year prior to this October day I invited Peter Eager and Rosemary Watson, two friends from San Diego, California, to experience the wall. Neither had ever cast for walleyes at night, nor were they prepared for the vicious easterly that chilled the evening. Peter and Rosemary are adaptable people, however. They fished seriously and endured the discomfort like Oneida Lake veterans. The lake rewarded them with two hefty walleyes. It was a fine fishing–great camaraderie, a taste of nature's power, and successful angling to sweeten the time.

Several weeks later Rosemary, a teacher and freelance writer, sent me a poem in which she captured elements of that North Wall trip. Let me share her work with you.

Ode to a Walleye

Dark waves beat the shore
White capped with foam
New York winds that gust
  with gale force
As I balance on the rocks.
Night storms in
on Oneida Lake.

Do you see them?
He says
As I search the dark torrent
  of water in search of a
  mound of fish
  that breaks the surface
Grasping at minnows
  darting this way and that
Out of the jaws of
Walleye.

Cast your line like this
He says
Throwing the lure with a
Practiced flick of the wrist.
I can only vainly attempt
His artistry in motion
I reel in (as I fight the wind)
A clump of seaweed.
You'll feel a tug, then jerk the pole
  to set the hook
He says
But I only set
A clump of sea weed.

Here, I'll do the casting
He says
You just reel in the fish.
I feel it, that gentle tug
the tension on the line
that signals a bite
I reel in (as I fight the wind)
It pulls back...the battle is on
Between the fish and me
Dark fins flapping the water
Trying to pull away
Twisting and grappling
With life on a thin line
Taut with the stress of the fight
I win (as I fight the wind).

I've got the net
He says.

– Chapter 33 –

Running Through Sylvan Beach History

They rendezvoused on an early summer's morn at the spot where the Barge Canal met Oneida Lake. Here, the canal widened into a harbor and a few boats were tied to its concrete banks. The ancient Sylvan Beach pier protected the harbor and stretched westward into the lake. The first section of the old breakwater was intact and open to the public, but the lake had eroded the rest of the half-mile long jetty beyond safety's realm. Two diehard anglers walked their offerings along the pier and canal. In seasons past these places would be crowded with the fishing fraternity, but this year's bumper crop of baitfish curtailed the walleyed pike "bite" before it ever began. A solitary walker, his swinging arms testifying to fitness's zeal, cruised past the fishermen in this sunrise tableaux.

They finished their requisite, almost ceremonial stretching and began the run. A thirty-yard jog along the old pier brought them to Sylvan Beach's lake front park. As usual, he led and established the rhythm. Since they were "doing 10K" today, he set a moderate pace, within her comfort zone. To the east, on their right, was the old Midway, a small amusement park. In the morn when all was quiet, one could imagine the mellow tunes of the carousel, a modern replacement of William Cottman's 1896 original, bubbling through the air. Ghostly melodies of entertaining hurdy-gurdy rhythms, those organ-grinding, monkey-dancing notes, rested within a few old carnival buildings. Hard rock sounds thundered perfectly with the crash of roller coaster cars and the accompanying screams of thrilled patrons. Sounds of "Laffland," a fun-house built from two sections of the 19th century's Rowe Brothers' Bath House, of "Fascination," a unique arcade of old-fashioned games, of bumper cars and bumping boats, of popping carmelcorn and sizzling fries melted together into a kind of carnival fugue that had played its merry melody for over a hundred years. Even in their run's early morning silence, one could imagine the music living, again.

The run angled from the lakefront to Park Avenue and followed that street northward past "Pfohl's," a Beach disco housed in a building that was home to "The Eagle Hotel" around 1900, "DiCastro's" in the 1950s and '60s, and "Bruno's" in the 1980s, all prominent nightspots in their eras. The runners jogged through the avenue's comforting shade, by scores of rental cottages whose vacationing cargoes were fast asleep at this early hour. They neared Union Chapel, the Beach's oldest church.

The chapel was a unique, New England-style building, sided with white clapboards, windowed with clear, rectangular panes that contrasted with a circle of stained glass that haloed its chancel. The church, built in 1887 on land donated by the Spencers, the Beach's founding family, was a Protestant sanctuary that was open for services every summer Sunday. When the crowd overflowed, the chapel's walls were propped out and the congregation sat on the sandy ground that bordered the building. Old pulleys that testified to this ancient expansive practice sat idle above the paneled lower walls. Plain benches contrasted with great gilded chandeliers in the Chapel's interior, the latter perhaps a reminder of the Beach's first golden era, a time around 1900 when railroads carried thousands to the "Coney Island of Central New York" on every summer weekend. The Chapel had even been used as a set for a Liza Minelli film, "The Sterile Cuckoo," shot at the Beach in 1968. The saying, "Teach Us Thy Way, Oh Lord," inscribed above the altar, spoke to the faithful. Union Chapel's sacred hymns had flowed through the village for over a century.

Onward they ran through Sylvan Beach's numbered street progression...14th, 15th and the parking lot of the "Beach Buffet," a restaurant that occupied a building that the year prior had housed a nightclub called the "T-Rex." On evening runs past they jogged by the T-Rex when music cranked from jukeboxes and live bands created a fast, moving rhythm that energized their running. In the near silence of early morning, however, the club was closed and a dog's barking provided the sole melody.

The Beach Buffet occupied another historic musical site. Its parking lot once contained the Saint Charles Hotel, a magnificent structure that was built by Louis Chesebrough, owner of the Vaseline Company, in 1899. The hotel, which burned in 1914, regularly held "balls," where music that graced a more elegant dancing than Sylvan Beach has ever known filled the 15th Avenue air. The Saint Charles was a grand hotel that hired chefs to prepare unique lakeside cuisine and uniformed coachmen to meet its patrons at the Ontario and Western Railroad Station, where Eddie's Restaurant is today.

The Beach Buffet itself was once named the "Kon-Tiki" and, during the 1970s, this business brought "big band style" music to the Beach. John Newton's "one man band" piped the tunes made popular by Harry James, the Dorsey Brothers, and Lawrence Welk to an adoring, slow-dancing crowd. Every Sunday the Tiki hosted "amateur night" and some fine local musicians, whose talents reflected the brassy, big sound of the '30s and '40s, brought their notes to the club's stage. It was a microcosmic reincarnation of "Russell's Hotel and Danceland," a Beach big band emporium of the Depression/World War II era. Located at the corner of Akehurst and Main, Russell's once hosted name performers that drew tremendous crowds. When the Dorseys played Russell's, cars jammed Main Street from the hotel south to the intersection of Routes 31 and 13–three miles away! From Ellington to Caloway to Sinatra, the musical elite played the Russell's scene.

They continued northward to Edgewater Drive, where Oneida bordered the roadway and reached for the runners every time they passed. Today, a slight easterly breeze flattened the lake, this being the East Shore. The wind made for fine angling conditions. A dozen boats drifted and trolled in the twenty-foot depths about a mile out. He was a fisherman before he became a runner and Edgewater brought his love for angling to focus. He had fished the lake since he was a teenager and had always been awed by the water's productivity. Later, he researched the lake's past and was amazed at how old-time fish dealers measured catches in tons. Fish like landlocked Atlantic salmon and lake whitefish once thrived in Oneida's depths. Biological changes brought on these fish's demise and the walleyed pike and smallmouth bass now swam atop the complex food web. Recently, the proliferation of zebra mussels, small bivalves that feed on algae, had changed patterns in that web. The walleye population had taken a hit during the last decade from another exotic creature–a bird, of all things!–the double crested cormorant. Research proved that a few hundred cormorants could devour hundreds of thousands of fish annually. In the last year, however, good hatches of walleyes and perch, coupled with increased cormorant controls, promised a renaissance for the lake's fish numbers. He thought of a close friend, a sports writer from Utica, who once characterized the lake as an "aquatic Garden of Eden" and he smiled, knowing that Oneida had weathered some severe ecological tests in its history and always emerged as the productive victor.

"Lost in thought again, are you?" Her comment jarred him from his morning daydream. She had taken advantage of his Edgewater preoccupation and stealthily increased her pace until she ran just behind. "You might run better if you concentrated," she jabbed.

"Thanks for the advice," he answered, "But remember that historians often run with the past."

She smiled as they began to climb North Bay's hill, a gentle and beautiful incline. He looked back at the lake and the hills to the south and recalled Oneida County historian Samuel Durant's words, penned in 1878. Describing the moving scene, the chronicler wrote, "Oneida Lake, viewed from the promontory at North Bay, when a fresh wind is blowing and the sky is clear or partly cloudy, is long remembered. Stretching away to the west and south, the blue waters of the lake appear magnificent, with their curling waves and caps of foam, and on the opposite shore the distant hills of Madison County rise bold and free, a fitting background for an exquisite picture." The image, one of many romantic portrayals penned during the 19th century, captured a few brush strokes of a lake panorama that had moved observers throughout recorded history.

Durant's vision had stayed with him ever since he began researching the lake's past and he was still absorbed by it as they descended North Bay's hill. They passed along Edgewater again, parallel to the old bed of the Ontario and Western Railroad, and started the Sylvan Beach avenue countdown. McClanathan Avenue, named for farmers Elmer and Francis McClanathan, who worked the sandy soil long before people thought of tans and designer bathing suits, formed the village's northern border. They passed camps built by the Gregory, Powers, Bates, Keiffer, and Foley families, pioneering cottagers in the early twentieth century. Then came 29th, 28th, 27th...they ran along Main Street until they got to 21st, where they turned lakeward and headed south on Park. Some older cottages lined the upper part of Park Avenue, venerable, warm dwellings whose sides had weathered Oneida's furies for decades. The buildings bore older names like "Sylvaneida," "Lake Breeze Repose," and "Sandsoftime."

He imagined many of the cottages in their turn of the century splendor, adorned with gingerbread ornamentation like that found on their counterparts in Nantucket, Martha's Vineyard, and Chautauqua. His mind returned to happy Sylvan Beach photographs he had seen, pictures of smiling families posed on their cottage porches, framed in an antiquarian splendor by their buildings' gingerbread gothic style. Early twentieth century Sylvan and Verona Beaches boasted scores of these beautiful dwellings, buildings girdled by expansive verandas, peaked with steepled finials, and eaved by carved bargeboard that bore witness to their creators' skills and patience. Now, little of the fragile architectural frills remained and many cottages were gone, but a precious few existed along the East Shore. In these, he found reassurance that some people still cared about preservation, about keeping the best of the past alive.

"Like those buildings, don't you?," she said, as she once again pulled next to his right shoulder. "Just imagine restoring one."

"I'd love to do it," he answered. "Restoration would be beautiful. The cost, however...but it would be worth every penny. How can you put value on beautiful buildings? Clapboard Van Goghs. The Beach was so rich with them." He shook his head. Perhaps in another time and place.

Down Park Avenue they ran. When they came to 13th he temporarily lost his musicality and simply pointed to a big building labeled "The Oneida," on their right. Playing pedagogue, he asked, "What do you think that structure originally was?"

"A hotel, " she responded. "They still use it like one. I think it's kind of a 'bed & breakfast' place."

"You were close, my friend," he complimented. "It was Dr. Martin Cavana's 'Sanitarium, Private Hospital, and School For Nurses.' Cavana was an interesting fellow and a pretty significant guy in the Beach's story. He came from Oneida and built this place in 1891. His reputation attracted patients from all over the Northeast. Cavana treated Louis Chesebrough, who owned the Vaseline Company and built the St. Charles Hotel. The doctor convinced him to build his great hotel in the Beach. Cavana was the village's leader during its first 'heyday,' if you will. He organized the merchants and, together, they attracted gatherings called 'picnics.' The biggest of these, the annual 'hop growers' picnic' sometimes brought over 50,000 people here for one-day extravaganzas. Cavana's Sylvan Beach had hotels that could accommodate hundreds of patrons and its midways quadrupled the size of the one today. It had bath houses, fleets of fishing vessels, steamboats docked along its piers...in short, it was a hopping commodity, no pun intended. Newspapers portrayed the village as an Inland Coney Island and in this region it had no equal.

This lasted until 1924, when Cavana died and his sanitarium closed. In the '20s automobiles replaced railroads and Sylvan Beach lost a lot of its uniqueness. People became more mobile. They went elsewhere and the Beach changed. The hotels lost business, some folded, but the village endured as a nice, blue collar resort."

"I wonder if couples ran through the village then," she mused as the runners entered the park, and shifted to a grassy pathway. The sandy soil was soft and cushioned their tired muscles. Tall beach pines, their curved trunks testaments to their hardiness, and powerfully rooted oaks, descendants of the trees that gave the Beach its "sylvan" name, canopied their footsteps. Village founder James D. Spencer's first resort venture was a large picnic grove on land that included part of the park. A benevolent man, Spencer deeded the park to the village, insuring that a verdant oasis would always flourish in the Beach's hub.

They jogged through the green and Eddie's Restaurant loomed ahead. Eddie's was one of their favorite Beach places. On many an evening they relaxed in one of the restaurant's cozy booths. They enjoyed the cross-section of people who shared their comfort in Eddie's. They liked the family atmosphere that lent welcome warmth to the place. He had savored the Eddie's scene for over three decades. When he first came to Sylvan Beach he delighted in bringing friends there, taking particular pride in being able to explain the story behind each of Lorraine Clark's and Iva Money's historical paintings that decorated the dining rooms. Now, he shared them with her and he liked that. He had been taught that history belonged to all and that sharing it was a warm, bonding act. Several years ago Eddie's celebrated its 60th anniversary and photos commemorating the restaurant's fine past added character to its walls. Eddie's was built on an important spot in village history–the site of the Ontario and Western Railroad Station. Here the trains discharged their eager touristy cargo in Cavana's time, and picked up the fatigued vacationers who had reveled in the village's vibrant offerings. On peak picnic days, passenger trains slowly backed down Railroad Avenue, Main Street's pre-auto title, and ended their journey by emptying vacationers aplenty at the station by the park. He imagined the sounds...whistles blowing...car doors sliding open...a conductor shouting "Sylllll Vanbeach" at the top of his lungs...trunks dragged from baggage compartments...the milling, excited banter of the newly arrived.

"Too bad they aren't open," she said. "You could use a cup of strong coffee."

"I don't believe so," he protested. Drenched with sweat, fatigued by the miles, the runners smiled with the feeling that the end was approaching, and coming fast. They ran through scenes they had been a part of just minutes before. The Chapel, the Midway, the lake front park reappeared through their cantering gait. All were peopled with morning souls tentatively beginning this summer day. The easterly breeze had shifted to the west in the hour their run took and it seemed to increase as they neared the canal. Westerlies embodied Oneida's power and he savored their force, respecting and enjoying nature's gusting airs. The lake almost seemed to be helping him to the finish.

Now, the canal rested before them and their run became history. Tired, yet happy, they slapped their customary high-fives. They felt a satisfying fatigue that, paradoxically, energized them for the day's tasks. She talked about the run's details, of the refreshing breezes and the warming conversation that kept them moving.

They started their post-run walk, a mile trek in which their bodies adapted to a slower pace. They walked along the pier and passed "Yesterday's Royal," a restaurant housed in a restored hotel. An old-time touring vessel, its wooden parts shining in their sunrise polish, complemented the Royal and caught their interest.

He recalled a popular song from thirty years past that seemingly played on every Beach jukebox during his first month of research. He explained the song's significance and, then, quietly recited two favorite lines.

> Something touched me deep inside,
> The day…the music…died…

"Nice run," she said. "Nice history."

Ruth Rogers

The old Brewerton Bait Shop, on Route 11 in downtown Brewerton, was a fountainhead of fishing supplies and knowledge for Oneida Lake's West End anglers.

Marv Ladd

Many of the Bait Shop's patrons fished the Oneida River, photographed here from its north bank in Oswego County. Chuck Rogers netted baitfish in the river and guided northern pike anglers along the Oneida's docks.

Jim Donlon

The 1950s Midway from the air. Note the number of large trees. The "sylvan" (meaning "wooded") nature of the Beach gave the village welcome, cooling shade.

Mike Wameling

The Midway was very popular during the 1950s.

Jim Donlon

Powerboat racing fans jammed the beach on a beautiful summer day in the late 1950s.

The Money family's Midway gave tons of fun to Beach patrons throughout the decade. This building faced the Barge Canal.

John Clements

The nautical bar at Ron-Nells' Restaurant, owned by Ron and Nell McKenzie, was a classy Sylvan Beach attraction in the 1950s.

Ann Hopkins

Bait dealers like Mose Poppleton, Bill Krahl, and Ray Sawner often netted emerald shiners ("buckeye" minnows in Beach vernacular) in the shallows along the lakefront in the 1950s.

A Verno flutter spoon and one of its fans–an Oneida Lake "jack perch."

Tony and Sally Verno

Tony Verno, the "flutter spoon king," enjoys his favorite pastime.

Fort Brewerton Historical Society

Part of North Wall was created as a breakwater for the second Oneida Lake Canal's entrance to the lake. The steamboat, *Lottie,* emerges from the canal's lakeside lock in this photo from 1900. The picture was taken on the approximate site of the wall today.

A section of the old canal breakwater can be viewed from North Wall when lake levels are lowered in late fall.

Jean Kowalski

Bathers enjoy Oneida Lake's surf and the toboggan slide at Sylvan Beach, around 1910.

Ann Hopkins

Union Chapel–built in 1887 on land donated by James D. Spencer and sons, the Beach's founding family.

Mike Wameling

The grand St. Charles Hotel, that operated from 1899 - 1914, was built by Louis Chesebrough, manufacturer of Vaseline.

Mike Wameling

Patients and staff enjoy comforting shade on the lakefront side of Dr. Cavana's Sanitarium, around 1905.

– Chapter 34 –

Rhythms of the Lake

John Cronin, a conservationist whose job entailed checking for polluters of the Hudson River (his official title is "river keeper") described his position in 1999:

"My job allows me to be in touch with the rhythms of the river and to understand what it means to fit the rhythms of your life around those other rhythms. When you are a fisherman, one of the rhythms is the tide, but every day the hours change. One week you're having breakfast at 7 A.M., the next at two in the afternoon. All this extends to life on the shore, to the people who come down to watch the boats come in. The whole community participates in the rhythms of the river."

In the past people have blended beautifully with Oneida Lake's rhythms. Many anglers, especially, developed an amazing, almost uncanny unity with their lake. The lake became a friend and benefactor as their lives intertwined in celebration.

ONEIDA CREEK BAY
March 1975

The warm spring rain fell for almost a full day and melted the remaining snow and ice that once wintered the Stockbridge Valley. Vapors rose from the hillsides and spread across pastures and roads, fogging the area with mists of seasonal change. Two aqueous inches showered the valley and the cornfields and hay lots freshened with March's awakening odors. Everywhere was liquid. Ground water spurted from ubiquitous pores in the hillsides and merged with the runoff, cascading over rock ledges. Water rivuleted along last autumn's corn rows, muddying into a seasonal coloring as it dropped from the valley's heights to Oneida Creek below. The creek, Oneida Lake's third largest tributary, collected the hillsides' runoff as it drained the valley. The small stream's spring-swollen volume burst through gardens, lawns, and brush lands as it rushed northward toward the lake. It powered through the Indians' territory and caromed off concrete and riprap in Oneida City before meandering over its banks through the gentle farm fields by Route 31 that they call "Oneida Valley." These acres and the adjoining wetlands of the Verona Beach State Park absorbed much overflow, enough to prevent flooding along the lakeshore. Its force somewhat calmed, the creek's browned waters entered Oneida and continued surging, leaving a half-mile trail the locals called a "mud rile." Currents and waves swirled and mixed the creek's and lake's deep tans, browns, olive greens, and blues, as the two life forces joined rich hues in their annual vernal blending.

Most upstaters remained indoors during the downpour, grumbling about the rain, the air's omnipresent dampness, the cold winds, and their self-imposed isolation. To Canastota fishermen like the Cesarios, Fabrizis, Cerios, and Marchettis, however, the rains signaled an angling renaissance that heralded the beginning of the lake's annual bullhead "run," a long-anticipated sporting thaw that occurred at Oneida Creek's bay. Rains and stream runoff warmed the recently ice-freed lake and fish quickly responded to temperature. Many of the fishermen were proud descendants of Italian-American farmers who came to Canastota to raise onions, potatoes, and peppers in the rich muck lands north of that village. Like their ancestors, they were hard-working men and they looked upon the lake more as a provider than playground. They relished bullhead dinners, shared their bounty with family and friends, fertilized their gardens with entrails, and even sold a few fish for "beer money." They fished for Oneida's other species, but the bullhead run began their year and, as such, it was an important rite of spring.

The fishermen collected bait prior to their bullhead pilgrimage. On the afternoon of the rains the Canastotans walked through corn fields near the Thruway, pulling remnant stalks, shaking free the small worms that clustered around the decaying roots. It was a dank, dirty task, but it was an established prelude to the upcoming fishing and it was repeated every year. The fishermen swore that several of these worms, "gobbed" together on a hook, were unbeatable bullhead bait. They boasted that their offerings were much superior to the larger, fatter night crawlers that other anglers used. The men pried stalk after stalk and they didn't stop until their bait cans squirmed with enough slimy delicacies to last several days.

Many Canastotans docked their boats at Al Beickert's marina, a small lakefront harbor on Oneida Creek's south bank. Others took advantage of Beickert's livery, where a fisherman could rent a fourteen-foot aluminum boat for $3 a day. Each boat contained two rugged, eight-foot galvanized iron pipes that, when driven into the creek mouth's mud bottom, provided a stable mooring. One pipe was tied to a bowline, the other lashed to the stern. Stability was critical in spring bullheading because the fish bit lightly and rods had to be kept still for anglers to detect bites. Each fisherman used two rods and rested them against the boat's side. The fish fed on the bottom and one-ounce sinkers were needed to keep the bait there. Anglers attached more weight to their lines if a strong current flow bumped the bait downstream. Typically, a bullheader cast his rig, allowed the sinker to hit bottom, set his rod in a secure boat position, and then reeled to tighten the line. Fishermen watched their rods' tips for the telltale movement that indicated a feeding fish. They often used towels to grasp the slippery bullheads and took care removing hooks from the fish. Bullheads have three "horns," one behind each gill and another on the dorsal fin. These sharp spikes easily puncture human skin and the resulting wounds sting for several hours.

Beickert's marina hummed during the annual run. He and his wife, Millie, started the marina in the early 1950s. They were equal partners who pulled minnow seines, cleaned boats, and managed the marina together. Millie ran the business while her husband worked at Oneida Limited, and Al took over after he returned home. The Beickerts' son, Ed, loved to fish for bullheads and Al sold Ed's catches for 35¢ per pound, live weight. Anglers like Leo Vella and Gordon Klock pursued bullheads every day after the run began and marketed their delectable harvests.

Anglers from Oneida, Chittenango, Rome, even the hill country of Southern Madison County bullheaded with the Canastotans at Oneida Creek. Fishermen lined the banks in front of the Harbor Bar, a colorful, popular after-angling stop where bullhead outings were recounted with spirit and imagination. Others crowded the rusted Lehigh Valley railroad bridge that crossed the creek here. Locals nicknamed the span the "Peace Bridge" because a graffiti artist had spray painted "peace" in large letters across the bridge's east side during the Vietnam War.

Despite spring's inclement conditions, bullhead-fishing days were festive outings. An angling camaraderie thrived. The Canastotans, in their rowboats and on shore, where they sat atop the traditional five-gallon plastic buckets, laughed and joked as they referred to each other with lively nicknames. A Syracuse journalist once called Canastota the "village of nicknames" and, as the fishermen experienced Oneida Creek's bay, lines like "'Teet,' you've missed so many fish it looks like you're exercisin'!" "'Bosco'–a five-year-old woulda' caught that one!" and "'Chet,' whaddyadoin'? Catchin' fish or shootin' the breeze?" laced the air.

Every year...every spring...bullhead time at the creek mouth. People cajoled, cursed, and commented within the life that they loved. They braved the elements, caught their fish, and lived with the rhythms of Oneida Lake's rebirth.

A Three-Day Blow at the Sylvan Beach Pier
May 1955

"West wind's been up for two days now," mused the fishermen in the diners and taverns of this East Shore village on a chilly late spring night, "And it should stay up tomorrow. They were sayin' on the news that the wind's between fifteen and twenty-five miles per hour, with some gusts hittin' thirty. That's a good 'three-day blow.' Best we've seen this year. And you know what winds like that do."

An Oneida Lake three-day blow raised the spirits of the Beach's anglers because the winds meant walleyes and very productive fishing. The Sylvan Beach pier was a focal point for "pike" angling. Its story flows like this.

Sylvan Beach's shore-bound walleye anglers lived for the west wind. Teens cut school, businessmen locked their doors, and workdays were abbreviated during three-day blows. The Beach's pier, a concrete breakwater, extended about a half-mile westward into the lake. A mass of boulders, locally nicknamed "the rock pile," stretched for another 200 yards at a northwesterly angle, at the end of the pier. Built in 1917 as a part of New York State's Barge Canal project, the pier sheltered Sylvan Beach harbor and prevented sand from clogging the canal. Erosion and weathering have reduced the pier today to a jumbled mess of broken concrete slabs, but the breakwater was solid in 1955. Vast schools of emerald shiners, called "buckeye minnows" in lake vernacular, provided walleyes with a major source of food during the '50s and strong west winds drove these baitfish eastward. The minnows congregated along the pier and rock pile. Predator fish such as walleyes and silver bass naturally followed their buckeye forage. The population of these species was extremely high in the 1950s. Consequently, the waters bordering the pier teemed with game fish when the west wind roared.

And the pier itself teemed with anglers...sometimes hundreds of them...a unique fishing fraternity within Oneida Lake's history. A typical pier fisherman wore hip boots, warm clothing, and some sort of rain slickers, because spring and fall westerlies were usually cool breezes and the waves sprayed water everywhere when they crashed into the pier. Anglers tied ropes around their waist and let the rope dangle to the pier's surface. They attached a fish stringer to the end of the rope. The stringer had to be a long, rugged one because fishermen were allowed to keep fifteen walleyes in the 1950s. Anglers dragged their rope-stringer combos as they walked the pier. Water that flowed over the pier kept the fish cool and fresh.

A pier angler's outfit was a primitive, yet effective, fish catching apparatus. Most rods were bamboo "cane poles," usually about ten feet long. There was no reel. Instead, two knobs were attached to the pole's thicker end and spaced about eight inches apart. These knobs were usually wooden, but nails also sufficed. Braided linen line was wrapped around the knobs and passed through three or four small metal guide loops that were attached to the rod. When a fisherman wanted to let out more line he merely had to unwrap it from the knobs and wiggle the pole. A sinker at the end of the line pulled it down and out. Anglers tied long shank hooks at the line's end. These hooks were ideal for impaling buckeye minnows. A small lead sinker was placed about a foot above the hook. Many sportsmen bought their "pier poles" at Victor Serby's "Sylvan Beach Department Store," a "mom and pop" general merchandise operation on Main Street, or at "Head's Store," a grocery run by Isaiah "Ike" and Minnie Head at the corner of 5th and Main. Most pier poles marketed locally were the creations of "Doc" Nichols, a veteran Beach angler, boatman, and tackle crafter who also fashioned metal tip-ups for ice fishing in his shop on 10th Avenue. A few utilitarian fishermen made their own pier rods out of limbs that they cut from trees. Tom Sawyer and Huck Finn would have been comfortable fishing with a pier man's gear.

Anglers usually hooked buckeyes through both lips and "walked" the bait along the pier. There was a definite order of walking in pier fishing. When the pier was crowded, fishermen lined the breakwater's north (lake) side, about ten feet apart. They walked westward...very slowly...gradually releasing more line as the lake deepened. In effect, they trolled their bait along the bottom. When a pier man reached the end of the concrete, he lifted his buckeye and walked back toward shore, reentering the line of anglers wherever possible. If the pier wasn't crowded, fishermen would walk slowly out and when the leading angler reached the rock pile the whole line of fishermen would turn around and walk back. More walleyes were taken on the walk out, however, than on the return. Although anglers theorized that fish faced shoreward when they pursued bait, catch discrepancies remained a mystery.

Walleyes weren't the only fish caught along the Sylvan Beach pier. Smallmouth bass inhabited the pier's sides in summer and yellow perch, locally called "jack perch," lurked there in all seasons. Fish pirates set chicken-wire funnel traps for perch on the pier's canal side when "jacks" spawned in April. Anglers caught bullheads at night, and large carp and catfish snapped many pier poles.

The pier's rock pile was the center for a unique form of fly-fishing. Now, Oneida Lake bears no resemblance to the Beaverkill or Esopus, but a few lovers of the rise have discovered angling pleasure there. The lake's silver bass population boomed during the 1950s. Although these fishes' true name is "white bass," they are silver-toned and resemble saltwater striped bass. Fly fishers discovered that silvers loved light-colored streamers. They fashioned these flies from deer tails and named them "bucktail streamers." Most pier fly casters used two bucktails and cast only when gulls telegraphed the silvers' position. Two flies gave anglers a better chance to experience a wild silver bass fight. After a silver hit a streamer, fishermen allowed the fish to swim away while keeping pressure on it. Since silvers traveled in huge schools, a second bass almost always engulfed the other fly. "Feed bag filling" catches of silver bass regularly occurred during the '50s.

Silver bass pursued baitfish with a bluefish's reckless abandon. When the bass cornered buckeyes, gulls and terns screamed and dove for the jumping, terrified prey. The birds were incredibly aggressive. Glenn Chesebrough, an old-time Beach angler, loved to fly fish for silvers at the rock pile. He always enjoyed telling how he once caught a seagull that mistook his bucktail for a minnow. "I knew how to play a big fish in the water," Glenn told, "But reeling a bird out of the air was an entirely different matter. Getting it off the hook was even more challenging!"

Landing fish on the pier was as unique as pier fishing itself. After a walleye struck the minnow, most fishermen simply set the hook and lifted their pike into the pier. Sometimes a dozen pike would fly through the air simultaneously if a group of fishermen "walked through" a big walleye school. Ed McCarthy, a life-long Beach resident, likened the pike-lifting scene to Mediterranean tuna fishermen hauling albacore into their boats. "It was wild...fish were everywhere," he recalled, "And it was fun. In my opinion, it was the neatest kind of fishing that people around here ever experienced."

There were other methods for bringing fish atop the pier. Conservative pier men brought their pike alongside and then waited for a big wave to lift the fish onto the concrete. Large walleyes, northern pike, and catfish had to be netted, however, and this provides a nice side bar of pier history. Water drained through several large, circular holes in the pier. The holes were ideal spots to prop "pier nets," wooden-handled, metal-rimmed tools of the angling trade. These large nets were perfect for landing oversized fish. Pier men fondly recall how the nets were "always there" for public use. No one stole or vandalized them; a spirit of trust and friendship thrived on the pier. Anglers seldom carried their own nets because they knew that these examples of "common pier property" would rest in their customary places.

Fishing spawns camaraderie and the pier sported a close angling fraternity. "You usually didn't know people's last names, " recalled John Clements of Sylvan Beach, "But you knew their first names or nicknames. You saw the same people every day. Bill Krahl and Ray Sawner, who ran bait shops in the Beach, were always on the pier. Then there was Joe from Chittenango, Red from Durhamville, Sammy from North Bay. They'd always greet you with a smile and say, 'How ya hittin' 'em?'" Clements was a student in Oneida High School during the 1950s and he and his friends missed many a day of classes when they contracted the very contagious "pier fever."

Companionship contributed to camaraderie, but so did the dangers that all who shared the Beach breakwater faced. The pier's concrete surface, constantly exposed to Oneida's rich, algae-laden water, became mossy and slippery. Sub-freezing temperatures in late fall ice-coated the pier. The biggest waves broke across the pier with a force that could wash unsteady anglers into the water. While the breakwater's lakeside depth was shallow for much of the pier's length, the Barge Canal side was deep. Pier men often dressed in heavy, easily soaked wool clothing, and wore hip waders that had the buoyancy of concrete blocks. If an angler was pushed into the chilled water in spring or fall and didn't have another person nearby to offer quick assistance, he was in serious trouble. Several anglers perished in the '50s and early '60s and these tragedies prompted New York State to close the pier.

A short section of the pier was lined with chain-link fence and reopened in the mid-1970s. The better part of the breakwater, however, lies in a state of extreme disrepair. Talk of rebuilding and restoring the pier has surfaced intermittently during the past quarter-century. Much of this discussion was merely political wind, but recent studies initiated by the Village of Sylvan Beach and conducted by the United States Army Corps of Engineers have breathed life into hopes for restoration. People with vision realize that a new Sylvan Beach pier would be an economic boon to the area and an unparalleled social and recreational asset in Central New York.

App's Boat Livery, Cleveland Harbor
July 1965

It is evening and Clarence App rests at his customary place, sitting on his wooden chair on the front porch of his boat livery's office-storehouse-bait shop building of all trades. Clarence and his wife, the former Lucy Abel, live there, too. He designed the structure himself. In fact, he and his brother Elliott designed and built everything in their marina when they started it in the late 1920s. Every dock, mooring post, light fixture, and board had Clarence's and Elliott's signatures on them. The brothers even dug the original marina harbor, by hand of course, calculating all the required depths and angles. Oneida Lake anglers could rent a boat, dock a boat, launch a boat, buy bait and tackle, and acquire some unique fishing expertise at "App's Boats and Bait," Clarence's realm.

Design came easy for Clarence. The self-described "engineer, veteran fisherman, and boat livery operator" earned degrees in civil, mechanical, and electrical engineering from Syracuse University. Despite his impressive education, Clarence was a modest, easy-going man. Even the tie that he wore every hour of every working day added to his aura of rumpled informality. Mechanically gifted, he could repair virtually anything and, in the off-season, he did odd construction jobs for Cleveland folk. He helped his neighbors by working cheaply, and earned the affectionate nickname, "the two-dollar man." Although some credited Clarence with wiring "three-quarters of Cleveland's houses," he never practiced his engineering professions full time. Another force exerted a greater influence on his life. People said, "The lake got him." He loved Oneida and no drawing board, drafting table, or lush corporate salary could tempt him to leave.

The App family's history parallels Cleveland's past. Martin App, Clarence's grandfather, emigrated to the United States from Wurtenburg, Germany, around 1850. He moved upstate and settled in Cleveland at an opportune time. The village was growing rapidly. Ample waterpower from Black Creek provided the impetus for factory construction. The village's tannery, gristmill, sawmill, and stores served the needs of neighboring farmers. The glass industry started in 1840 and fueled Cleveland's economy throughout the nineteenth century. European craftspersons settled there and worked in the glass factories. Cleveland's population mushroomed and other businesses such as stores and hotels sprouted.

Martin took advantage of Cleveland's economic growth and built the "App Block," a large, subdivided commercial structure on Division Street. He operated a general store and funeral parlor downstairs (he was also the village's undertaker). A dancehall, upstairs, gave hard-working Clevelanders a welcome place to unwind. Later, the hall was used as a theater. App also leased space to other businesses. The block was a village landmark until 1993, when fire destroyed it.

Martin's son, George, continued the family's businesses. George and his wife, Eva Weber App, raised two daughters and three sons and stressed the merits of higher education to each of them. Helen studied nursing at Oswego, but never practiced, electing instead to help her mother manage the store after George died. Katherine became an English instructor and taught in the Syracuse Public Schools for eleven years before marrying Robert Bennett and moving to Philadelphia. John Weber App, the oldest son, was graduated from Syracuse University and its law school. He became an attorney in Manhattan. Elliott attended the Simmons School of Embalming in Syracuse and assisted with the family's undertaking enterprise. He was also a partner in App's Boats and Bait until just before he passed away in 1942. And then there was Clarence....

He had had a tiring summer day, sweating through temperatures that topped ninety sweltering degrees. The smallmouth bass and yellow perch were biting and business filled Clarence's waking hours. This morning was particularly hectic. Up at 4:30 A.M., first rental customer at 5:00, boats to be bailed from the previous eve's cloudburst, second patron at 5:10, more bailing, eight more anglers before 6:00, worm counting for the baitless, still more bailing, sell a couple fish-killing "June Bug Spinners," give angling advice to everyone, collect launching fees from Pennsylvania sportsmen, finish the bailing, rent two more boats, sell 200 additional crawlers, ten dozen crabs, five dozen "bass bugs," grab a cup of coffee and, good Lord, it was 9:00! When the fish went on a feeding binge, Clarence's life got awfully busy.

Taking a breather, he walked into his office, refilled his cup, and extracted a stack of postcards from his desk's glorious clutter. People chuckled at Clarence's office organization, but he knew where everything was and that's all that mattered. Clarence sat down and scribbled this message on the back of four cards:

"Cleveland, N.Y. Oneida Lake. Dear Fisherman, Yesterday the Bass and Perch bit the best of all season. Many good catches came in. Bait used–worms & bugs. Pike catches at night are increasing. We trust you now can catch your share. App's Boat Livery–C.G. App." He addresses the cards to customers in Syracuse, Utica, Buffalo, and Rochester and set them aside. Lucy would mail them when she made her daily post office pilgrimage.

Clarence's day passed quickly, like all Oneida Lake summer days. Its hours melted away in a rich, filled rhythm that is the lake's warm season. A dribbling of customers, a bit more bait, some additional advice in the latter morning hours. Clarence took another break around noon, lunched on a sandwich, and retired for a two-hour nap. Harold "Sonny" Morse, a local kid, had arrived at the livery to take care of what little mid-day business occurred. Clarence liked children and many Cleveland boys, drawn to the waterfront by their outdoorsy upbringing, do odd jobs around the marina. They bail boats, count bait, pick crawlers at night, handle the rentals, and help him with heavy tasks such as hauling the wooden rowboats. He pays the boys a few dollars and throws in a nice fringe benefit–the use a boat. A stickler for promptness and detail, Clarence always blows a loud, shrill whistle when the boys' "lake time" expires.

Clarence's seasons pass quickly and, as he and the livery age together, the seasons seemingly pass faster still. Spring thaws brought welcomed anticipation of the year's good fishing, but every year's first warmth heralded major marina overhauls. Months of icy imprisonment lifted and twisted the docks so that each one had to be reset in the livery's lakebed. Every board had to be checked because prolonged exposure to Oneida's harsh environs cracked and rotted the untreated wood. Black Creek flowed into the lake at App's Harbor and it carried debris that, combined with Oneida's jetsam, sometimes clogged the marina. Limbs, scrap wood, assorted trash, and even an ice fishing shanty found their way into Clarence's cove. Everything had to be cleared.

Spring was also buoy time. Clarence took pride in an intricate buoy system that he devised to mark time-tested angling "hot spots" near the marina. He made twenty-five buoys, each a large plastic jug or aluminum can, and set them in the lake. The buoys were numbered and a small red flag attached to a light rod enhanced their visibility. Apps' patrons received a copy of Clarence's hand-sketched lake map, which showed "fishing grounds available from App's Boat Livery." Clarence wrote on the map "the favorite fishing grounds of the old timers are marked with numbered buoys of this livery. This system gives all an equal chance. No guides are necessary. You are fishing at spots where the fish have been and will cavort." A circle noted each buoy's placement. The buoy's number was inscribed within it. The buoys marked spots such as the "bubbling springs" of Cleveland's "inner bar," the "grass beds" south of Bernhard's Point, and "App's Sunken Barge," a Barge Canal casualty. The map also noted the location of prominent shore points, state navigational buoys in the lake's channel, and the ever-productive Shackelton Shoals in mid-lake. Clarence added a touch of ethos to his cartographic creation by noting "commercial fishermen bring their catches into this harbor daily. We know from them where and how to fish. They also go by our buoys. This information is yours for the asking."

Every year, autumn's chills warmed Oneida Lake's fishing and App's Livery bustled through September. Late October's and early November's snows warned of winter's imminent freeze and Clarence prepared the livery for hibernation. He pulled the buoys, dried their lines, detached their holding weights, removed the flags, and stored them in his barn on the other side of Route 49. He and the boys pulled the heavy Emmons boats from the water and placed each boat on a trailer and towed it to the barn. Clarence rigged an electric winch to lift the boats to a loft where he repaired them during winter. Emmons boats, built by Nearing Emmons in Brewerton, were rugged, ribbed wooden vessels that could handle most Oneida storms. They needed yearly care, however. Each watercraft had to be thoroughly dried in the loft. Then, Clarence methodically scraped the boats' sides and seams. He allowed time for additional drying and then recaulked every seam. When the caulk hardened, he repainted his Emmons boats with next season's protective coats. The process took time, but winter afforded Clarence the maintaining hours that his fleet required. Aside from his handyman's projects and a bit of ice fishing, he had time during the frosted months to prepare for the upcoming season.

But it is summer now and a hot summer day besides. Clarence naps uncomfortably and awakens sweaty and tired. "No sense staying in bed," he muses as he walks downstairs and thanks Sonny for watching the marina. "Take a boat tomorrow morning if I've got one," he says. "You're bound to catch some fish. And bring a friend with you. Might's well share the fun." Sonny nods and leaves Clarence alone on the livery's main dock. A passing friend toots his car's horn and Clarence waves, the sound shaking a frustrated slumber's grogginess from his clearing thoughts. He strolls to a telescope mounted atop a tripod. He placed this "spying scope" where the view commanded the widest panorama of the lake and, boat-by-boat, he checks on his anglers. No one was reeling but it was 3 P.M. and the heat's intensity probably slowed the fishing. "Let the sun settle a bit," Clarence thinks. "There'll be an evening feed, just as there always is. Light gets less, temperature falls, and fish hit more. This lake doesn't disappoint those who know it very often."

So Clarence settles back into his chair, surveys his harbor, and awaits his fishermen. They return by 8 P.M., all with fish, all happy with the day. Clarence stacks oars, checks anchor lines for tightness, and admonishes two surprised anglers that, while they were welcome to return, they had best maintain that welcome by taking the food wrappers and soda cans they left in their boat with them. Duly chastised, the fishermen comply.

Then it is evening, summer's welcome cooling time, when comfort soothes all. It's evening and Clarence App rests at his customary place, sitting on his wooden chair on the front porch of his office-storehouse-bait shop building of all trades. Weather-permitting, every evening, he sits there and every evening a few neighbors gather with him, gabbing away, exchanging news but, especially, listening to Clarence tell story after story. App is an adept raconteur who can spin tales on end without repeating himself. "Chunky" is there on this summer eve. He is a welder from Little Falls, and he owns a camp a short distance away. Lawrence Bullard and his son-in-law, Richard Griesmyer, sit on Clarence's steps. They dock their boat in the marina and keep company with Oneida regularly. Martin Auer from Syracuse is there, too. He's a State Senator and his family summers at Cleveland. Like Clarence, he loves to fish and feels comfortable with the people who gather at App's.

And so, amidst the day's cooling time, the engineer and veteran fisherman spins his web of tales. The others pause and listen, never interrupting because to do so would "rile Clarence's crick" and no one wants to anger this entertaining storyteller.

"Let me tell you about Jake Kyser, boys," Clarence begins. "Jake was a fish pirate the likes of which the lake has never seen. Had nets everywhere, even near Cleveland, though he lived at Upper South Bay. Owned a hotel there, too. Anyway, Jake once had to spend a few days in jail after the game wardens confiscated his nets. Didn't slow him down one bit. His wife tended his other nets every night, taking the fish, resetting the nets. During the day she wove twine and replaced the nets that the wardens got. Lord, she was one fast lady in a boat, rowed like a member of the Syracuse crew, but I don't think she belonged to the university's alumni association. Perfect partner for Jake. They say some marriages are made in heaven, but this one was made for Oneida Lake.

Heck, Jake was arrested for selling pike one time and had to appear in Cleveland's court. When the judge asked him who he sold the fish to, Jake pointed to Warden Travis, one of our local enforcers of the game laws! Now this Travis, there's a story for you. His family operated a meat market in my father's block over on Division Street. The Travis kids got nicknames from that market. They used to call the warden "Chicken" Travis. He had brothers who were known as "Ham" and "Pike." Nothing like a few meaty nicknames to make a family noteworthy.

Speaking of Cleveland, did I ever tell you that, in the old days, this town was so small that they had to shoot a man to start the local cemetery? Thank the good Lord that we don't live in times like those.

But times now can be tough, too. Take taxes, for instance. Laws today compel me to pay a merchant tax, capital stock tax, excise tax, income tax, real estate tax, school tax, carpet tax, auto tax, flight tax, cigar tax, street tax, and, if I tell too many stories, syntax. In addition to those taxes, people request that I contribute to every organization and society that the inventive mind of man can organize. Listen to them...the Society of Saint John the Baptist, bless him; the Navy Relief; the Children's Home; the Gold Diggers' Home; the Policemen's Benefit; the YMCA; the Boy Scouts; the hospitals; the Red Cross; the White Cross; the Purple Cross; and the Double Cross. If I keep contributing they just might enroll me in the moron's society, and good Lord, I'd sure as heck deserve it.

Used to be a farmer that lived on the road to Panther Lake and this farmer had an interesting thing happen to him. He had an outhouse located on a hillside, just above the springhouse in which he cooled his milk. The milk inspector came by one day and ordered the farmer to demolish the outhouse. The old man grumbled, as only farmers can, but he complied with the order. Had to keep selling milk, support the missus and the little ones, you know. In any case, the milk inspector came back one week later to check on the farmer. First thing he saw, when he pulled into the driveway, was a sign posted on the front lawn. It said, 'Dairy Closed.' He walked to the house, knocked on the door, and soon the farmer answered. 'What's going on?' inquired the inspector. 'Had to get out of the milk business,' responded the farmer. 'Can't cool the milk any more. My spring dried up.'

I remember this other North Shore farmer who believed in Christian Science. Nothing against the Scientists, now. They're good, God-fearing people. This farmer had a wife who was going into labor for the first time. He was worried about her and wanted to make her delivery as painless as possible. So, he went to a Christian Science minister and asked what he could do. The minister advised the farmer to 'Get on your knees and pray to God that some of your wife's pain be transferred to the baby's father's stomach.' The farmer went home and prayed for one hour. Nothing happened. He prayed for another hour. Again, no results. The farmer shook his head and wondered what went wrong. Since it was time for evening chores, he walked to the barn. There, on the milk house floor, was his hired man, doubled over with violent stomach cramps.

We used to show what they called 'flicker pictures' in App's Hall, upstairs in the App Block. These were silent movies, with a few subtitles. My father hired a pianist to play while the film was showing. There used to be a local fellow, a big flicker fan, who had bright red hair that stuck up like hay grass in a meadow. He wore a hat with a hole in the middle of it and his hair protruded in a strikingly comical way. He was a sociable chap and liked to drink. One night, after a session with John Barleycorn, this gentleman staggered upstairs in the hall and burst into the flicker picture show. He looked at one of the horrified local ladies and kept saying to her, 'C'mon honey, let's go home.' Swaying back and forth, he repeated this line over and over until gravity and inebriation overpowered his equilibrium. He crashed to the floor and rolled around, scattering chairs and people all over the hall. The pianist even stopped playing, though I can't imagine why. I was young then and

I thought it was all a part of the show.

Now, let's get serious here. You know that you have to be careful when you're out on Oneida Lake. Respect the lake. Don't fear it. It can be a great friend, but a vicious foe. One of our local ice fishermen found that out. He spent hours on the lake, in what he thought was a comfortable day. His hands got cold, but then they turned warm. He lost feeling in the hands when he walked to shore. The feeling didn't return. He went to the doctor and the doc said two words, "severe frostbite." Those hands had to be amputated.

You take your chances when you live with the lake but, when you know the water, it can become your trusted friend. You wake up with it, work with it, and rest when it rests. The lake's seasons tell you what to do and when to do it. Your days are determined by its moods. When it smiles in summer you're busy, like today, very busy because lots of people want to share the lake with you. Other days, times when it's choppy and a little cantankerous, you see different people–the old fishermen, people who know the lake like you do and know that the fish bite best when the waves kick up. They kind of feel the lake, sense its moods, know when it gives–that's when they fish. They know when it can take...they stay off it then. Whether the lake welcomes or warns, they listen–very, very intently. They can sense Oneida and they love this water; they wouldn't want to be anywhere else. You might say that Oneida Lake has a rhythm in every day and every season...almost like a heartbeat. And when you spend your life with the lake, as those old fishermen and I have, you come to realize that its rhythms and yours are the same."

– Chapter 35 –

Different Rhythms

The Twenty-First Century

Significant problems, challenges, and conflicts face Oneida Lake and its people today. These difficulties emanate from human encroachments on the lake's well-founded rhythms. All of the issues share a commonality–they vie with the lake's established patterns and threaten its environmental and physical integrity.

Ecological Disturbances: New Species Invade the Lake

The movement of exotic (non-native) species into Oneida Lake's watershed during the past two decades has dramatically altered the lake's biological rhythms. Historically, the lake has proven to be a tough, enduring entity and has adjusted to every ecological disturbance. Dam construction on tributary streams doomed the lake's migratory Atlantic salmon in the nineteenth century. A dramatic drop in oxygen within the lake's bed around 1960, brought on by extremely hot weather, eradicated the "eel fly," a mayfly important to the food web. Other organisms filled the vacated niches in each of these cases and the lake continued to produce prodigiously. Fish pirates netted exponential catches up to the middle of the twentieth century, yet these mega-harvests never permanently hurt fish populations. Lumbering practices and farmland-clearing during the nineteenth century removed most of the lake's forest periphery and temporarily muddied the tributaries, but the lake's broad, absorbent plain minimized any permanent damage. By 1985, after nearly two centuries of intense human use, Oneida Lake's fishery remained a crown jewel of New York's environment and nourished a vibrant local economy.

The lake's superlative walleye and perch angling, however, experienced a dramatic setback in the 1990s. Cornell University biologists from the lake's Shackelton Point Field Station reported that the average annual adult walleye population had fallen from about 675,000 (from 1958 to 1990) to 215,000 (in 1999), and adult yellow perch numbers dropped from over 2,000,000 to 750,000. Alarmed citizens, led by the Oneida Lake Association, demanded explanations. Much of the answer lay with an exotic species that arrived at Oneida not by water, but in the air.

Cormorants: A Threat From Above

Double-crested cormorants were once abundant throughout the Atlantic Seaboard, Mississippi Valley, and Great Lakes regions. Cormorants are fish-eating birds that consume over a pound per day. Common pesticides, used by farmers up to the mid-twentieth century, reduced their numbers severely. Unrestricted hunting also impacted populations. The birds rebounded after pesticides were banned in the 1960s and they were protected by the Federal Government's "endangered species" list.

Ornithological accounts showed that cormorants seldom used Oneida Lake in the past. One nesting pair of adults was observed on the lake, however, in 1984. There were forty pairs in 1989, 200 in 1996, and over 300 by 1998. Between one and two hundred younger, non-nesting birds swelled the population and, by the end of the twentieth century, from 600 to 800 cormorants made the lake their home during spring and summer. Attracted by resident birds and bountiful fish, migratory cormorants from the Great Lakes and Canada began stopping on Oneida in the 1990s. These birds arrived in mid-August and expanded the lake's existing cormorant population to over 2,000. Oneida Lake was clearer in the 1990s because another exotic, the zebra mussel (an algae-eating bivalve) had entered through the canal system and proliferated. Clarity abetted cormorant predation.

Biologists at the Cornell Field Station warned that cormorants could become major players in the lake's ecosystem. Cornell's statistics, released in 1999, proved beyond a shadow of a doubt that the birds had a devastating impact on Oneida Lake's fishery.

Cormorants consumed millions of walleyes and yellow perch from the 1990s through 2002. This ichthyologic holocaust coincided directly with the severe decline in the lake's walleye and yellow perch fisheries. Angling for these fish once drew thousands annually to the lake. Discouraged by poorer catches, many fishers abandoned Oneida in the latter 1990s. The economic ramifications were felt throughout the lake basin. Marinas lost customers, boat liveries' rental income plummeted, bait and tackle stores saw revenues fall by over 50%, and businesses such as diners, restaurants, motels, and grocery stores, all of which catered to fishermen, suffered in turn. Losses totaled in the millions of dollars.

Cornell's Field Station statistics showed that from the spring of 1996 to the spring of 1997 cormorants ate around 100,000 walleyes and 1,100,000 yellow perch. The birds consumed about 355,000 walleyes and 2,000,000 yellow perch during a similar time frame in 2001. In addition, biologists estimated that year classes of walleyes (fish born in a particular year) were losing two-thirds of the fish that would normally become adults.

Cormorants were also adversely affecting Lake Ontario's once-famous smallmouth bass fishery. Huge colonies of the birds nested on the Galoo Islands, west of Henderson Harbor. Faced with a critical situation, New York State convened a "cormorant task force" in September of 1994. Among the group's recommendations was a non-lethal harassment of Oneida Lake's birds. The New York State Department of Environmental Conservation, commonly known as the DEC, officials obtained a permit from the United States Fish and Wildlife Service to annually "haze" the lake's cormorants following Labor Day Weekend. Cormorants are subject to Federal Government control because of their migratory nature. Hazing included placing noisemakers and reflectors on islands inhabited by the birds, exploding fireworks over the islands, and chasing birds with watercraft. The Fish and Wildlife Service granted New York permission to harass cormorants because expanding populations had been negatively impacting common terns, a threatened species that also used Oneida Lake's islands. The DEC hired the Animal and Plant Health Inspection Service (APHIS) of the United States Department of Agriculture to chase birds off the lake. APHIS often addresses complaints regarding nuisance wildlife.

Oneida Lake's cormorant harassment program began in September 1998. About 3,000 birds were on the lake when hazing started and, after five days, few remained. Similar results occurred in subsequent years, reducing the birds' fish take by thirty to forty-five per cent. Cormorants, however, still consumed huge quantities of the lake's sport fish. Cornell's statistics for 2001, previously cited, were recorded in a year when hazing occurred.

Pressed by public and private forces, the Fish and Wildlife Service announced in November of 1999 that it intended to prepare an Environmental Impact Statement about double-crested cormorants. The Service uses these statements to change official policies. Public fact-finding sessions were held throughout the country. The Oneida Lake Association, which had been actively involved with the issue from the beginning, presented a detailed report that documented the ecological and economic harm that cormorants brought to the lake's region. Cornell Field Station biologists contributed statistical documentation of the birds' adverse effects and projected how the lake would recover if cormorant populations were reduced or removed.

The 2001 Fish and Wildlife Services Preliminary Environmental Impact Statement recommended that states be given the opportunity to apply for "depredation permits" that allow reduction of cormorant populations in cases where the birds "are injurious to public resources." Public resources were defined as "fish, wildlife, plants, and other wild species occurring on public lands and waters." States would have to work closely with the Service to win approval for their goals and methods for cormorant population reduction plans and results would be closely monitored.

Despite harassment, cormorants were killing millions of fish and the Oneida Lake Association decided to push New York's DEC for more effective controls. A massive lobbying campaign aimed at Central New York's legislators began in early 2003. Thousands of letters, e-mails, and calls flooded Assemblypersons' and Senators' offices. The area's elected representatives responded positively and pressed the DEC. The Conservation Department convened another task force in the spring of 2003 and charged the committee with developing an official cormorant policy for Oneida Lake.

The task force, which included groups such as the Audubon Society and the Oneida Lake Association, recommended that Oneida Lake's annual cormorant population be limited to one hundred birds. This was a positive departure from *status quo*. APHIS, in cooperation with the DEC, expanded their harassment plan. Hazing began on August 16, 2003, and over 2,000 cormorants left Oneida within a week. APHIS biologists resumed hazing in the spring of 2004, with the one hundred cormorant limit as their goal.

Oneida Lake's fishery's future rests in the DEC's hands. The department must continue to champion the lake and resist pressure to compromise its cormorant reduction policy. By removing these birds, the DEC has taken a giant step toward restoring New York's most productive freshwater fishery. Good fishing creates jobs and the Oneida Lake region's recessed economy will doubtless receive a welcome stimulus. Children who have been brought up listening to their parents' and grandparents' stories about the lake's fabled fishing will again experience that rich legacy. On the other hand, a future DEC compromise of the one-hundred bird limit could allow cormorants to return and ravage a uniquely blessed aquatic resource. A DEC regression would constitute environmental negligence of the most grotesque order.

Zebra Mussels

Oneida Lake is connected to the Great Lakes through New York State's canal system. This creates a positive economic climate because recreational boating abets businesses in lakeside communities, Sylvan Beach and Brewerton especially. However, the connection has become an environmental curse because exotic organisms from Lakes Erie and Ontario can easily reach Oneida Lake through the canals.

Zebra mussels are bivalves that resemble small clams. The mussels are native to the Black, Caspian, and Aral Seas' basins of Eastern Europe and Central Asia. Ships from European ports dumped ballast water that contained these mussels into the Great Lakes during the 1980s. The mussels thrived in their new North American home. Both larval and adult mussels readily attach to boats. They spread from Lakes Erie and Ontario through the Barge Canal system to Oneida Lake. Zebras became well established in the lake by 1992. Oneida contains high levels of shell-nourishing calcium. The mussels needed solid objects on which to attach and the lake's extensive rock reefs provided ideal sites. Perhaps most importantly, however, the mussels feed on algae and Oneida Lake is rich in these tiny plants.

One zebra mussel can consume algae from up to a quart of water every day. Oneida Lake supports mussel densities that occasionally exceed 100,000 per square meter. The lake contains billions of mussels. The feeding of these bivalves has, at certain times of the year, clarified the lake's water. Cornell scientists determined that the lake was considerably clearer during the 1990s and even measured visibility to a depth of thirty feet, an amazing statistic for a murky, algae-rich lake like Oneida.

Some scientists worried that zebra mussels' algae consumption might severely disrupt the lake's rhythms by altering the bottom step of the food web. Algae provide a major source of nutrition for aquatic insects and small fish. Less algae, so the reasoning flowed, meant fewer insects, fewer juvenile and bait fish and, thus, fewer large fish. Oneida Lake, however, adjusted to its bivalve newcomer and, to date, those apprehensions have proved to be unfounded. Because of zebras, Oneida is clearer and light penetrates to greater depths. Since algae needs light to grow, much more lake water is capable of producing algae and summer "blooms" occur with regularity, though they begin later and are not as long-lasting as in the past. More algae grow on the lake's bed, where the plants nourish invertebrates. The bottom level of Oneida Lake's food web remains secure despite the zebra "invasion."

In addition to stimulating algae production, the clearer lake water engendered by zebra mussels' feeding has also abetted the growth of aquatic vegetation, commonly known as "weeds" or "weed beds." The lake's vast, expanded weed beds provide habitat for large and smallmouth bass, pickerel, pumpkinseed sunfish, and bluegills, all of which thrive in a zebra-musselled Oneida. The weeds create a protective nursery where juvenile fish find sanctuary, nutrition, and life. Invertebrates such as daphnia (usually called "freshwater shrimp") and aquatic insects thrive in the weeds. Indeed, the bottom levels of the lake's food web are so rich that Cornell biologists have concluded that conditions currently exist that would support a recovery of the walleye population.

The Need for Effective Legislation

Zebra mussels became a part of American ecosystems largely because effective legislation that would protect our country's environs from water-transported exotic creatures has been sorely lacking. The Ballast and Water Law, passed in the mid-1990s after the zebra mussel invasion, requires foreign ships to exchange their freshwater ballast for saltwater prior to entering American inland navigational channels. The Coast Guard inspects vessels and tests their holds' waters for salinity. The law incorporates the theory that saltwater will kill the holds' freshwater organisms. Some aquatic creatures, however, thrive in both salt and fresh water and these can pass into our ecosystems. Moreover, the law only applies to the American side of the Great Lakes–Saint Lawrence system. The fresh for salt exchange is voluntary for ships using the Canadian sector. Consequently, foreign freshwater organisms can easily invade the lakes. Furthermore, the world's merchant marine includes many older ships that contain compartments that are sealed from the saltwater flushing. These miniature holds, whose hidden natures elude inspection, can be discharged into our waters. To complicate matters, over ninety per cent of ships entering the Great Lakes' system carry cargoes, with a minimal amount of ballast water below. Thus, on inspection, their holds appear to be environmentally safe. However, even this ballast, brought from Europe or Asia, can contain exotic organisms–fish, invertebrates, shellfish, and the like. After unloading cargoes at American or Canadian ports, the ships often fill their holds with Great Lakes' water and discharge into the lakes.

Round Gobies and Water Chestnuts

Another exotic destined for Oneida Lake is a small fish called the "round goby." Adult gobies are about five inches long. Ships originating in the Black Sea basin brought these fish to the Great Lakes in the mid-1990s. Presently, gobies are common in Lake Ontario and the western part of the Barge Canal. Thus, it's merely a matter of time before they reach Oneida Lake.

Gobies consume zebra mussels and will probably thrive in Oneida. Small and largemouth bass relish gobies and the lake's robust bass populations will benefit. However, gobies will be competing with established forage fish such as emerald shiners, gizzard shad, and young perch and this could disrupt the lake's food web.

Water chestnuts are exotic plants that reached Oneida Lake in the past five years. Originating in Asia, the plants spread rapidly during the 1990s. They grow in masses that clog waterways, limit navigation, and destroy native vegetation. Their seeds, called "nutlets," have sharp spines that easily pierce human skin. When the plants appeared near Brewerton's Route 81 Bridge in 1999, the Oneida Lake Association alerted government agencies and the general public. The Oswego County Soil and Water Conservation Department, Cornell Cooperative Extension of Onondaga County, and local Boy Scout groups joined the association in organizing plant-pulling days, where vast quantities of chestnuts were removed. Water chestnuts were treated with the chemical Aqua-Kleen during the summer of 2003 and this process eliminated several large beds. Publicity campaigns notified lakeside property owners of the impending peril and, to date, the plants have been contained. Their threat continues, however, because removal programs cannot eradicate all chestnuts, and seeds that break off and sink to the lake's bed may eventually germinate. Public vigilance may be the best method for keeping chestnuts in check.

Zebra mussels, double-crested cormorants, round gobies, and water chestnuts–exotics all–changing, threatening Oneida Lake's biological rhythms. Unless strong Federal legislation reforms conditions that allow foreign organisms to enter American environments, there will be more unwanted invaders, and more problems.

Phosphorus: Indispensible to the Food Web

Another factor relating to algae production and total productivity is the concentration of phosphorus in the lake. The construction of waste water facilities in lakeside communities, and refined farming techniques, have reduced Oneida's phosphorus levels to about twenty to thirty parts per billion (twenty to thirty ounces of phosphorus in every billion ounces of water). Phosphorus is *the* essential element for plant production and less phosphorus translates to less vegetation. Cornell Field Station Director Edward Mills has determined that twenty to thirty parts per billion is the minimum amount of phosphorus needed to maintain the lake's current high level of fish production. "If phosphorus in Oneida Lake were reduced to the levels reached in Lake Ontario (around ten parts per billion)," Mills stated, "The lake's superb warm water fishery would be at risk." Oneida is plenty clean at status quo and no further tampering with existing sewage treatment or farming practices should occur. Keep the phosphorus, keep the fish. It's that clear.

The Lake's Flood Plain: Drainage, Development, and Discord

Human alterations to Oneida's environment have directly conflicted with the lake's established rhythms.

Generally speaking, the lake region's residents adapted their lives to Oneida's rhythms throughout all the nineteenth and most of the twentieth centuries. Past generations were raised to respect the lake as a great provider and to know its ways and secrets because this knowledge was a "good" that enhanced life. The old-time lake anglers, boatmen, and farmers seldom tested the lake because they knew problems would arise.

Modern society, however, has sometimes ignored its ancestors' wisdom. The case of flooding provides a perfect example. Older generations of Oneida Lakers didn't build permanent structures within the lake's flood plain. Barns, farmhouses, and other homes were usually situated on high ground, well away from danger's path. When lakefront cottages and camps became fashionable in the latter 1800s and early 1900s, however, a building boom occurred. Waterfront homes again became a hot item during the prosperous 1980s and 1990s. Old camps received expensive renovations. New homes materialized and properties were touted as "lakefront," "lake view," and even "near lake."

In the spring of both 1993 and 1994, heavy rains melted an unusually thick snowcap (a late winter blizzard in March 1993 buried Upstate). Oneida's tributaries overflowed and widespread flooding followed. The lake rose five feet above its normal waterline in 1993 and three feet above that level in 1994. Driveways became navigable channels and lawns transformed into bays as the lake engulfed its ancient flood plain. Home owners sandbagged in what was often a futile attempt to check rising waters. Damage estimates ran into the millions of dollars.

Disasters like these were bound to foster controversies. The New York State Thruway Authority controls the lake's level and reduces it three feet every fall to safeguard against flooding. Some lakeshore property owners petitioned the authority to permanently reduce Oneida's water level. Opponents of these proposals, led by the Oneida Lake Association, argued that permanently lowering the lake would produce disastrous environmental and economic effects. The cost of redredging the scores of marinas that surround Oneida would be exorbitant. Exposed acres of mud flats would severely damage the lake's aesthetics. In addition, eliminating acres of shallows would liquidate prime spawning grounds for walleyes, bass, and perch, and habitat for invertebrates that are key creatures in the lake's food chain. Scientists backed these arguments. State officials realized the potential harm and kept the lake's water level at *status quo*.

People who bought or built within the lake's flood plain risked the consequences of Oneida's well-established rhythms. More development has occurred in the lake's immediate area within the past decade. The environmental repercussions of these changes remain undetermined. Suburban sprawl spreads every year through the Towns of Cicero, Hastings, West Monroe, and Constantia. Brewerton, a sleepy river village when I first met the lake in 1972, is now home to McDonalds, Burger King, a shopping plaza, and housing projects aplenty. The Towns of Sullivan and Lenox in Madison County have been steadily gaining population. At the East End of the lake, the Oneida Indian Nation has acquired several marinas, a bait and tackle shop, two "quick stop" markets, and acres of farmland. The Nation's extensive purchases spark conjecture as to what development plans may be in the offing. The Pyramid Corporation may soon be building "Destiny U.S.A.," a mega-mall on Syracuse's North Side–only ten miles from the lake. Projections state that the mall will attract millions of visitors annually and one cannot help but wonder what impact that may have on Oneida's environs.

Growth can be a positive process, but development near a major body of water leads to concerns. Drainage in the land surrounding the lake can be dramatically upset. The lake's watershed, cut by additional roads, driveways, ditches and the like, loses a part of its capacity to retain water. Runoff from rains gets to the lake quicker, accentuating flooding and related problems. Highways separate wetlands from the lake, impeding their productivity. More lawn chemicals, garden pesticides, and salts drain into the lake. Development alters the aesthetics of the lake's immediate environs. Fields and forests are replaced by homes and businesses, waterfowl and shore birds are displaced, and noise increases. The lake's rhythms change and that can create problems.

Landmark Preservation

A fair number of historic structures remain near the lake and some preserved in fine period style. The Oneida Lake Congregational Church, on Route 31 east of Lakeport, is a superb example. Completed in 1847, the church exhibits a modified, conservative Greek Revival architecture and has been cited in books about notable Madison County buildings. Across from the church is "Orchard Cottage," erected by John Chapman and his family in 1847. Designed like an English country house, the two-story brick structure was once part of Chapman's estate. Chapman was a noted hunter, wrote a book about marksmanship, and even sponsored formal fox hunts on his south shore lands. Charles Dickens met Chapman and his wife Mary on a voyage to the United States and described the couple in the book, "American Notes." Trinity Episcopal Church in Constantia, built by the Scriba family in 1832, is a fine example of rustic frontier architecture and, along with its churchyard, is beautifully maintained. At Sylvan Beach, Union

Chapel's board of trustees perpetuates their church in its beautiful New England colonial style. Erected in 1887 on land donated by the Beach's founding Spencer family the chapel, with its expanding sidewalls and great chandeliers, is an architectural gem. The carousel building in the Sylvan Beach Midway, LaBella's Greek Revival "Pancake House," Cavana's Sanitarium (now called "The Oneida" and used for vacation rentals), and the Cottman House (at the mouth of Snug Harbor Resort's backset in Verona Beach) remind visitors of the village's vibrant past. "Yesterday's Royal," an old Beach restaurant-hotel restored by the Aubeuf family, is an exuberant, refreshing example of historic revival that gives its patrons lively tastes of the village in its heyday. The Sylvan Beach village board did their part to enhance the village's historical flair in 2000 by demolishing the New York State Troopers' Barracks in the park and replacing it with a structure that closely resembles the former Ontario and Western Railroad Station.

Major examples of architectural preservation catch the eye, but less noteworthy buildings symbolize other eras of Oneida's past. The functional brick structure that once housed the Brewerton Bait Shop still stands at the corner of Library Street and Route 11. Two fieldstone houses, superb examples of nineteenth century farmers' utilitarian philosophy, impress the passersby on Route 49 west of Cleveland. A unique, two-story home, built from stones used to line the Erie Canal's banks, is located on the south side of Route 31 east of Bridgeport, across from the entrance for the South Shore State Boat Launch. And, on the side streets of virtually every lakeside community, the small, humble cottages of upstate's blue collar majority, whose lives have been intrinsically intertwined with Oneida Lake's past and who continue to revel in the water's joys today, speak of their heritage. Camps labeled with titles like "Restabit," "Bigenuf," and family names such as "Hoen," "Armani," and "Yankovic" show pride of property ownership. The rhythms that play through these buildings are a far cry from the suburban beat that, every year, occupies more and more of the lake's prime landscape. Sometimes, the two types of structures exist in close proximity–a new $350,000 home within a quarter mile of a trim, blue-collar cottage. Different economic communities have always blended within the Oneida Lake region.

In an extremely positive note, several landmarks in the lake region that have suffered neglect will soon be restored. Carpenters and painters are giving new life to the scroll brackets, hooded moldings, and widow's walk of the former Elmer Johnson house, a splendid Italianate Revival home on Route 31 east of Lakeport. The structure is the best example of this architectural style in the lake area. The regional Episcopal diocese donated St. James Church in Cleveland to the village's historical society in 2003. The society's plans include an immediate re-roofing of this vintage English gothic sanctuary, with interior restoration to follow.

In a contrast, New York State's Barge Canal harbor at Cleveland, potentially a vital place, exists in a state of blatant disrepair. Ice has eroded the harbor's two sheltering breakwaters almost beyond recognition, the state's dock is a rough mooring at best, and the parking lot sometimes resembles a moonscape. The Village of Cleveland has been unsuccessfully lobbying the state to refurbish the facility. If properly developed, the harbor would give boaters access to Cleveland's businesses and would complement its sister facilities at Sylvan Beach and Brewerton.

Any construction or demolition near the lake needs to be carefully evaluated because errors can occur that negatively impact the environment or obliterate priceless history. Some areas of the lake have suffered from haphazard development that has, in places, produced strange mishmashes of buildings. Fortunately, the opposite holds true in other locales, where construction blends nicely with natural visual aesthetics. Lake Shore Road in Verona Beach, where homes and cottages intersperse among the East Shore's tall, dignified oaks, pines, and maples, and sections of the North Shore along Route 49, where commercial development has, by and large, been separated from neatly-kept, shaded lakefront dwellings, are excellent examples of human adaptation to Oneida's rhythms.

Preservation for the Public: the Lake's Parks

It is in the lake's parks and public access points that the greatest triumphs of development and preservation have occurred. The Verona Beach State Park on the East Shore is an underused gem. The park's broad, sandy beach, arboreally-cathedralled picnic groves, and trails that explore lush, vital wetlands delight its relatively few visitors. Onondaga County's Oneida Shores Park at Brewerton connects thousands with hiking, cross-country skiing, swimming, and boating, and sponsors many family-oriented events. The park guards a large section of the Muskrat Bay woodland-wetland biome and its rustic, "great camp-styled" Arrowhead Lodge functions as an events' center. The Godfrey Point Boat Launch east of Cleveland and the South Shore Launch between

Lakeport and Bridgeport are aesthetically pleasing facilities that accommodate thousands annually. State Canal Development monies have transformed Brewerton and Sylvan Beach harbors into bustling ports, reminiscent of the days when barges and tugs crowded these popular anchorages. Refurbished canal banks provide easy docking, and walkways along the wharves attract hundreds. New businesses have sprouted near and along the canal. Although the rhythms of different boatmen hum through the harbors today, this restoration is an extremely positive move and will certainly engender future economic growth.

Proposed park and public access developments along the lake present contrasting scenarios. New homes will soon occupy the great Lakeport field that stretches a half-mile from Route 31 to the shore. This beautiful meadow, the last agricultural meadow bordering Oneida Lake, delighted viewers for decades. Development of this prime land, however, was inevitable. Thankfully, the Town of Sullivan demonstrated wisdom in planning the meadow's future. Although townhouse apartments, a boat basin, and a restaurant will occupy the bulk of the field, about twelve acres that border the lake will be set aside as a semi-wild "passive park," crisscrossed with walking trails. The shoreline will remain in its virgin state–a preserved slice of Oneida's environmental past.

In another positive example, the Sylvan Beach Barge Canal breakwater, locally nicknamed "the pier," extends about half a mile into Oneida Lake. Once an anglers' Mecca, the pier has suffered from erosion, weathering, and neglect and exists in a dilapidated state. Ninety percent is closed to the public. In 2001, the United States Army Corps of Engineers began testing the existing pier structure and the surrounding lakebed as part of a study that may lead to restoration. Estimates for rebuilding the jetty range to ten million dollars. As a tourist attraction, however, a reconstructed Sylvan Beach canal pier would be an amazing success. Angling remains excellent in waters bordering the pier and fishers would flock to the breakwater. Joggers, bikers, bird watchers, and casual strollers would revel in the pier's offerings.

On the other side of the coin, a proposed historical-recreational park in Brewerton has sparked controversy despite its sound philosophical grounding. The Fort Brewerton Historical Society conceived the project in 1995 and developed a professionally designed master plan in 1998. The park included a restored Fort Brewerton, a new museum, a kiosk for visitors' information, basketball, volleyball, and tennis courts, a public amphitheatre for concerts, and moorings for restored steamboats. The plan entailed acquiring all the properties west of Route 11 along the Oneida River from the bridge to just beyond the Barge Canal Lighthouse, and north to Oswego County Route 37. The society presented their plan to the Town of Hastings and the Town's Board was initially enthusiastic. Problems arose, however, when a businessperson approached the board and asked for permission to build a restaurant-tavern in an existing commercial structure in the proposed park. The property was slated for acquisition and occupied part of the site of the original Fort Brewerton landing. It doubtless contained hundreds, perhaps thousands, of invaluable unearthed artifacts. Although the Historical Society fought the alteration vigorously, even enlisting help of the New York State Parks, Recreation, and Historic Preservation Department, economics prevailed as the Town Board opted for the restaurant. Tax dollars and revenues took priority over the restoration of priceless historical property.

Afterthoughts

Citizens possess considerable power to influence Oneida lake's future. There are effective courses of action that they can follow to help preserve and protect this great natural resource.

First, concerned persons can join the Oneida Lake Association. This environmental watchdog group, founded in 1945, is the only organization totally dedicated to the lake's conservation. The association aggressively confronts any threat to the lake's environmental integrity. Its history includes major victories such as securing cormorant control, the construction of the new Constantia hatchery, and the passage of legislation banning the sale of walleyed pike. No group defends Oneida Lake as vigorously as the "OLA." No group can exert as much positive influence.

People can closely monitor the Oneida Lake Watershed Advisory Council's activities. The council, which includes representatives from the lake area's county, town, and village governments, as well as other stakeholder groups, sets goals for Oneida's improvement and may have a big impact on future DEC policies. The council sponsors issues' hearings and publishes brochures describing its work. Members of the lake community can attend these meetings and read all publications produced by this potentially influential group. They can voice their opinions regarding the council's recommendations.

Residents and other property owners can participate in local governments. Villages and towns surrounding Oneida lake schedule monthly board meetings in which important public policies often emerge. Zoning issues, subdivision hearings, planning board actions, wetlands threats, and related environmental concerns are aired at these meetings. The lake's people can insist on strict ordinances governing these crucial topics.

Lake lovers can get involved in community clean-up and enhancement projects. Roadside trash removal events are common throughout the lake's basin. Cornell Cooperative Extension of Onondoga County sponsors water chestnut-pulling days in the Brewerton area that eliminate potentially expansive growths of this bothersome aquatic weed. The Cleveland Historical Society, Constantia Library Guild, and Fort Brewerton Historical Society actively recruit support for their worthwhile causes.

People who care about Oneida Lake can immerse themselves in a variety of efforts that directly enhance the lake's well being. Above all, however, they must speak out when problems occur. They can report polluters, inform game wardens about poaching, and object to landscape-scarring development. They can notify the DEC about threatened wetlands or alert sheriffs' departments to boating violations. They can editorialize in letters to newspapers or their elected representatives. If they disdain individually, they can find strength in numbers through organizations like the OLA.

But they must speak out. Different rhythms will continue to disrupt Oneida Lake's natural harmonies. History has shown that the challenges these problems pose can be conquered, but only if people who care take the time to act.

Postlude

Messenger's Bay is my favorite spot to relax and quietly think about Oneida Lake and my relationship with it. I love to sit by the bay and, shaded by the Faulkner willows, encouraged by an aqueous vista flowing to Dunham's Island, Constantia, and beyond, muse about my work's focus. Rachel Carson's moving environmentalist classic, *The Sea Around Us*, often comes to mind. Carson discussed how life began in the sea and how human beings depend on the ocean not only for sustenance, but also for employment, transportation, recreation, health, and even spirituality. She warned that spoiling the sea would imperil life itself because of the overall importance of the oceans to human existence.

I've often thought of Oneida Lake as a sea in miniature, vitally significant to the littoral world it borders. The lake has given life to millions of people–it continues in this role today. An examination of this book's stories dramatizes this point. The tales show how the lives of steamboat captains, North Shore loggers, Cleveland glass workers, and farmers in all lakeside communities were inextricably intertwined with Oneida during the 1800s and early 1900s. The lake's economic benefits are evident in stories that demonstrate how families like the Miltons tapped a market for their rugged hand-crafted boats, how the lake's tributaries furnished power for Constantia's small industries, how the lake's magnificent shelving beaches helped spur Sylvan and Verona

Beach's genesis, and how Oneida's vast fish populations supported pirates and sport anglers in every community. Other tales portray Oneida Lake's surface as a crucial highway for armies during the colonial and revolutionary eras and for boatmen after the lake became a part of the Barge Canal System in 1917. Businesspersons took advantage of the lake area's robust twentieth century tourist economy and accounts of enterprises like Chuck and Millard Rogers' "Brewerton Bait Shop" and Edward and Florence Stewart's "Eddie's Restaurant" reflect that trend.

The lake's biological evolution can be tracked through the book's tales. John Humphrey Noyes and his followers documented bountiful schools of pike and perch in the 1870s in "Perfectionists in Paradise." Arnold Armani's memories in "An Unforgettable Duck Hunt" rekindle images of the vast flights of waterfowl that once darkened Oneida's skies. The lake's sturgeons' tragic decline and jubilant renaissance emerges from "Dinosaurs of the Depths." The joys that accompany Oneida Lake angling burst from stories about Clarence App and Tony Verno.

Oneida Lake has been a source of inspiration throughout its history. Documents reveal how writers were impressed by the lake's aesthetics and potential as early as the 1790s. This book's stories showcase authors like Welcome Spencer, the "Lakeport Philosopher," and members of the utopian socialist Oneida Community who marveled at the beauty of Oneida Lake's surroundings. Enterprising people acted on those visions and built lakeside communities–this fact emerges clearly in the lake's lore. In contrast, Oneida's environs can be harsh and threatening and these qualities surface in stories like "Blizzard" and "Shipwrecks." The lake can be a powerful force that inspires respect and awe.

The Sea Around Us underscored the importance of safeguarding the world's oceans. I cannot stress enough the absolute necessity of protecting Oneida Lake. The lake is vital to Central New York's economic, social, and recreational health. Seldom in the course of American history has a large body of clean, fresh water blessed with Oneida Lake's resources been placed so close to so many people. All stakeholders in the lake's environs–sportspersons, local government officials, research scientists, merchants, and residents alike–should realize that the preservation of the lake as the productive wonder that it is, and always has been, must be an uncompromised priority, because Oneida Lake is too valuable to lose.

Al Beickert's marina at Oneida Creek's mouth was a focal point for spring bullheading. A mooring pole, used for stabilization, is visible by the boat in the lake proper.

Jean Kowalski

Nattily-dressed strollers pause to chat with anglers on the Sylvan Beach pier during the 1920s.

Sylvan Beach's hotels loom in the far distance as Oneida's surf laps against the pier.

Richard Griesmyer

Rugged wooden boats await customers in App's harbor.

Richard Griesmyer

Clarence App–engineer, veteran fisherman, and one of the most famous boat livery owners in Oneida Lake history.

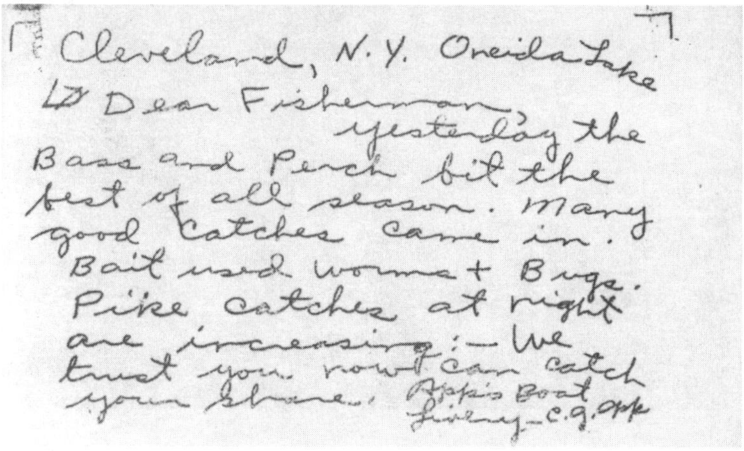

Cleveland, N.Y. Oneida Lake
Dear Fisherman,
yesterday the
Bass and Perch bit the
best of all season. Many
good catches came in.
Bait used worms + Bugs.
Pike catches at night
are increasing:— We
trust you now can catch
your share. App's Boat
Livery—C.G. App

Katherine App Bennett

Clarence App mailed these postcards to regular customers when the "bite was on."

Double-crested cormorants consumed millions of Oneida Lake fish since 1989. Their predation was the major cause of the lake's fishery's decline during the 1990s. New York State finally instituted aggressive cormorant control in 2004. This photo was shot on Wantry Island in 1995.

Ann Hopkins

Cleveland harbor can be successfully restored to what it was when this photo was shot in the 1950s–but only if New York State will invest in this worthy project.

Oneida Lake is a Mecca for power boaters, jet skiers, and sunbathers.

With diligent conservation, Oneida Lake will be a source of joy for generations to come.

My Debts

History books are not solo endeavors and I will be forever grateful to the many good people who helped make this volume a reality. Sheila Orlin, the book's primary editor, enhanced my work considerably. Theresa Ann Cardinal, Robert Igoe, Jr., Jeromy Mikuszewski, and Kurt Snyder critiqued parts of the manuscript. Lynne Browne coordinated many of the technical aspects of this book. John Mahaffy and Amanda Adkison's map artistry graces the endpapers. Zach Steffen coordinated the book's final layout. Guy Danella and his crew lent their expertise to restoring and enhancing many of this book's photos. My thanks go to all.

The book's stories come from many sources. I have listed the tales in this bibliographical chapter and credit the sources that influenced each.

I extend my sincere gratitude to all who helped and I apologize to anyone that I might have inadvertently excluded.

A LITTLE GEOGRAPHY: Data about the Lake's geography comes from "The Limnology of Oneida Lake–An Interim Report," by Philip E. Greeson and George S. Meyers, U.S. Geological Survey, 1969, and from a table included with the article "Oneida Lake: Undergoing Ecological Change," by Edward L. Mills and Kristen T. Holeck, published in Clearwaters, v. 31, no.4, winter 2001.

I thank Cornell University Field Station Director Edward Mills, who granted permission to use the Oneida Lake watershed map.

PICTURES: This story conveys images I encountered during walks that Karen Howlett and I took along Sylvan and Verona Beaches.

I interviewed my friend Charlie Hamlin for the Messenger's Bay part of the story. I first met Charlie when I was a teenager. My grandfather Stanley Osterhout and I rented boats at Hamlin's Marina. These angling excursions began my journey into Oneida Lake's history. Charlie and old-time Hamlin's patrons like Sam Spangler and Bill Taylor always had some fishing lore to share with Gramps and me. Each story made our Oneida Lake outings richer.

I am indebted to William Faulkner, and to his style that I loosely used in my Messenger's Bay anthem, for his images of the Deep South that have lived with me since I met them at Hamilton College in the early 1970s. When I saw the great willows that grow by Messenger's shore, I immediately thought of them as the "Faulkner trees." easily transplanted to Yoknapatawpha County, Mississippi.

ARMIES ON THE LAKE: Elet Milton in a paper, "Some Army Movements Through Oneida Lake." It is a part of the collection of the Brewerton Historical Society, headquartered in the Oliver Stevens Blockhouse Museum, Brewerton.

The Horatio Gates letter from *The Papers of Sir William Johnson*, by Milton W. Hamilton, The University of the State of New York, Albany, 1951, v. X.

OF FECKIES, GLOBULES, AND AN EMETIC, TOO: This story was recorded in the Milton Papers, on file at Brewerton Historical Society. I am grateful to Lynn Mayo, reference librarian at Hamilton College, who translated the Latin phrases in this letter, and in other chapters.

RAFTING LOGS ACROSS ONEIDA: This story was recorded in the Milton Papers, on file at Brewerton Historical Society.

A TAMMANY MAN AT LOWER SOUTH BAY: Asa Eastwood's diaries are a part of the special collections of the E.S. Bird Library of Syracuse University. My thanks to the university for granting permission to use excerpts and to Public Services Librarian Carolyn Davis for securing me that permission.

CAPTAINS, PIRATES, AND MAIDENS–A LOWER SOUTH BAY FANTASY: From the Onondaga Historical Association's superb collection of local history material. They have been most generous in allowing me to use it. Recorded in the *Syracuse Daily Standard*, July 17, 1854 this story is in the association's file.

DINOSAURS FROM THE DEPTHS: Richard Colesante, former Director of New York State's Oneida Fish Cultural Station at Constantia, sent me excerpts from these three books that provided background for this story:

Carlander, Kenneth D., *Handbook of Freshwater Fishery Biology*, The Iowa State University Press, Ames, Iowa, 1970.

Crossman, E.J., and Scott, W.B., *Freshwater Fishes of Canada*, Fisheries Research Board of Canada, Ottawa, 1973.

Evermann, Barton Warren, and Jordan, David Starr, *American Food and Game Fishes*, General Publishing Company, Ltd., Toronto, 1969.

Two articles from the files of the Onondaga County Historical Association, Syracuse, proved to be extremely useful. They are:

Anonymous, "Big Fish," *Syracuse Standard*, May 5, 1856.

Hunter, Rod, "Sportsman's Corner," *Syracuse Post-Standard*, May 18, 1973.

William R. Daly, of Sherrill wrote me a wonderful letter in which he recounted a story about Oneida Lake's sturgeons.

Tony Van De Valk and James R. Jackson, biologists at the Cornell University Field Station at Shackelton Point, have provided clear, detailed explanations to all my questions about lake sturgeons.

CLEVELAND STYLE PATRIOTISM: The article is from the *Syracuse Courier and Union* and was published in July 1861. Terry Prior, Director of the Oswego County Historical Society, helped track down the paper's origin.

Information about Thomas Deans and the Grand Army of the Republic Posts at Cleveland and Constantia was gleaned from articles collected by Norman and Colleen Goodale, Cleveland. Corky Winn, of Bernhard's Bay, provided information about his grandfather George Clough, an officer in the 5th New York Volunteer Cavalry, Grand Army of the Republic. Geoffrey Gursky, of Cleveland, has been very helpful with information and photos about his area's history.

PERFECTIONISTS IN PARADISE: These lively stories are recorded in the *Oneida Circular*, a paper published by the Oneida Community. Editions of this paper are on file in the local history room of the Oneida City Library, Oneida.

TALES FROM THE NORTH SHORE: Several of these stories were sent to me by Joni Hines, of Cleveland.

Laurence Cottet's son, Jack, gave me additional information about his father.

The Constantia stories appeared in the *Syracuse Herald*, April 6, 1919. Zinah Fuller's obituary was included in the *Utica Morning Herald*, November 11, 1878. These items are a part of the collection of the Onondaga Historical Association, Syracuse.

The account of the fox chase ran in the *Brookfield Courier* on March 30, 1892. The Brookfield Historical Society owns bound volumes of this newspaper.

Corky Winn provided photos, captioning data, and reference for my North

Shore stories. "Cork" has been a valued source of information and friendship.

ELOPING ON THE WAVES: The original article from the *New York Morning Journal* appeared in the late 1880s. Elet Milton's notes helped me complete the story. It is a part of the Milton Papers in the Fort Brewerton Historical Society.

A CONSTANTIA VISIT, ANYONE?: The Onondaga Historical Association owns a copy of an article in the *Syracuse Journal* of August 17, 1881, used here.

THE LAKEPORT PHILOSOPHER: Welcome Spencer's writings appeared in the *Madison County Times* in the 1870s and 1880s. Carol Green and Clara Houck, Town of Sullivan historians, connected me with microfilmed files of that paper.

Information about Welcome Spencer's family came from the Madison County Census of 1880, on microfilm at the Onondaga County Library, The Galleries, Syracuse. Spencer's obituaries, published in the *Madison County Times* on January 12, 1894, and the *Oneida Democrat Union*, January 10, 1894, were also useful.

MESSAGES: Jean and John Kowalski, owners of the Canal View Restaurant in Sylvan Beach, gave me access to their marvelous postcard and photo collection. Mike Wameling, of Verona Beach, also opened his collection for my use.

Messages were also taken from postcards that I examined at various antique and card shows that are held annually in Central New York.

BLIZZARD!: The story appears in a "Just Around the Corner" column, written by "Bertrande" for the *Syracuse Post Standard* in 1947. The Milton Papers in the Brewerton Library contain this article.

THE FIRST ONEIDA LAKE HATCHERY: The staff at the Oneida Lake Fish Cultural Station, Constantia, display an article from the *Oswego Palladium*, April 12, 1897, that is used in this story.

THE COTTAGERS' LIFE: Margaret Cullen, of Utica and Verona Beach, sent me a copy of "Diamond Jubilee, 1890–1965," a history of "Seven Oaks," the Verona Beach cottage owned by the John Forbes Tuttle family. This paper, written by Annie Tuttle Rush and Cornelia Tuttle Bowe, highlights the family's experiences at the Oneida Lake retreat. Conversations with Ms. Bowe revealed information that enhanced the story.

BEACONS IN TRIPLICATE: Bill Orzell, Director of the Canal Society of New York State allowed me to use his article about Oneida Lake's lighthouses.

MURPHY'S COWS STAYED IN THE BARN: William "Buddy" McCarthy granted me several interviews during the summer of 2000, from which I gleaned material in this story.

DOLLARS THROUGH THE ICE: These stories came from the *Syracuse Herald* of January 26, 1930, sent to me by Lona Flynn, Historian of the Town of Cicero.

"BESTING" THE FISH PIRATES: The central article for this story came from the Brewerton Library and was included in a Syracuse paper on July 26, 1936.

I supplemented this story with information gathered from Colleen Goodale, of Cleveland, Harry Best's daughter, and from Paul Brown, of Leonardsville, a retired New York State Environmental Conservation Officer.

BOATS BUILT IN BREWERTON:The Brewerton Library has a copy of the Syracuse newspaper article, dated August 2, 1931, that described Thomas Milton's craft. John F. Cook authored the article.

Chris Stallknecht sent me information about "Emmons boats," manufactured just north of Brewerton by Nearing Emmons. Carol Greene mailed me data about "Damon Boats," built by the Damon family near Bridgeport.

A BEACH FAMILY TRADITION: An interview with Eddie Stewart, Sr. generated most of the story's narration.

In addition, Ed McCarthy, Carol McCarthy, Patti McCarthy, Eddie Stewart, Jr., Leslie Stewart, and John DePerno gave me information that enriched the story. I also talked with several of the Stewarts' employees and, of course, supplemented the tale with many calorie-saturated trips to this venerable restaurant.

SHIPWRECKS: The Samuel Kirkland quote comes from *The Journal of Samuel Kirkland*, edited by Walter Pilkington, a former librarian of Hamilton College. Charles Lafayette "Lafe" Todd, my teacher, friend, and angling partner during and after my years at Hamilton, gave me a copy of this book. Lafe continues to communicate with and encourage his students decades after they graduate. He embodies the Hamilton philosophy and spirit.

Margaret Cullen, of Utica, sent me a copy of the article from June 30, 1925.

James Allen, of Central Square, mailed me documentation of his efforts at locating the *Thomas H.* Conversations with Jim revealed further details. I also researched the tragedy in the microfilmed records of the *Syracuse Post-Standard* in the Onondaga County Library.

The articles about the shipwrecks in November 1930 and October 1936 came from the Milton Papers of the Brewerton Historical Society.

Margaret Dobson Druse, Easton, Pennsylvania, shared memories of a childhood spent, in part, on Oneida Lake's southeast shore, and provided details about Nabor's Grove and the grounded barges on the lake's eastern beaches. An accomplished historian, She is a co-author of *Our Hidden Heritage– Pennsylvania Women in History*, the American Association of University Women, 1984.

AN UNFORGETTABLE DUCK HUNT: Many thanks to my friend Arnold Armani for sharing his memories of this notable occasion, and details about his family's history.

INSIDE XANDRIA: Paul Laible was a gracious host for a lengthy interview, conducted during the summer of 1997.

Dr. Edward Mills, Director of the Cornell University Field Station at Shackelton Point, the former Xandria Estate of Charles Brown, has enriched my work by granting me access to the Station's historical and biological resources. Ed has dedicated his life to researching Oneida Lake's biological secrets and to protecting the aquatic bounty that is Oneida's essence.

LIFE WITH POP: The late Milt Kellogg of Long Point, who spent a great portion of his life with Oneida Lake, sent me these stories. Milt was a frequent correspondent, caller, and friend. I hope that they're biting in the next world, and that Saint Peter doesn't mind listening to some well-embellished tales.

BREWERTON'S BAIT SHOP: Chuck Rogers allowed me to enter his life for several delightful hours of Oneida Lake memories.

Steve Rogers, Charlie Engel, and Ruth Rogers provided additional material.

The article about the old Brewerton Bait Shop, by Fred David, came from the *Syracuse Herald-American* of September 15, 1996.

THE FLUTTER SPOON KING: I interviewed the late Tony Verno during the summers of 1995 and 1996. Great interviews. Great guy.

Tony's nephew and fishing partner, retired Conservation Officer Mike Mitchell, of Canastota, provided additional data about his talented uncle.

Tony and Sally Verno, Tony's son and daughter-in-law, sent me the photo.

A FABULOUS FIFTIES FANFARE: I interviewed George Sawner, Ed McCarthy, Carol Heinz McCarthy, John Deperno, Ernie Money, Phyllis Grieco Money, Eddie Stewart, Sr., and the late Lilian Esengard Sawner to gather material for this story. Their candor and warmth brought life to this chapter.

Frank Tomanio of the *Utica Observer-Dispatch* helped me obtain photos.

NORTH WALL: Rosemary Watson wrote the wonderful "Ode To A Walleye" and Peter Eager invited her to join me for a North Wall evening. Ron Renslow, owner of the Oneida Lake Marina, maintains this neat place.

RUNNING THROUGH SYLVAN BEACH HISTORY: This is a conglomerate of images taken from many "Beach runs" that Karen Howlett and I have enjoyed.

RHYTHMS OF THE LAKE: Ed Beickert told me details about his father's marina, once known as the "bullhead capital of the East Shore." Francis Fabrizi and Mike Mitchell helped me identify the nicknames of the men who fished there.

John Clements, Ed McCarthy, Charlie Hamlin, and Richard "Red" Devan brought me back to the days of "pier fishing for pike" at Sylvan Beach.

Richard Griesmyer, Corky Winn, Parker Stone, Tom Pierce, Mrs. Elliott App, and the late Catherine App Bennett shared their memories of Clarence and his marina. May the lake's rhythms bless their lives forever.